matplotlib Plotting Cookbook

Learn how to create professional scientific plots using matplotlib, with more than 60 recipes that cover common use cases

Alexandre Devert

BIRMINGHAM - MUMBAI

matplotlib Plotting Cookbook

First published: March 2014

Production Reference: 1200314

Published by Packt Publishing Ltd.
Livery Place
35 Livery Street
Birmingham B3 2PB, UK.

ISBN 978-1-84951-326-5

www.packtpub.com

Cover Image by Prashant Timappa Shetty (sparkling.spectrum.123@gmail.com)

Credits

Author
Alexandre Devert

Reviewers
Francesco Benincasa
Valerio Maggio
Jonathan Street
Dr. Allen Chi-Shing Yu

Acquisition Editor
Rebecca Youe

Commissioning Editor
Usha Iyer

Content Development Editor
Ankita Shashi

Technical Editors
Shubhangi Dhamgaye
Pratik More
Humera Shaikh

Copy Editors
Dipti Kapadia
Aditya Nair
Kirti Pai

Project Coordinator
Sanchita Mandal

Proofreaders
Ameesha Green
Paul Hindle

Indexer
Tejal Soni

Production Coordinator
Manu Joseph

Cover Work
Manu Joseph

About the Author

Alexandre Devert is a scientist, currently busy solving problems and making tools for molecular biologists. Before this, he used to teach data mining, software engineering, and research in numerical optimization. He is an enthusiastic Python coder as well and never gets enough of it!

I would like to thank Xiang, my amazing, wonderful wife, for her patience, support, and encouragement, as well as my parents for their support and encouragement.

About the Reviewers

Francesco Benincasa, Master of Science in Software Engineering, is a designer and developer. He is a GNU/Linux and Python expert and has vast experience in many languages and applications. He has been using Python as the primary language for more than 10 years, together with JavaScript and framewoks such as Plone or Django.

He is interested in advanced web and network developing as well as scientific data manipulation and visualization. Over the last few years, he has been using graphical Python libraries such as Matplotlib/Basemap and scientific libraries such as NumPy/SciPy, as well as scientific applications such as GrADS, NCO, and CDO.

Currently, he is working at the Earth Science Department of the Barcelona Supercomputing Center (`www.bsc.es`) as a Research Support Engineer for the World Meteorological Organization Sand and Dust Storms Warning Advisory and Assessment System (`sds-was.aemet.es`).

Valerio Maggio has a PhD in Computational Science from the University of Naples "Federico II" and is currently a Postdoc researcher at the University of Salerno.

His research interests are mainly focused on unsupervised machine learning and software engineering, recently combined with semantic web technologies for linked data and Big Data analysis.

Valerio started developing open source software in 2004, when he was studying for his Bachelor's degree. In 2006, he started working on Python, and has since contributed to several open source projects in this language. Currently, he applies Python as the mainstream language for his machine learning code, making intensive use of matplotlib to analyze experimental data.

Valerio is also a member of the Italian Python community and enjoys playing chess and drinking tea.

I wish to sincerely thank Valeria for her true love and constant support and for being the sweetest girl I've ever met.

Jonathan Street is a well-known researcher in the fields of physiology and biomarker discovery. He began using Python in 2006 and extensively used matplotlib for many figures in his PhD thesis. He shares his interest in Python data tools by giving lectures and guiding educational sessions for regional groups, as well as writing on his blog at `http://jonathanstreet.com`.

Dr. Allen Chi-Shing Yu is a postdoctoral researcher working in the field of cancer genetics. He obtained his BSc degree in Molecular Biotechnology from the Chinese University of Hong Kong in 2009, and obtained a PhD in Biochemistry from the same university in 2013. Allen's PhD research primarily involved genomic and transcriptomic characterization of novel bacterial strains that can use toxic fluoro-tryptophans but not canonical tryptophan for propagation, under the supervision of Prof. Jeffrey Tze-Fei Wong and Prof. Ting-fung Chan. The findings demonstrated that the genetic code is not an immutable construct, and a small number of analogue-sensitive proteins are stabilizing the assignment of canonical amino acids to the genetic code.

Soon after his microbial studies, Allen was involved in the identification and characterization of a novel mutation marker causing Spinocerebellar Ataxia—a group of genetically diverse neurodegenerative disorders. Through the development of a tool for detecting viral integration events in human cancer samples (ViralFusionSeq), he has entered the field of cancer genetics. As the postdoctoral researcher in Prof. Nathalie Wong's lab, he is now responsible for the high-throughput sequencing analysis of hepatocellular carcinoma, as well as the maintenance of several Linux-based computing clusters.

Allen is proficient in both wet-lab techniques and computer programming. He is also committed to developing and promoting open source technologies, through a collection of tutorials and documentations on his blog at `http://www.allenyu.info`. Readers wishing to contact Dr. Yu can do so via the contact details on his website.

www.PacktPub.com

Support files, eBooks, discount offers and more

You might want to visit www.PacktPub.com for support files and downloads related to your book.

Did you know that Packt offers eBook versions of every book published, with PDF and ePub files available? You can upgrade to the eBook version at www.PacktPub.com and as a print book customer, you are entitled to a discount on the eBook copy. Get in touch with us at service@packtpub.com for more details.

At www.PacktPub.com, you can also read a collection of free technical articles, sign up for a range of free newsletters and receive exclusive discounts and offers on Packt books and eBooks.

http://PacktLib.PacktPub.com

Do you need instant solutions to your IT questions? PacktLib is Packt's online digital book library. Here, you can access, read and search across Packt's entire library of books.

Why Subscribe?

- Fully searchable across every book published by Packt
- Copy and paste, print and bookmark content
- On demand and accessible via web browser

Free Access for Packt account holders

If you have an account with Packt at www.PacktPub.com, you can use this to access PacktLib today and view nine entirely free books. Simply use your login credentials for immediate access.

Table of Contents

Preface

matplotlib is a Python module for plotting, and it is a component of the ScientificPython modules suite. matplotlib allows you to easily prepare professional-grade figures with a comprehensive API to customize every aspect of the figures. In this book, we will cover the different types of figures and how to adjust a figure to suit your needs. The recipes are orthogonal and you will be able to compose your own solutions very quickly.

What this book covers

Chapter 1, First Steps, introduces the basics of working with matplotlib. The basic figure types are introduced with minimal examples.

Chapter 2, Customizing the Color and Styles, covers how to control the color and style of a figure—this includes markers, line thickness, line patterns, and using color maps to color a figure several items.

Chapter 3, Working with Annotations, covers how to annotate a figure—this includes adding an axis legend, arrows, text boxes, and shapes.

Chapter 4, Working with Figures, covers how to prepare a complex figure—this includes compositing several figures, controlling the aspect ratio, axis range, and the coordinate system.

Chapter 5, Working with a File Output, covers output to files, either in bitmap or vector formats. Issues like transparency, resolution, and multiple pages are studied in detail.

Chapter 6, Working with Maps, covers plotting matrix-like data—this includes maps, quiver plots, and stream plots.

Chapter 7, Working with 3D Figures, covers 3D plots—this includes scatter plots, line plots, surface plots, and bar charts.

Chapter 8, User Interface, covers a set of user interface integration solutions, ranging from simple and minimalist to sophisticated.

What you need for this book

The examples in this book are written for Matplotlib 1.2 and Python 2.7 or 3.

Most examples rely on NumPy and SciPy. Some examples require SymPy, while some other examples require LaTeX.

Who this book is for

The book is intended for readers who have some notions of Python and a science background.

Conventions

In this book, you will find a number of styles of text that distinguish between different kinds of information. Here are some examples of these styles, and an explanation of their meaning.

Code words in text, database table names, folder names, filenames, file extensions, pathnames, dummy URLs, user input, and Twitter handles are shown as follows: "We can include other contexts through the use of the `include` directive."

A block of code is set as follows:

```
[default]
exten => s,1,Dial(Zap/1|30)
exten => s,2,Voicemail(u100)
exten => s,102,Voicemail(b100)
exten => i,1,Voicemail(s0)
```

When we wish to draw your attention to a particular part of a code block, the relevant lines or items are set in bold:

```
[default]
exten => s,1,Dial(Zap/1|30)
exten => s,2,Voicemail(u100)
exten => s,102,Voicemail(b100)
exten => i,1,Voicemail(s0)
```

Any command-line input or output is written as follows:

```
# cp /usr/src/asterisk-addons/configs/cdr_mysql.conf.sample
  /etc/asterisk/cdr_mysql.conf
```

New terms and **important words** are shown in bold. Words that you see on the screen, in menus or dialog boxes for example, appear in the text like this: "clicking on the **Next** button moves you to the next screen."

Warnings or important notes appear in a box like this.

Tips and tricks appear like this.

Reader feedback

Feedback from our readers is always welcome. Let us know what you think about this book—what you liked or may have disliked. Reader feedback is important for us to develop titles that you really get the most out of.

To send us general feedback, simply send an e-mail to `feedback@packtpub.com`, and mention the book title via the subject of your message.

If there is a topic that you have expertise in and you are interested in either writing or contributing to a book, see our author guide on `www.packtpub.com/authors`.

Customer support

Now that you are the proud owner of a Packt book, we have a number of things to help you to get the most from your purchase.

Downloading the example code

You can download the example code files for all Packt books you have purchased from your account at `http://www.packtpub.com`. If you purchased this book elsewhere, you can visit `http://www.packtpub.com/support` and register to have the files e-mailed directly to you.

Downloading the color images of this book

We also provide you a PDF file that has color images of the screenshots/diagrams used in this book. The color images will help you better understand the changes in the output. You can download this file from `https://www.packtpub.com/sites/default/files/downloads/3265OS_Graphics.pdf`.

Errata

Although we have taken every care to ensure the accuracy of our content, mistakes do happen. If you find a mistake in one of our books—maybe a mistake in the text or the code—we would be grateful if you would report this to us. By doing so, you can save other readers from frustration and help us improve subsequent versions of this book. If you find any errata, please report them by visiting `http://www.packtpub.com/submit-errata`, selecting your book, clicking on the **errata submission form** link, and entering the details of your errata. Once your errata are verified, your submission will be accepted and the errata will be uploaded on our website, or added to any list of existing errata, under the Errata section of that title. Any existing errata can be viewed by selecting your title from `http://www.packtpub.com/support`.

Piracy

Piracy of copyright material on the Internet is an ongoing problem across all media. At Packt, we take the protection of our copyright and licenses very seriously. If you come across any illegal copies of our works, in any form, on the Internet, please provide us with the location address or website name immediately so that we can pursue a remedy.

Please contact us at `copyright@packtpub.com` with a link to the suspected pirated material.

We appreciate your help in protecting our authors, and our ability to bring you valuable content.

Questions

You can contact us at `questions@packtpub.com` if you are having a problem with any aspect of the book, and we will do our best to address it.

1
First Steps

In this chapter, we will cover:

- Installing matplotlib
- Plotting one curve
- Using NumPy
- Plotting multiple curves
- Plotting curves from file data
- Plotting points
- Plotting bar charts
- Plotting multiple bar charts
- Plotting stacked bar charts
- Plotting back-to-back bar charts
- Plotting pie charts
- Plotting histograms
- Plotting boxplots
- Plotting triangulations

Introduction

matplotlib makes scientific plotting very straightforward. matplotlib is not the first attempt at making the plotting of graphs easy. What matplotlib brings is a modern solution to the balance between ease of use and power. matplotlib is a module for Python, a programming language. In this chapter, we will provide a quick overview of what using matplotlib feels like. Minimalistic recipes are used to introduce the principles matplotlib is built upon.

Installing matplotlib

Before experimenting with matplotlib, you need to install it. Here we introduce some tips to get matplotlib up and running without too much trouble.

How to do it...

We have three likely scenarios: you might be using Linux, OS X, or Windows.

Linux

Most Linux distributions have Python installed by default, and provide matplotlib in their standard package list. So all you have to do is use the package manager of your distribution to install matplotlib automatically. In addition to matplotlib, we highly recommend that you install NumPy, SciPy, and SymPy, as they are supposed to work together. The following list consists of commands to enable the default packages available in different versions of Linux:

- **Ubuntu**: The default Python packages are compiled for Python 2.7. In a command terminal, enter the following command:

  ```
  sudo apt-get install python-matplotlib python-numpy python-scipy
  python-sympy
  ```

- **ArchLinux**: The default Python packages are compiled for Python 3. In a command terminal, enter the following command:

  ```
  sudo pacman -S python-matplotlib python-numpy python-scipy python-
  sympy
  ```

  If you prefer using Python 2.7, replace `python` by `python2` in the package names

- **Fedora**: The default Python packages are compiled for Python 2.7. In a command terminal, enter the following command:

  ```
  sudo yum install python-matplotlib numpy scipy sympy
  ```

There are other ways to install these packages; in this chapter, we propose the most simple and seamless ways to do it.

Windows and OS X

Windows and OS X do not have a standard package system for software installation. We have two options—using a ready-made self-installing package or compiling matplotlib from the code source. The second option involves much more work; it is worth the effort to have the latest, bleeding edge version of matplotlib installed. Therefore, in most cases, using a ready-made package is a more pragmatic choice.

You have several choices for ready-made packages: Anaconda, Enthought Canopy, Algorete Loopy, and more! All these packages provide Python, SciPy, NumPy, matplotlib, and more (a text editor and fancy interactive shells) in one go. Indeed, all these systems install their own package manager and from there you install/uninstall additional packages as you would do on a typical Linux distribution. For the sake of brevity, we will provide instructions only for Enthought Canopy. All the other systems have extensive documentation online, so installing them should not be too much of a problem.

So, let's install Enthought Canopy by performing the following steps:

1. Download the Enthought Canopy installer from `https://www.enthought.com/products/canopy`. You can choose the free Express edition. The website can guess your operating system and propose the right installer for you.
2. Run the Enthought Canopy installer. You do not need to be an administrator to install the package if you do not want to share the installed software with other users.
3. When installing, just click on **Next** to keep the defaults. You can find additional information about the installation process at `http://docs.enthought.com/canopy/quick-start.html`.

That's it! You will have Python 2.7, NumPy, SciPy, and matplotlib installed and ready to run.

Plotting one curve

The initial example of Hello World! for a plotting software is often about showing a simple curve. We will keep up with that tradition. It will also give you a rough idea about how matplotlib works.

Getting ready

You need to have Python (either v2.7 or v3) and matplotlib installed. You also need to have a text editor (any text editor will do) and a command terminal to type and run commands.

How to do it...

Let's get started with one of the most common and basic graph that any plotting software offers—**curves**. In a text file saved as `plot.py`, we have the following code:

```
import matplotlib.pyplot as plt

X = range(100)
Y = [value ** 2 for value in X]

plt.plot(X, Y)
plt.show()
```

Downloading the example code

You can download the sample code files for all Packt books that you have purchased from your account at `http://www.packtpub.com`. If you purchased this book elsewhere, you can visit `http://www.packtpub.com/support` and register to have the files e-mailed directly to you.

Assuming that you installed Python and matplotlib, you can now use Python to interpret this script. If you are not familiar with Python, this is indeed a Python script we have there! In a command terminal, run the script in the directory where you saved `plot.py` with the following command:

```
python plot.py
```

Doing so will open a window as shown in the following screenshot:

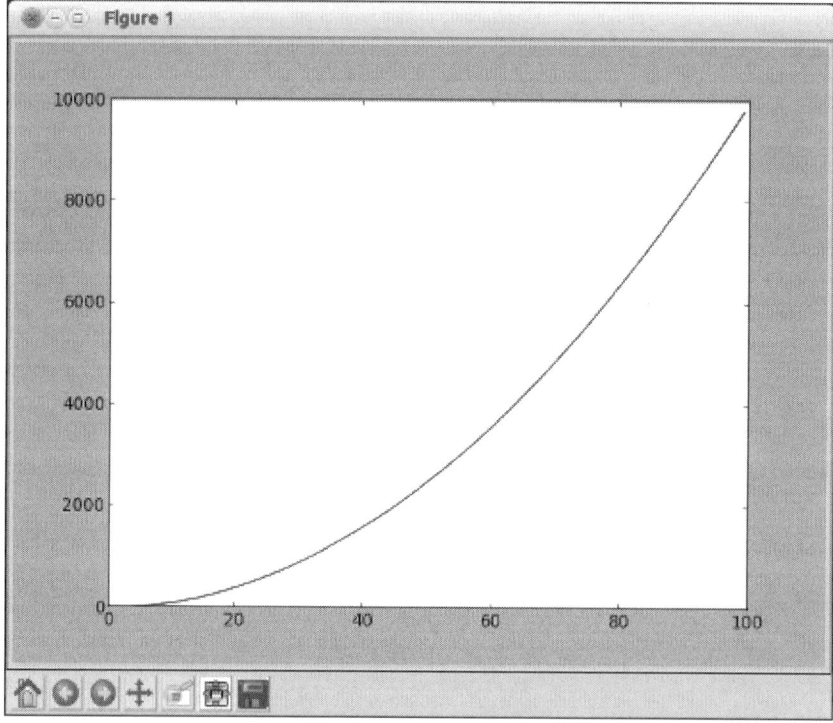

The window shows the curve *Y = X ** 2* with `X` in the [0, 99] range. As you might have noticed, the window has several icons, some of which are as follows:

- : This icon opens a dialog, allowing you to save the graph as a picture file. You can save it as a bitmap picture or a vector picture.

- [icon]: This icon allows you to translate and scale the graphics. Click on it and then move the mouse over the graph. Clicking on the left button of the mouse will translate the graph according to the mouse movements. Clicking on the right button of the mouse will modify the scale of the graphics.
- [icon]: This icon will restore the graph to its initial state, canceling any translation or scaling you might have applied before.

How it works...

Assuming that you are not very familiar with Python yet, let's analyze the script demonstrated in the previous section.

The first line tells Python that we are using the `matplotlib.pyplot` module. To save on a bit of typing, we make the name `plt` equivalent to `matplotlib.pyplot`. This is a very common practice that you will see in matplotlib code.

The second line creates a list named `X`, with all the integer values from 0 to 99. The range function is used to generate consecutive numbers. You can run the interactive Python interpreter and type the command `range(100)` if you use Python 2, or the command `list(range(100))` if you use Python 3. This will display the list of all the integer values from 0 to 99. In both versions, `sum(range(100))` will compute the sum of the integers from 0 to 99.

The third line creates a list named `Y`, with all the values from the list `X` squared. Building a new list by applying a function to each member of another list is a Python idiom, named **list comprehension**. The list `Y` will contain the squared values of the list `X` in the same order. So `Y` will contain 0, 1, 4, 9, 16, 25, and so on.

The fourth line plots a curve, where the x coordinates of the curve's points are given in the list `X`, and the y coordinates of the curve's points are given in the list `Y`. Note that the names of the lists can be anything you like.

The last line shows a result, which you will see on the window while running the script.

There's more...

So what we have learned so far? Unlike plotting packages like gnuplot, matplotlib is not a command interpreter specialized for the purpose of plotting. Unlike Matlab, matplotlib is not an integrated environment for plotting either. matplotlib is a Python module for plotting. Figures are described with Python scripts, relying on a (fairly large) set of functions provided by matplotlib.

Thus, the philosophy behind matplotlib is to take advantage of an existing language, Python. The rationale is that Python is a complete, well-designed, general purpose programming language. Combining matplotlib with other packages does not involve tricks and hacks, just Python code. This is because there are numerous packages for Python for pretty much any task. For instance, to plot data stored in a database, you would use a database package to read the data and feed it to matplotlib. To generate a large batch of statistical graphics, you would use a scientific computing package such as SciPy and Python's I/O modules.

Thus, unlike many plotting packages, matplotlib is very orthogonal—it does plotting and only plotting. If you want to read inputs from a file or do some simple intermediary calculations, you will have to use Python modules and some glue code to make it happen. Fortunately, Python is a very popular language, easy to master and with a large user base. Little by little, we will demonstrate the power of this approach.

Using NumPy

NumPy is not required to use matplotlib. However, many matplotlib tricks, code samples, and examples use NumPy. A short introduction to NumPy usage will show you the reason.

Getting ready

Along with having Python and matplotlib installed, you also have NumPy installed. You have a text editor and a command terminal.

How to do it...

Let's plot another curve, `sin(x)`, with x in the *[0, 2 * pi]* interval. The only difference with the preceding script is the part where we generate the point coordinates. Type and save the following script as `sin-1.py`:

```
import math
import matplotlib.pyplot as plt

T = range(100)
X = [(2 * math.pi * t) / len(T) for t in T]
Y = [math.sin(value) for value in X]

plt.plot(X, Y)
plt.show()
```

Then, type and save the following script as `sin-2.py`:

```
import numpy as np
import matplotlib.pyplot as plt
```

```
X = np.linspace(0, 2 * np.pi, 100)
Y = np.sin(X)

plt.plot(X, Y)
plt.show()
```

Running either `sin-1.py` or `sin-2.py` will show the following graph exactly:

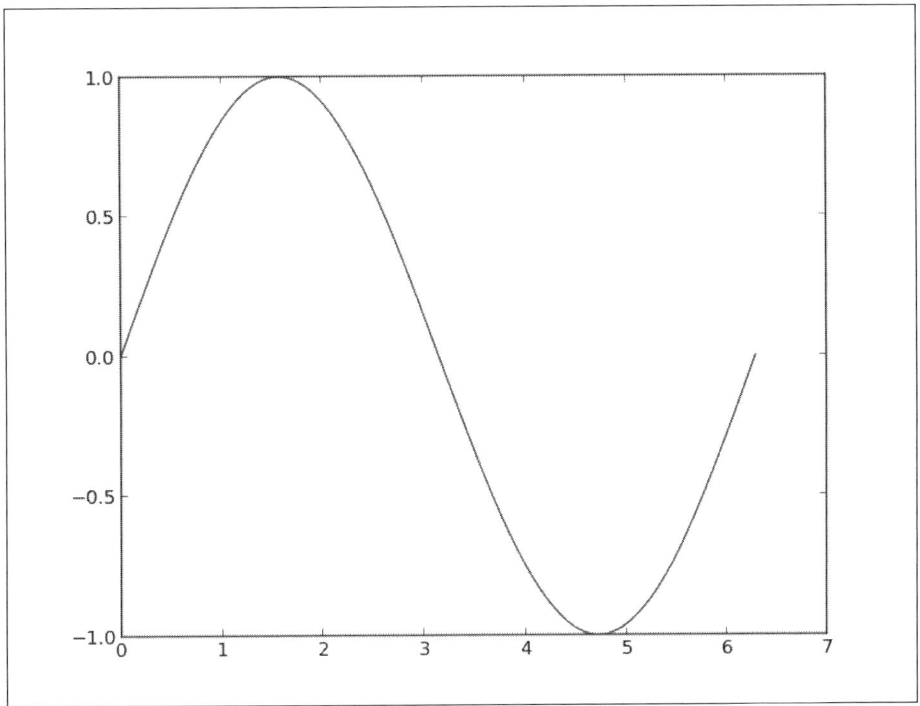

How it works...

The first script, `sin-1.py`, generates the coordinates for a sinusoid using only Python's standard library. The following points describe the steps we performed in the script in the previous section:

1. We created a list `T` with numbers from 0 to 99—our curve will be drawn with 100 points.
2. We computed the x coordinates by simply rescaling the values stored in `T` so that x goes from 0 to 2 pi (the `range()` built-in function can only generate integer values).
3. As in the first example, we generated the y coordinates.

The second script `sin-2.py`, does exactly the same job as `sin-1.py`—the results are identical. However, `sin-2.py` is slightly shorter and easier to read since it uses the NumPy package.

NumPy is a Python package for scientific computing. matplotlib can work without NumPy, but using NumPy will save you lots of time and effort. The NumPy package provides a powerful multidimensional array object and a host of functions to manipulate it.

The NumPy package

In `sin-2.py`, the `X` list is now a one-dimensional NumPy array with 100 evenly spaced values between 0 and 2 pi. This is the purpose of the function `numpy.linspace`. This is arguably more convenient than computing as we did in `sin-1.py`. The `Y` list is also a one-dimensional NumPy array whose values are computed from the coordinates of `X`. NumPy functions work on whole arrays as they would work on a single value. Again, there is no need to compute those values explicitly one-by-one, as we did in `sin-1.py`. We have a shorter yet readable code compared to the pure Python version.

There's more...

NumPy can perform operations on whole arrays at once, saving us much work when generating curve coordinates. Moreover, using NumPy will most likely lead to much faster code than the pure Python equivalent. Easier to read and faster code, what's not to like? The following is an example where we plot the binomial *x^2 -2x +1* in the `[-3,2]` interval using `200` points:

```
import numpy as np
import matplotlib.pyplot as plt

X = np.linspace(-3, 2, 200)
Y = X ** 2 - 2 * X + 1.

plt.plot(X, Y)
plt.show()
```

Running the preceding script will give us the result shown in the following graph:

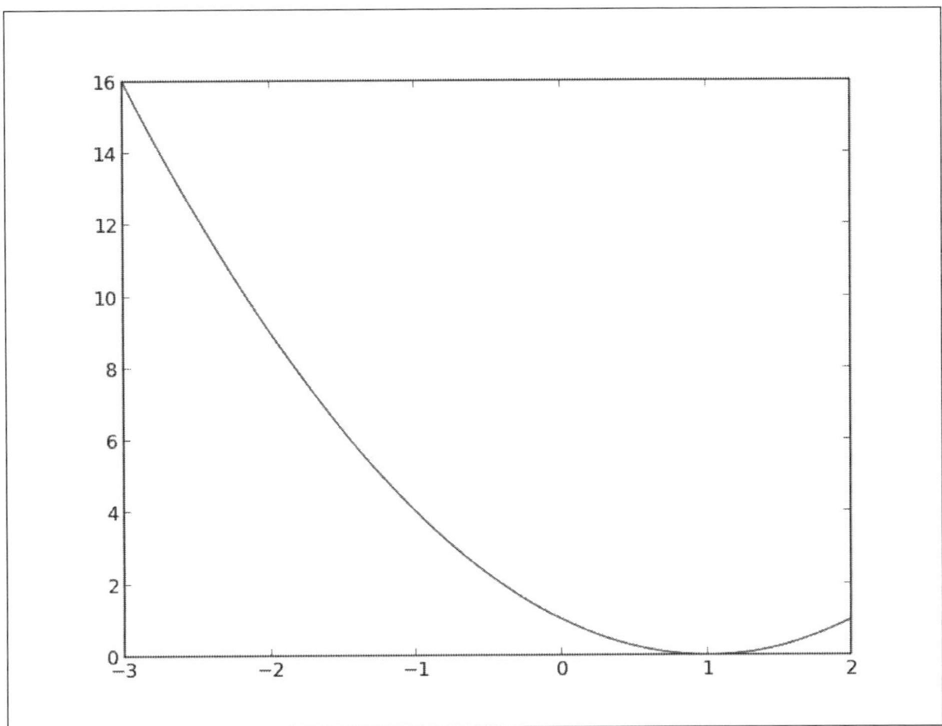

Again, we could have done the plotting in pure Python, but it would arguably not be as easy to read. Although matplotlib can be used without NumPy, the two make for a powerful combination.

Plotting multiple curves

One of the reasons we plot curves is to compare those curves. Are they matching? Where do they match? Where do they not match? Are they correlated? A graph can help to form a quick judgment for more thorough investigations.

How to do it...

Let's show both `sin(x)` and `cos(x)` in the [0, 2pi] interval as follows:

```
import numpy as np
import matplotlib.pyplot as plt

X = np.linspace(0, 2 * np.pi, 100)
```

```
Ya = np.sin(X)
Yb = np.cos(X)

plt.plot(X, Ya)
plt.plot(X, Yb)
plt.show()
```

The preceding script will give us the result shown in the following graph:

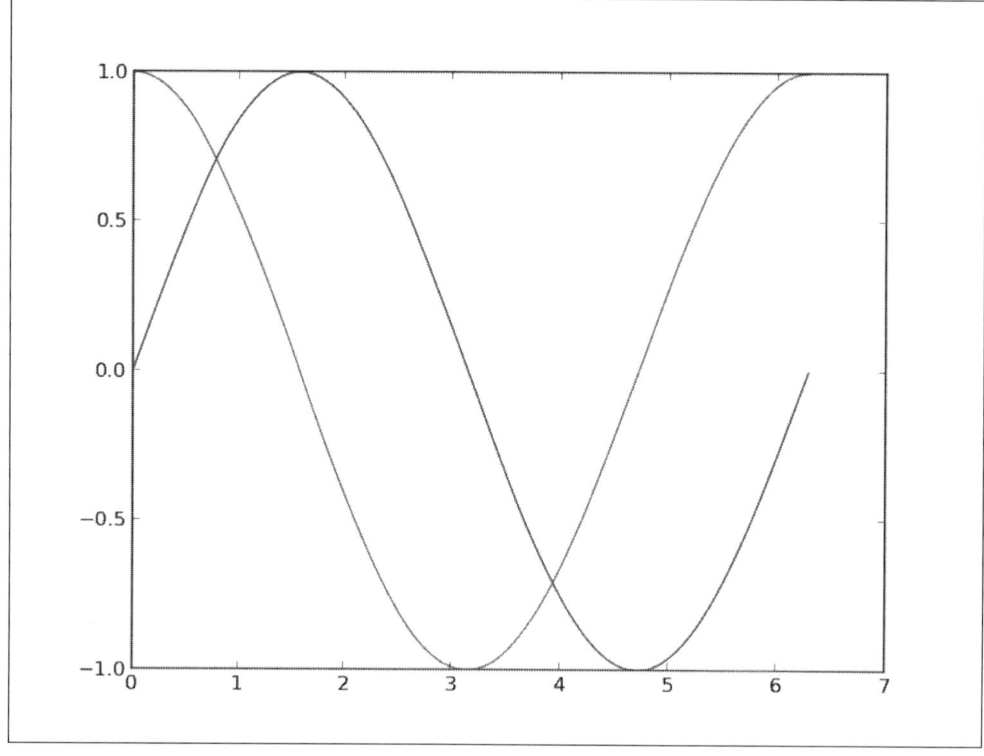

How it works...

The two curves show up with a different color automatically picked up by matplotlib. We use one function `call plt.plot()` for one curve; thus, we have to call `plt.plot()` here twice. However, we still have to call `plt.show()` only once. The functions `calls plt.plot(X, Ya)` and `plt.plot(X, Yb)` can be seen as declarations of intentions. We want to link those two sets of points with a distinct curve for each.

matplotlib will simply keep note of this intention but will not plot anything yet. The `plt.show()` curve, however, will signal that we want to plot what we have described so far.

There's more...

This **deferred rendering** mechanism is central to matplotlib. You can declare what you render as and when it suits you. The graph will be rendered only when you call `plt.show()`. To illustrate this, let's look at the following script, which renders a bell-shaped curve, and the slope of that curve for each of its points:

```
import numpy as np
import matplotlib.pyplot as plt

def plot_slope(X, Y):
  Xs = X[1:] - X[:-1]
  Ys = Y[1:] - Y[:-1]
  plt.plot(X[1:], Ys / Xs)

X = np.linspace(-3, 3, 100)
Y = np.exp(-X ** 2)

plt.plot(X, Y)
plot_slope(X, Y)

plt.show()
```

The preceding script will produce the following graph:

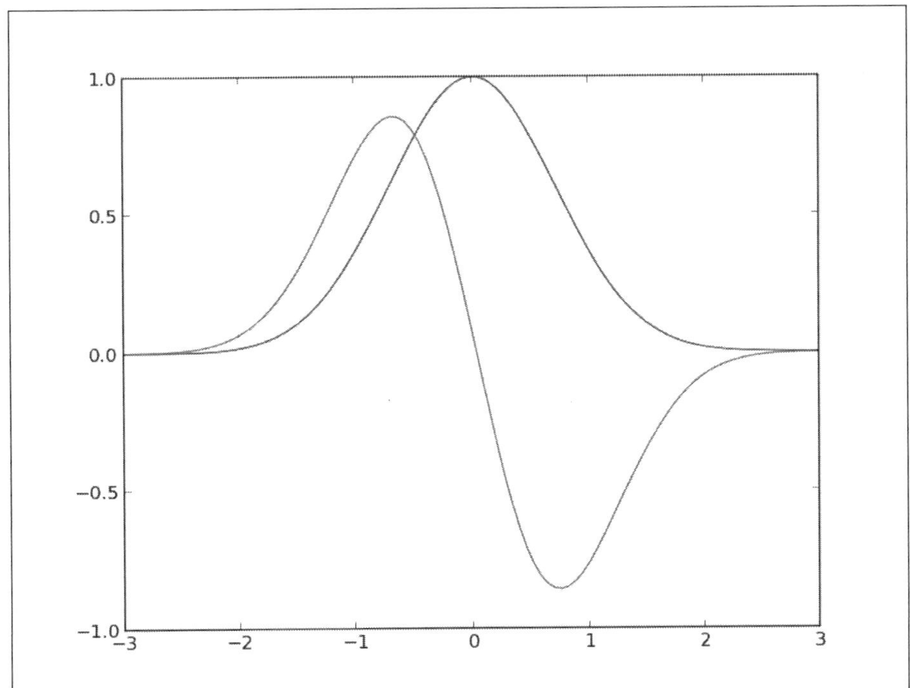

One of the function call, `plt.plot()`, is done inside the `plot_slope` function, which does not have any influence on the rendering of the graph as `plt.plot()` simply declares what we want to render, but does not execute the rendering yet. This is very useful when writing scripts for complex graphics with a lot of curves. You can use all the features of a proper programming language—loop, function calls, and so on— to compose a graph.

Plotting curves from file data

As explained earlier, matplotlib only handles plotting. If you want to plot data stored in a file, you will have to use Python code to read the file and extract the data you need.

How to do it...

Let's assume that we have time series stored in a plain text file named `my_data.txt` as follows:

```
0  0
1  1
2  4
4 16
5 25
6 36
```

A minimalistic pure Python approach to read and plot that data would go as follows:

```
import matplotlib.pyplot as plt

X, Y = [], []
for line in open('my_data.txt', 'r'):
  values = [float(s) for s in line.split()]
  X.append(values[0])
  Y.append(values[1])

plt.plot(X, Y)
plt.show()
```

This script, together with the data stored in `my_data.txt`, will produce the following graph:

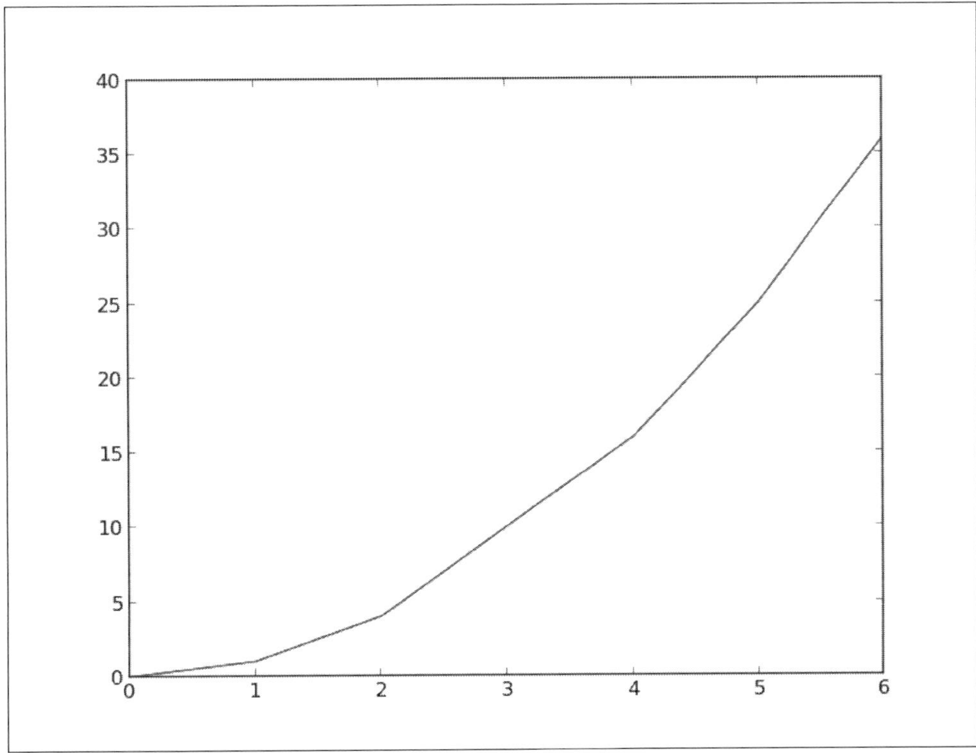

How it works...

The following are some explanations on how the preceding script works:

- The line `X, Y = [], []` initializes the list of coordinates `X` and `Y` as empty lists.
- The line `for line in open('my_data.txt', 'r')` defines a loop that will iterate each line of the text file `my_data.txt`. On each iteration, the current line extracted from the text file is stored as a string in the variable line.
- The line `values = [float(s) for s in line.split()]` splits the current line around empty characters to form a string of tokens. Those tokens are then interpreted as floating point values. Those values are stored in the list values.
- Then, in the two next lines, `X.append(values[0])` and `Y.append(values[1])`, the values stored in `values` are appended to the lists `X` and `Y`.

The following equivalent one-liner to read a text file may bring a smile to those more familiar with Python:

```
import matplotlib.pyplot as plt

with open('my_data.txt', 'r') as f:
  X, Y = zip(*[[float(s) for s in line.split()] for line in f])

plt.plot(X, Y)
plt.show()
```

There's more...

In our data loading code, note that there is no serious checking or error handling going on. In any case, one might remember that a good programmer is a lazy programmer. Indeed, since NumPy is so often used with matplotlib, why not use it here? Run the following script to enable NumPy:

```
import numpy as np
import matplotlib.pyplot as plt

data = np.loadtxt('my_data.txt')

plt.plot(data[:,0], data[:,1])
plt.show()
```

This is as short as the one-liner shown in the preceding section, yet easier to read, and it will handle many error cases that our pure Python code does not handle. The following point describes the preceding script:

- The `numpy.loadtxt()` function reads a text file and returns a 2D array. With NumPy, 2D arrays are not a list of lists, they are true, full-blown matrices.
- The variable `data` is a NumPy 2D array, which give us the benefit of being able to manipulate rows and columns of a matrix as a 1D array. Indeed, in the line `plt.plot(data[:,0], data[:,1])`, we give the first column of data as x coordinates and the second column of data as y coordinates. This notation is specific to NumPy.

Along with making the code shorter and simpler, using NumPy brings additional advantages. For large files, using NumPy will be noticeably faster (the NumPy module is mostly written in C), and storing the whole dataset as a NumPy array can save memory as well. Finally, using NumPy allows you to support other common file formats (CVS and Matlab) for numerical data without much effort.

As a way to demonstrate all that we have seen so far, let's consider the following task. A file contains N columns of values, describing N-1 curves. The first column contains the x coordinates, the second column contains the y coordinates of the first curve, the third column contains the y coordinates of the second curve, and so on. We want to display those N-1 curves. We will do so by using the following code:

```
import numpy as np
import matplotlib.pyplot as plt

data = np.loadtxt('my_data.txt')
for column in data.T:
  plt.plot(data[:,0], column)

plt.show()
```

The file `my_data.txt` should contain the following content:

```
0 0 6
1 1 5
2 4 4
4 16 3
5 25 2
6 36 1
```

Then we get the following graph:

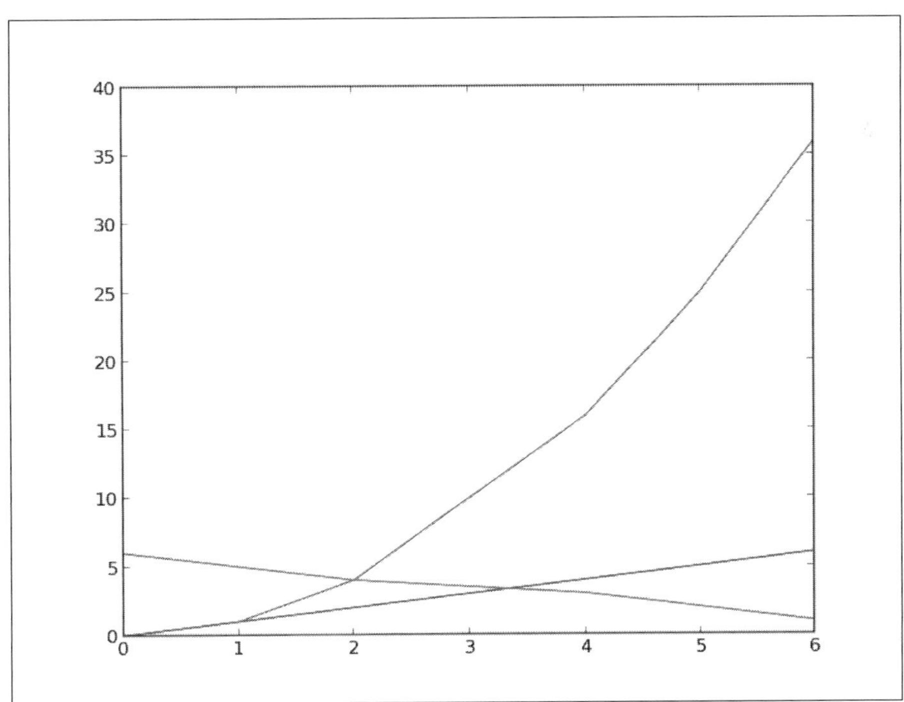

We did the job with little effort by exploiting two tricks. In NumPy notation, `data.T` is a transposed view of the 2D array data—rows are seen as columns and columns are seen as rows. Also, we can iterate over the rows of a multidimensional array by doing `for row in data`. Thus, doing `for column in data.T` will iterate over the columns of an array. With a few lines of code, we have a fairly general plotting generic script.

Plotting points

When displaying a curve, we implicitly assume that one point follows another—our data is the time series. Of course, this does not always have to be the case. One point of the data can be independent from the other. A simple way to represent such kind of data is to simply show the points without linking them.

How to do it...

The following script displays 1024 points whose coordinates are drawn randomly from the [0,1] interval:

```
import numpy as np
import matplotlib.pyplot as plt

data = np.random.rand(1024, 2)

plt.scatter(data[:,0], data[:,1])
plt.show()
```

The preceding script will produce the following graph:

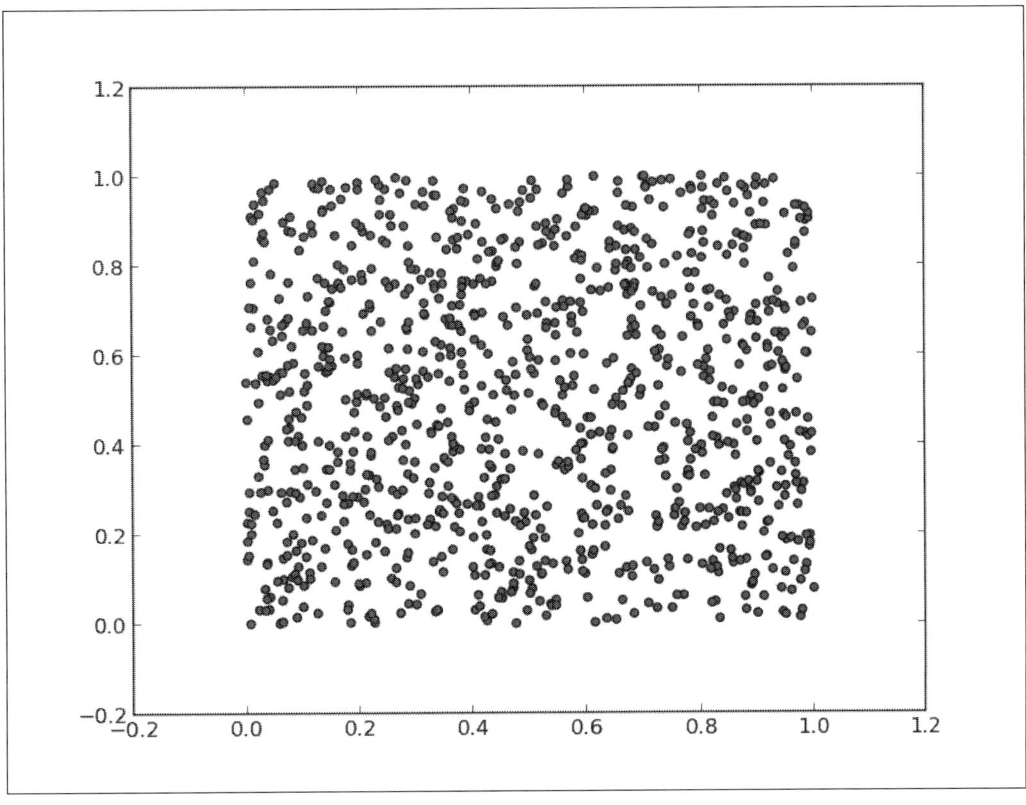

How it works...

The function `plt.scatter()` works exactly like `plt.plot()`, taking the x and y coordinates of points as input parameters. However, each point is simply shown with one marker. Don't be fooled by this simplicity—`plt.scatter()` is a rich command. By playing with its many optional parameters, we can achieve many different effects. We will cover this in *Chapter 2, Customizing the Color and Styles*, and *Chapter 3, Working with Annotations*.

Plotting bar charts

Bar charts are a common staple of plotting package, and even matplotlib has them.

How to do it...

The dedicated function for bar charts is `pyplot.bar()`. We will enable this function by executing the following script:

```
import matplotlib.pyplot as plt

data = [5., 25., 50., 20.]

plt.bar(range(len(data)), data)
plt.show()
```

The preceding script will produce the following graph:

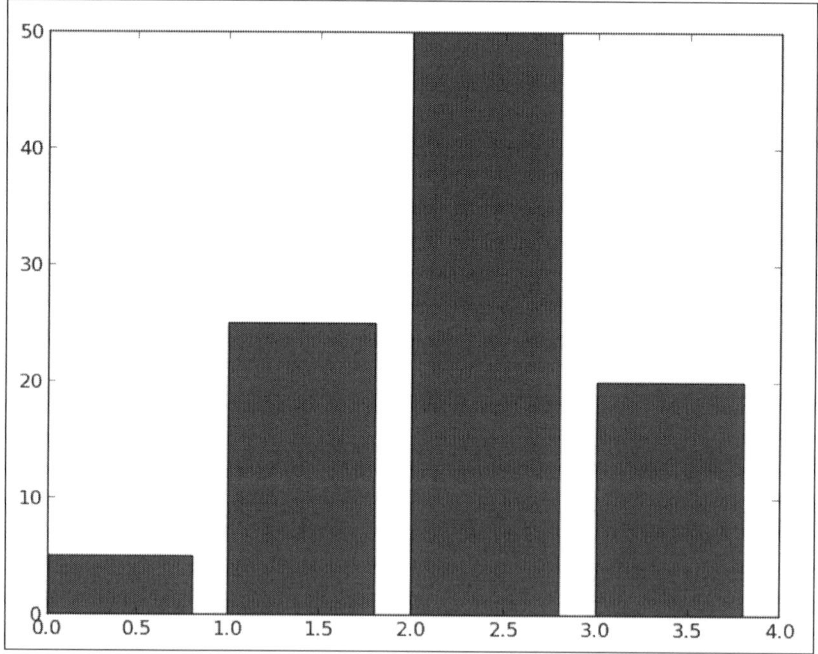

How it works...

For each value in the list data, one vertical bar is shown. The `pyplot.bar()` function receives two arguments—the x coordinate for each bar and the height of each bar. Here, we use the coordinates 0, 1, 2, and so on, for each bar, which is the purpose of `range(len(data))`.

There's more...

Through an optional parameter, `pyplot.bar()` provides a way to control the bar's thickness. Moreover, we can also obtain horizontal bars using the twin brother of `pyplot.bar()`, that is, `pyplot.barh()`.

The thickness of a bar

By default, a bar will have a thickness of 0.8 units. Because we put a bar at each unit length, we have a gap of 0.2 between them. You can, of course, fiddle with this thickness parameter. For instance, by setting it to 1:

```
import matplotlib.pyplot as plt

data = [5., 25., 50., 20.]

plt.bar(range(len(data)), data, width = 1.)
plt.show()
```

The preceding minimalistic script will produce the following graph:

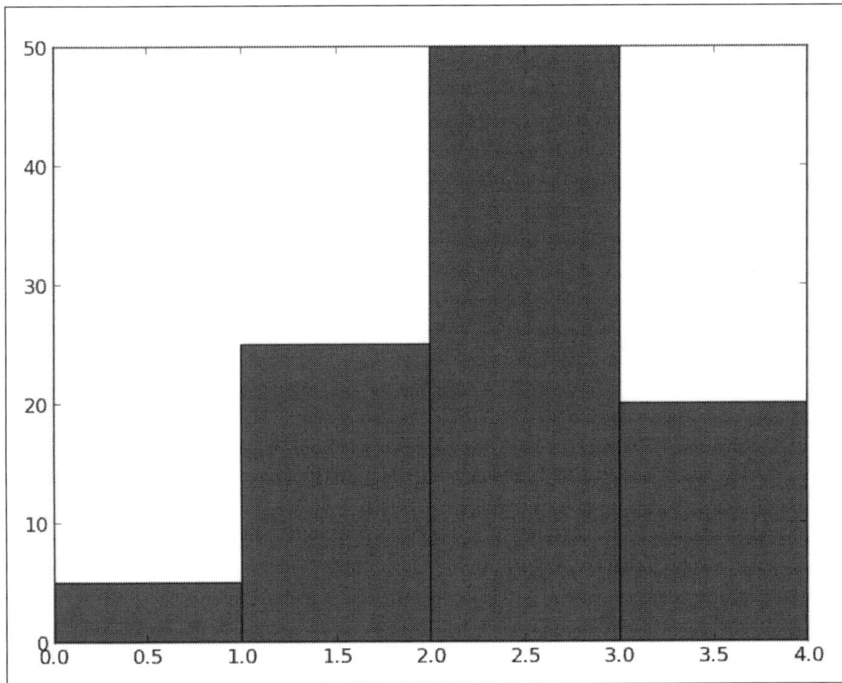

Now, the bars have no gap between them. The matplotlib bar chart function `pyplot.bar()` will not handle the positioning and thickness of the bars. The programmer is in charge. This flexibility allows you to create many variations on bar charts.

Horizontal bars

If you are more into horizontal bars, use the `barh()` function, which is the strict equivalent of `bar()`, apart from giving horizontal rather than vertical bars:

```
import matplotlib.pyplot as plt

data = [5., 25., 50., 20.]

plt.barh(range(len(data)), data)
plt.show()
```

The preceding script will produce the following graph:

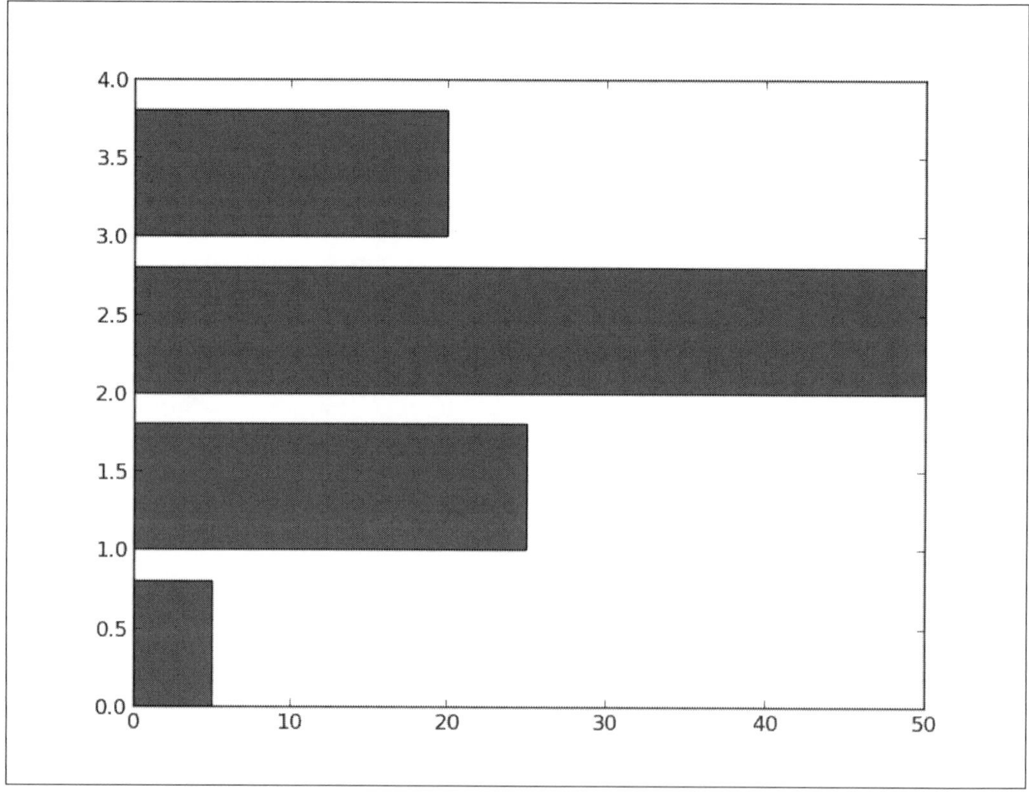

Plotting multiple bar charts

When comparing several quantities and when changing one variable, we might want a bar chart where we have bars of one color for one quantity value.

How to do it...

We can plot multiple bar charts by playing with the thickness and the positions of the bars as follows:

```
import numpy as np
import matplotlib.pyplot as plt

data = [[5., 25., 50., 20.],
  [4., 23., 51., 17.],
  [6., 22., 52., 19.]]

X = np.arange(4)
plt.bar(X + 0.00, data[0], color = 'b', width = 0.25)
plt.bar(X + 0.25, data[1], color = 'g', width = 0.25)
plt.bar(X + 0.50, data[2], color = 'r', width = 0.25)

plt.show()
```

The preceding script will produce the following graph:

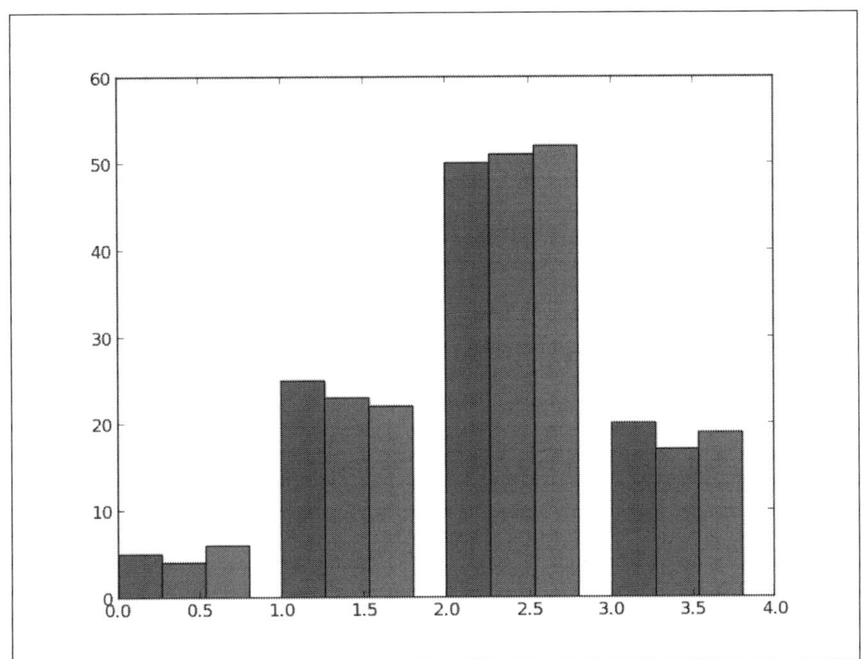

How it works...

The `data` variable contains three series of four values. The preceding script will show three bar charts of four bars. The bars will have a thickness of 0.25 units. Each bar chart will be shifted 0.25 units from the previous one. Color has been added for clarity. This topic will be detailed in *Chapter 2, Customizing the Color and Styles*.

There's more...

The code shown in the preceding section is quite tedious as we repeat ourselves by shifting the three bar charts manually. We can do this better by using the following code:

```
import numpy as np
import matplotlib.pyplot as plt

data = [[5., 25., 50., 20.],
  [4., 23., 51., 17.],
  [6., 22., 52., 19.]]

color_list = ['b', 'g', 'r']
gap = .8 / len(data)
for i, row in enumerate(data):
  X = np.arange(len(row))
  plt.bar(X + i * gap, row,
    width = gap,
    color = color_list[i % len(color_list)])

plt.show()
```

Here, we iterate over each row of data with the loop `for i, row in enumerate(data)`. The iterator `enumerate` returns both the current row and its index. Generating the position of each bar for one bar chart is done with a list comprehension. This script will produce the same result as the previous script, but would not require any change if we add rows or columns of data.

Plotting stacked bar charts

Stacked bar charts are of course possible by using a special parameter from the `pyplot.bar()` function.

How to do it...

The following script stacks two bar charts on each other:

```
import matplotlib.pyplot as plt

A = [5., 30., 45., 22.]
B = [5., 25., 50., 20.]

X = range(4)

plt.bar(X, A, color = 'b')
plt.bar(X, B, color = 'r', bottom = A)
plt.show()
```

The preceding script will produce the following graph:

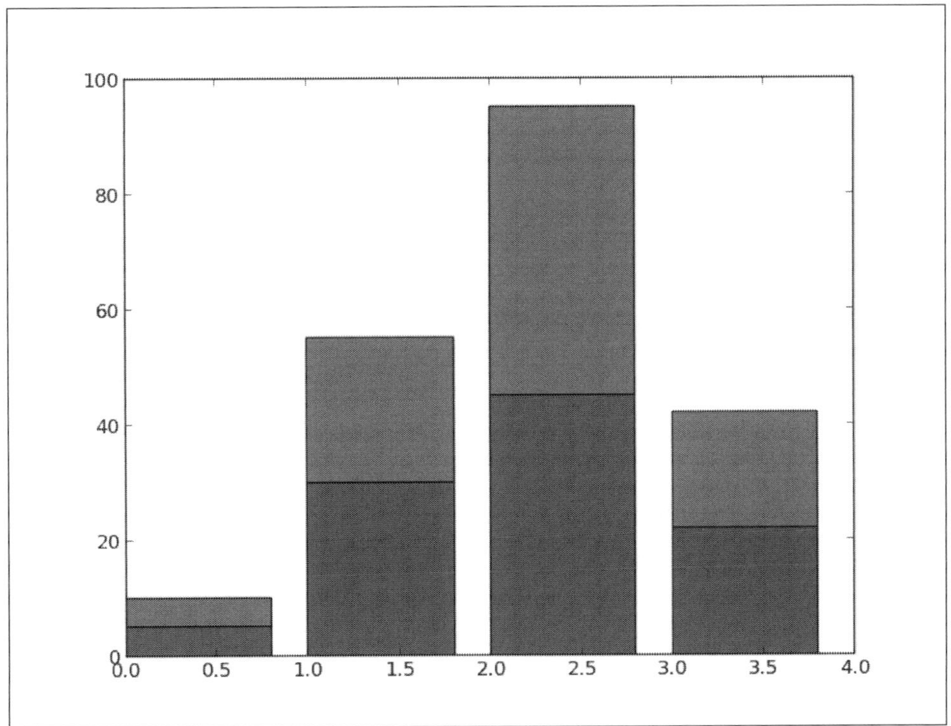

How it works...

The optional `bottom` parameter of the `pyplot.bar()` function allows you to specify a starting value for a bar. Instead of running from zero to a value, it will go from the bottom to value. The first call to `pyplot.bar()` plots the blue bars. The second call to `pyplot.bar()` plots the red bars, with the bottom of the red bars being at the top of the blue bars.

There's more...

When stacking more than two set of values, the code gets less pretty as follows:

```
import numpy as np
import matplotlib.pyplot as plt

A = np.array([5., 30., 45., 22.])
B = np.array([5., 25., 50., 20.])
C = np.array([1.,  2.,  1.,  1.])
X = np.arange(4)

plt.bar(X, A, color = 'b')
plt.bar(X, B, color = 'g', bottom = A)
plt.bar(X, C, color = 'r', bottom = A + B)

plt.show()
```

For the third bar chart, we have to compute the bottom values as `A + B`, the coefficient-wise sum of A and B. Using NumPy helps to keep the code compact but readable. This code is, however, fairly repetitive and works for only three stacked bar charts. We can do better using the following code:

```
import numpy as np
import matplotlib.pyplot as plt

data = np.array([[5., 30., 45., 22.],
  [5., 25., 50., 20.],
  [1.,  2.,  1.,  1.]]

color_list = ['b', 'g', 'r']

X = np.arange(data.shape[1])
for i in range(data.shape[0]):
  plt.bar(X, data[i],
    bottom = np.sum(data[:i], axis = 0),
    color = color_list[i % len(color_list)])

plt.show()
```

Here, we store the data in a NumPy array, one row for one bar chart. We iterate over each row of data. For the ith row, the `bottom` parameter receives the sum of all the rows before the ith row. Writing the script this way, we can stack as many bar charts as we wish with minimal effort when changing the input data.

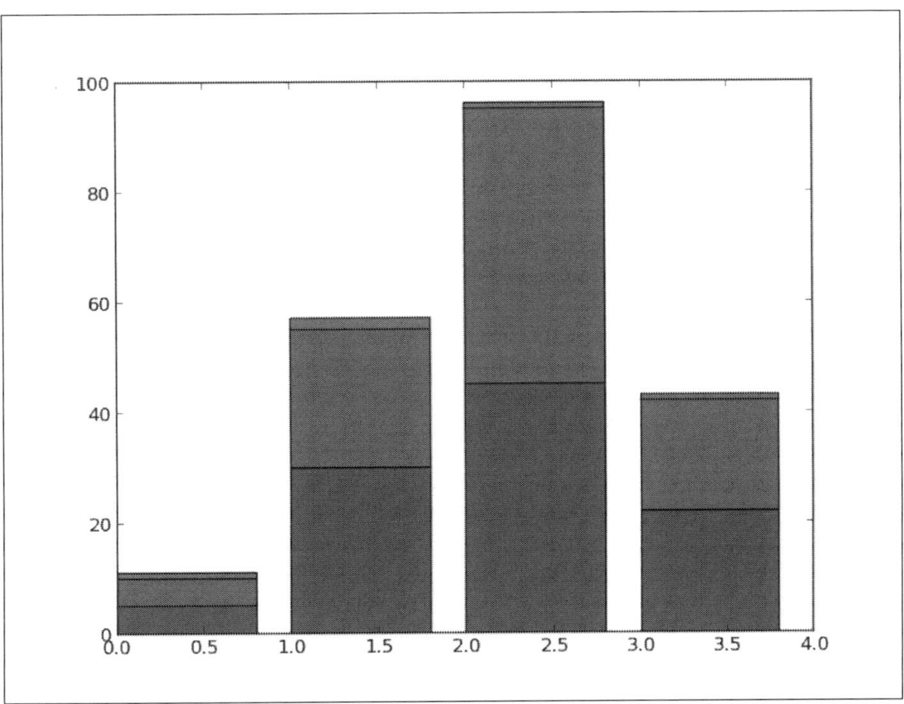

Plotting back-to-back bar charts

A simple but useful trick is to display two bar charts back-to-back at the same time. Think of an age pyramid of a population, showing the number of people within different age ranges. On the left side, we show the male population, while on the right we show the female population.

How to do it...

The idea is to have two bar charts, using a simple trick, that is, the length/height of one bar can be negative!

```
import numpy as np
import matplotlib.pyplot as plt

women_pop = np.array([5., 30., 45., 22.])
men_pop     = np.array( [5., 25., 50., 20.])
```

```
X = np.arange(4)

plt.barh(X, women_pop, color = 'r')
plt.barh(X, -men_pop, color = 'b')
plt.show()
```

The preceding script will produce the following graph:

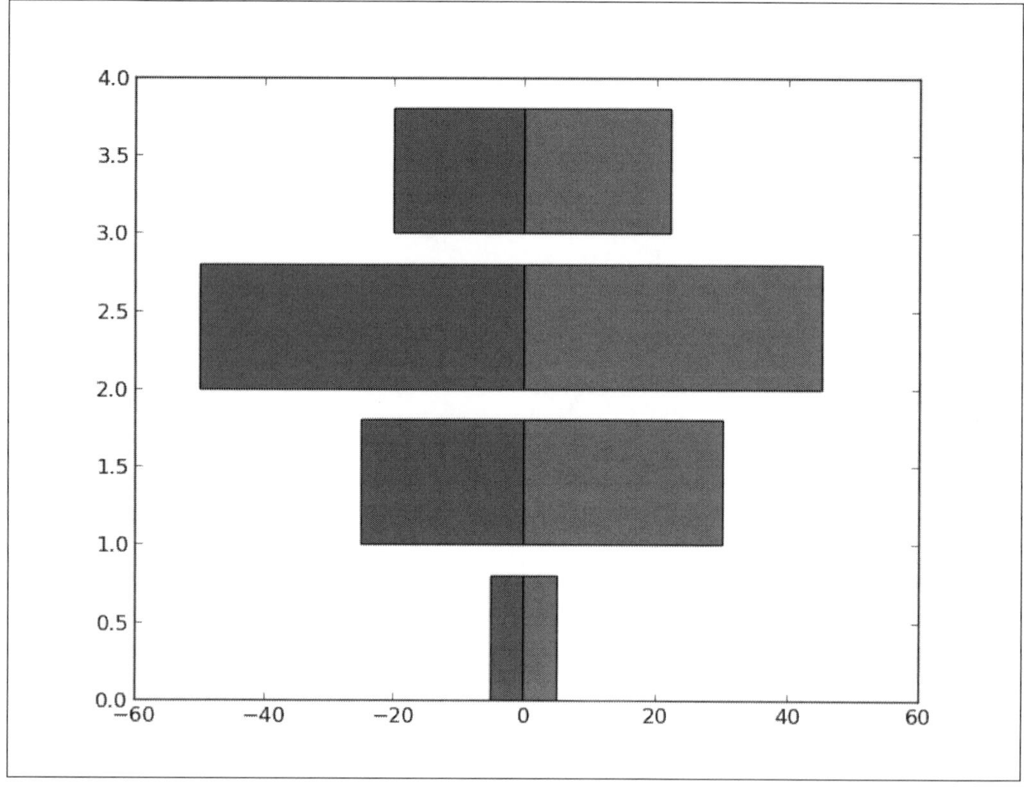

How it works...

The bar chart for the female population (in red) is plotted as usual. However, the bar chart for the male population (in blue) has its bar extending to the left rather than the right. Indeed, the lengths of the bars for the blue bar chart are negative values. Rather than editing the input values, we use a list comprehension to negate values for the male population bar chart.

Plotting pie charts

To compare the relative importance of quantities, nothing like a good old pie—**pie chart**, that is.

How to do it...

The dedicated pie-plotting function `pyplot.pie()` will do the job. We will use this function in the following code:

```
import matplotlib.pyplot as plt

data = [5, 25, 50, 20]

  plt.pie(data)
plt.show()
```

The preceding simple script will display the following pie diagram:

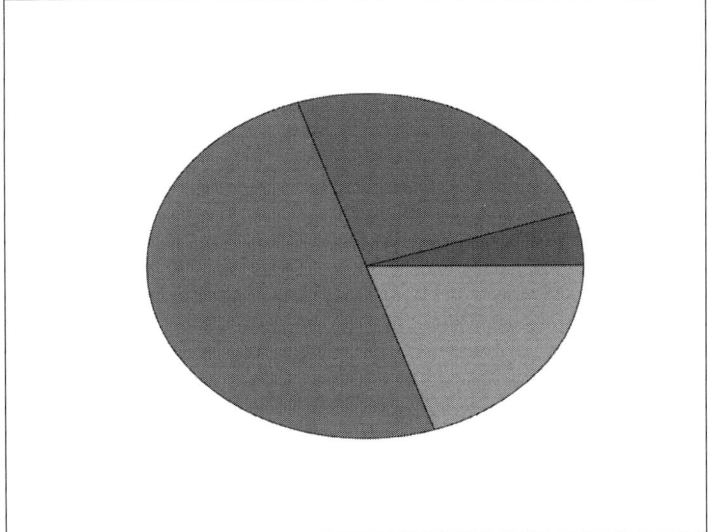

How it works...

The `pyplot.pie()` function simply takes a list of values as the input. Note that the input data is a list; it could be a NumPy array. You do not have to adjust the data so that it adds up to 1 or 100. You just have to give values to matplolib and it will automatically compute the relative areas of the pie chart.

Plotting histograms

Histograms are graphical representations of a probability distribution. In fact, a histogram is just a specific kind of a bar chart. We could easily use matplotlib's bar chart function and do some statistics to generate histograms. However, histograms are so useful that matplotlib provides a function just for them. In this recipe, we are going to see how to use this histogram function.

How to do it...

The following script draws `1000` values from a normal distribution and then generates histograms with 20 bins:

```
import numpy as np
import matplotlib.pyplot as plt

X = np.random.randn(1000)

plt.hist(X, bins = 20)
plt.show()
```

The histogram will change a bit each time we run the script as the dataset is randomly generated. The preceding script will display the following graph:

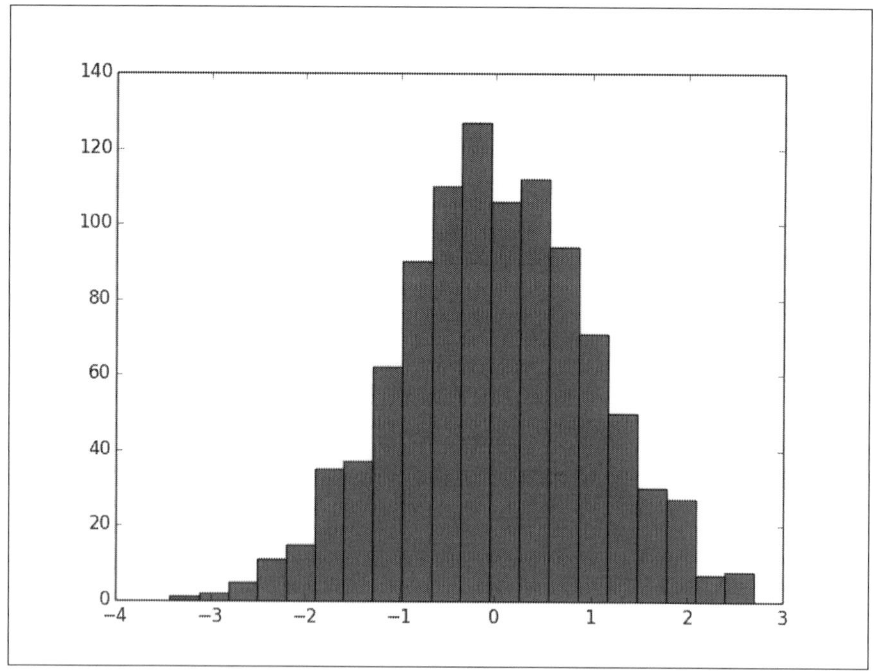

How it works...

The `pyplot.hist()` function takes a list of values as the input. The range of the values will be divided into equal-sized bins (10 bins by default). The `pyplot.hist()` function will generate a bar chart, one bar for one bin. The height of one bar is the number of values following in the corresponding bin. The number of bins is determined by the optional parameter bins. By setting the optional parameter `normed` to `True`, the bar height is normalized and the sum of all bar heights is equal to 1.

Plotting boxplots

Boxplot allows you to compare distributions of values by conveniently showing the median, quartiles, maximum, and minimum of a set of values.

How to do it...

The following script shows a boxplot for 100 random values drawn from a normal distribution:

```
import numpy as np
import matplotlib.pyplot as plt

data = np.random.randn(100)

plt.boxplot(data)
plt.show()
```

A boxplot will appear that represents the samples we drew from the random distribution. Since the code uses a randomly generated dataset, the resulting figure will change slightly every time the script is run.

The preceding script will display the following graph:

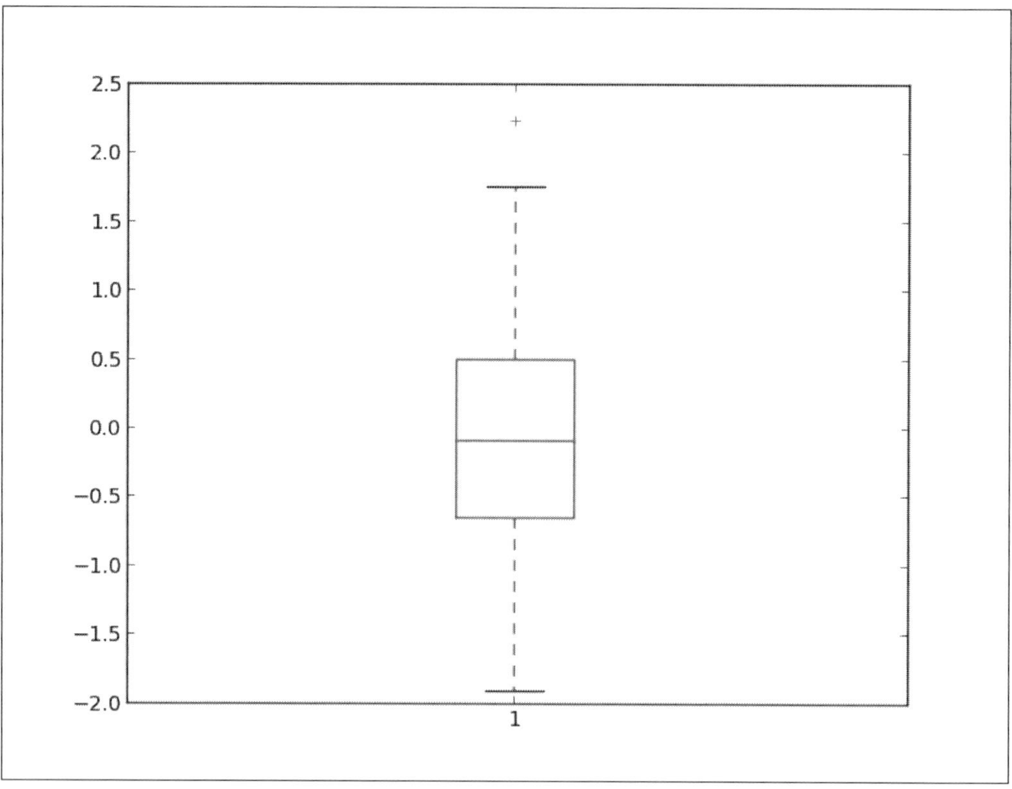

How it works...

The `data = [random.gauss(0., 1.) for i in range(100)]` variable generates 100 values drawn from a normal distribution. For demonstration purposes, such values are typically read from a file or computed from other data. The `plot.boxplot()` function takes a set of values and computes the mean, median, and other statistical quantities on its own. The following points describe the preceding boxplot:

- The red bar is the median of the distribution.
- The blue box includes 50 percent of the data from the lower quartile to the upper quartile. Thus, the box is centered on the median of the data.
- The lower whisker extends to the lowest value within 1.5 IQR from the lower quartile.
- The upper whisker extends to the highest value within 1.5 IQR from the upper quartile.
- Values further from the whiskers are shown with a cross marker.

There's more...

To show more than one boxplot in a single graph, calling `pyplot.boxplot()` once for each boxplot is not going to work. It will simply draw the boxplots over each other, making a messy, unreadable graph. However, we can draw several boxplots with just one single call to `pyplot.boxplot()` as follows:

```
import numpy as np
import matplotlib.pyplot as plt

data = np.random.randn(100, 5)

plt.boxplot(data)
plt.show()
```

The preceding script displays the following graph:

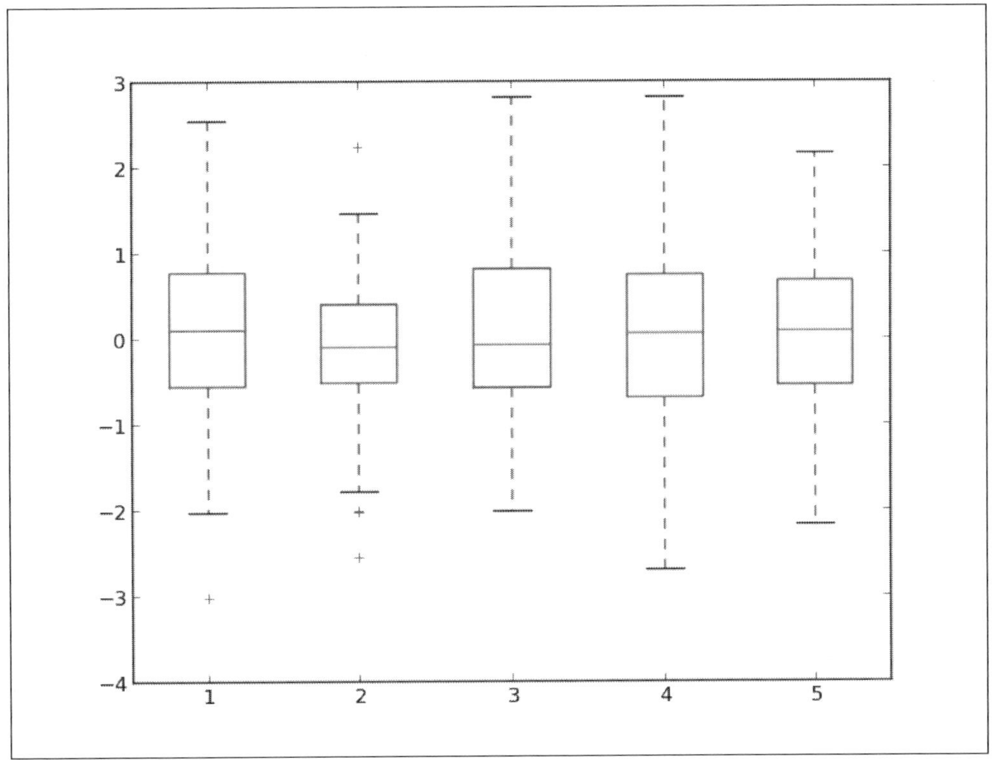

The `pyplot.boxplot()` function accepts a list of lists as the input, rendering a boxplot for each sublist.

Plotting triangulations

Triangulations arise when dealing with spatial locations. Apart from showing distances between points and neighborhood relationships, triangulation plots can be a convenient way to represent maps. matplotlib provides a fair amount of support for triangulations.

How to do it...

As in the preceding examples, the following few lines of code are enough:

```
import numpy as np
import matplotlib.pyplot as plt
import matplotlib.tri as tri

data = np.random.rand(100, 2)

triangles = tri.Triangulation(data[:,0], data[:,1])

plt.triplot(triangles)
plt.show()
```

Every time the script is run, you will see a different triangulation as the cloud of points that is triangulated is generated randomly.

The preceding script displays the following graph:

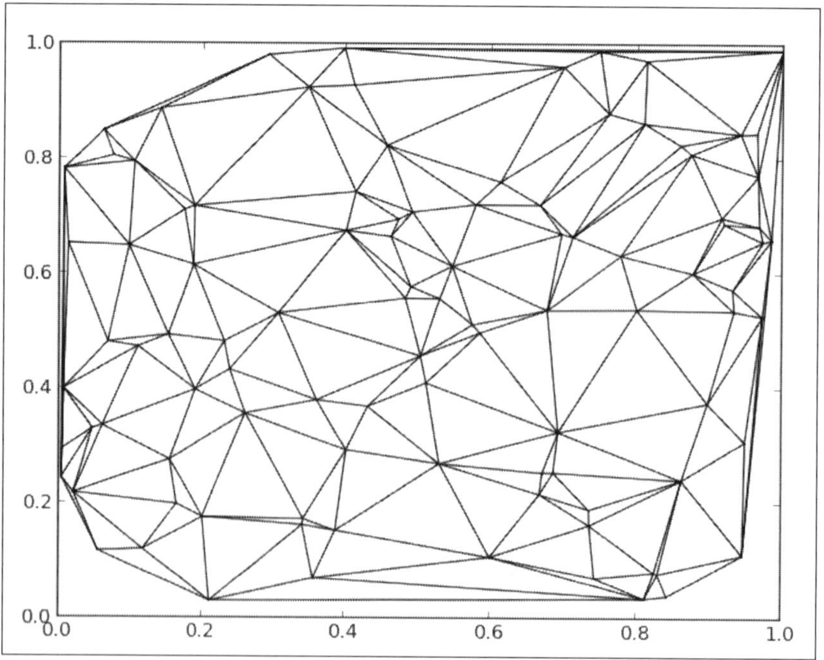

How it works...

We import the `matplotlib.tri` module, which provides helper functions to compute triangulations from points. In this example, for demonstration purpose, we generate a random cloud of points using the following code:

```
data = np.random.rand(100, 2)
```

We compute a triangulation and store it in the triangles' variable with the help of the following code:

```
triangles = tri.Triangulation(data[:,0], data[:,1])
```

The `pyplot.triplot()` function simply takes triangles as inputs and displays the triangulation result.

2

Customizing the Color and Styles

In this chapter, we will cover:

- Defining your own colors
- Using custom colors for scatter plots
- Using custom colors for bar charts
- Using custom colors for pie charts
- Using custom colors for boxplots
- Using colormaps for scatter plots
- Using colormaps for bar charts
- Controlling a line pattern and thickness
- Controlling a fill pattern
- Controlling a marker's style
- Controlling a marker's size
- Creating your own markers
- Getting more control over markers
- Creating your own color scheme

Introduction

All the plots available with matplotlib come with their default styles. While this is convenient for prototyping, our finalized graph will require some departure from the default styles. You might need to use gray levels only, or follow an existing color scheme, or more generally, an existing visual chart. matplotlib has been designed with flexibility in mind. It is easy to adapt the style of a matplotlib figure, as the recipes of this chapter will illustrate.

Defining your own colors

The default colors used by matplotlib are rather bland. We might have our own preferences of what convenient colors are. We might want to have figures that follow a predefined color scheme so that they fit well within a document or a web page. More pragmatically, we might simply have to make figures for a document that will be printed on a black-and-white printer. In this recipe, we are going to see how to define our own colors.

Getting ready

There are multiple ways to define colors in matplotlib. Some of them are as follows:

- **Triplets**: These colors can be described as a real value triplet—the red, blue, and green components of a color. The components have to be in the [0, 1] interval. Thus, the Python syntax `(1.0, 0.0, 0.0)` will code a pure, bright red, while `(1.0, 0.0, 1.0)` appears as a strong pink.
- **Quadruplets**: These work as triplets, and the fourth component defines a transparency value. This value should also be in the [0, 1] interval. When rendering a figure to a picture file, using transparent colors allows for making figures that blend with a background. This is especially useful when making figures that will slide or end up on a web page.
- **Predefined names**: matplotlib will interpret standard HTML color names as an actual color. For instance, the string `red` will be accepted as a color and will be interpreted as a bright red. A few colors have a one-letter alias, which is shown in the following table:

Alias	Colors
b	Blue
g	Green
r	Red
c	Cyan
m	Magenta

Alias	Colors
y	Yellow
k	Black
w	White

- **HTML color strings**: matplotlib can interpret HTML color strings as actual colors. Such strings are defined as `#RRGGBB` where RR, GG, and BB are the 8-bit values for the red, green, and blue components in hexadecimal.
- **Gray-level strings**: matplotlib will interpret a string representation of a floating point value as a shade of gray, such as `0.75` for a medium light gray.

How to do it...

Setting the color of a curve plot is done by setting the parameter color (or the equivalent shortcut `c`) of the `pyplot.plot()` function as follows:

```
import numpy as np
import matplotlib.pyplot as plt

def pdf(X, mu, sigma):
  a = 1. / (sigma * np.sqrt(2. * np.pi))
  b = -1. / (2. * sigma ** 2)
  return a * np.exp(b * (X - mu) ** 2)

X = np.linspace(-6, 6, 1000)

for i in range(5):
  samples = np.random.standard_normal(50)
  mu, sigma = np.mean(samples), np.std(samples)
  plt.plot(X, pdf(X, mu, sigma), color = '.75')

plt.plot(X, pdf(X, 0., 1.), color = 'k')
plt.show()
```

The preceding script will produce a graph similar to the following one, which displays five light gray, bell-shaped curves and a black one:

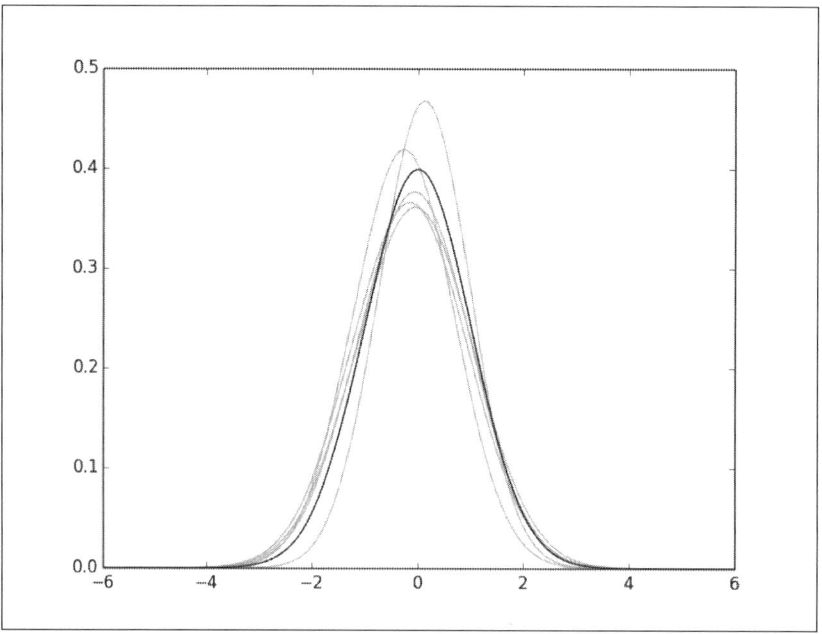

How it works...

In this example, we generate five sets of 50 samples from a normal distribution. For each of the five sets, we plot the estimated probability density in light gray. The normal distribution probability density is shown in black. There, the color is coded using the shortcut for black, that is, `k`.

Using custom colors for scatter plots

We can control the colors used for a scatter plot just as we do for a curve plot. In this recipe, we are going to see how to use the two ways to control the colors of a scatter plot.

Getting ready

The scatter plot function `pyplot.scatter()` offers the following two options to control the colors of dots through its color parameter, or its shortcut `c`:

- **Common color for all the dots**: If the color parameter is a valid matplotlib color definition, then all the dots will appear in that color.

- **Individual color for each dot**: If the color parameter is a sequence of a valid matplotlib color definition, the ith dot will appear in the ith color. Of course, we have to give the required colors for each dot.

How to do it...

In the following script, we display two sets of points, `A` and `B`, drawn from two bivariate Gaussian distributions. Each set has its own color. We call `pyplot.scatter()` twice, once for each point set, as shown in the following script:

```
import numpy as np
import matplotlib.pyplot as plt

A = np.random.standard_normal((100, 2))
A += np.array((-1, -1)) # Center the distrib. at <-1, -1>

B = np.random.standard_normal((100, 2))
B += np.array((1, 1)) # Center the distrib. at <1, 1>

plt.scatter(A[:,0], A[:,1], color = '.25')
plt.scatter(B[:,0], B[:,1], color = '.75')
plt.show()
```

The preceding script will produce the following graph:

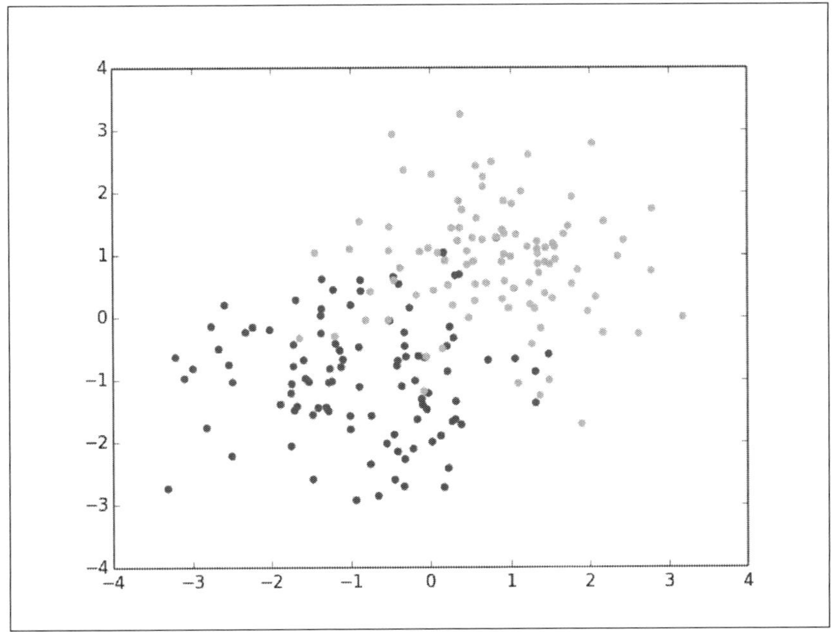

Thus, in this example, custom colors are used exactly like in `pyplot.plot()`. In the following script, things will be different. We load an array from a text file, the Fisher's iris dataset, available at `http://archive.ics.uci.edu/ml/datasets/Iris`. Its content looks like the following:

```
4.6,3.2,1.4,0.2,Iris-setosa
5.3,3.7,1.5,0.2,Iris-setosa
5.0,3.3,1.4,0.2,Iris-setosa
7.0,3.2,4.7,1.4,Iris-versicolor
6.4,3.2,4.5,1.5,Iris-versicolor
```

Each point of the dataset is stored in a comma-separated list of values. The last column that gives the label of each point is a string that can take three possible values—`Iris-virginica`, `Iris-versicolor`, and `Iris-Vertosa`. We read this file using NumPy's `numpy.loadtxt` function. The color of points will depend on their label, and we will display them with just one call to `pyplot.scatter()` as follows:

```
import numpy as np
import matplotlib.pyplot as plt

label_set = (
  b'Iris-setosa',
  b'Iris-versicolor',
  b'Iris-virginica',
)

def read_label(label):
  return label_set.index(label)

data = np.loadtxt('iris.data.txt',
                              delimiter = ',',
                              converters = { 4 : read_label })

color_set = ('.00', '.50', '.75')
color_list = [color_set[int(label)] for label in data[:,4]]

plt.scatter(data[:,0], data[:,1], color = color_list)
plt.show()
```

The preceding script will produce the following graph:

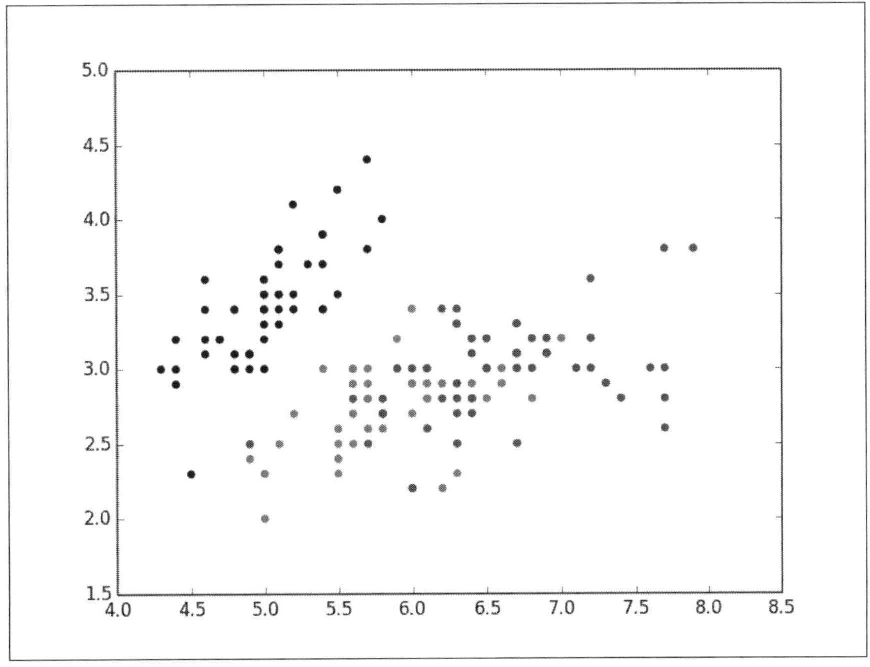

How it works...

For each of the three possible labels, we assign one unique color. The colors are defined in `color_set` and the labels are defined in `label_set`. The ith label in `label_set` is associated with the ith color in `color_set`.

We convert the list of labels, `label_list`, to a list of colors, `color_list`, with a list comprehension. We then need just one call to `pyplot.scatter()` to display all the points with their colors. We could have done this with three separate calls, but it would require more code for no tangible gain.

It's possible for two points to have the same coordinate and yet have a different label. In such a case, the color shown will be the color of the latest point drawn. Using transparent colors, the colors of overlapping points will be blended together.

There's more...

Just as the `color` parameter controls the color of the dots, the `edgecolor` parameter controls the color of the edge of the dots. It works strictly for the `color` parameter—you can set the same color for each dot edge or control the edge color individually as follows:

```
import numpy as np
import matplotlib.pyplot as plt

data = np.random.standard_normal((100, 2))

plt.scatter(data[:,0], data[:,1], color = '1.0', edgecolor='0.0')
plt.show()
```

The preceding script will produce the following graph:

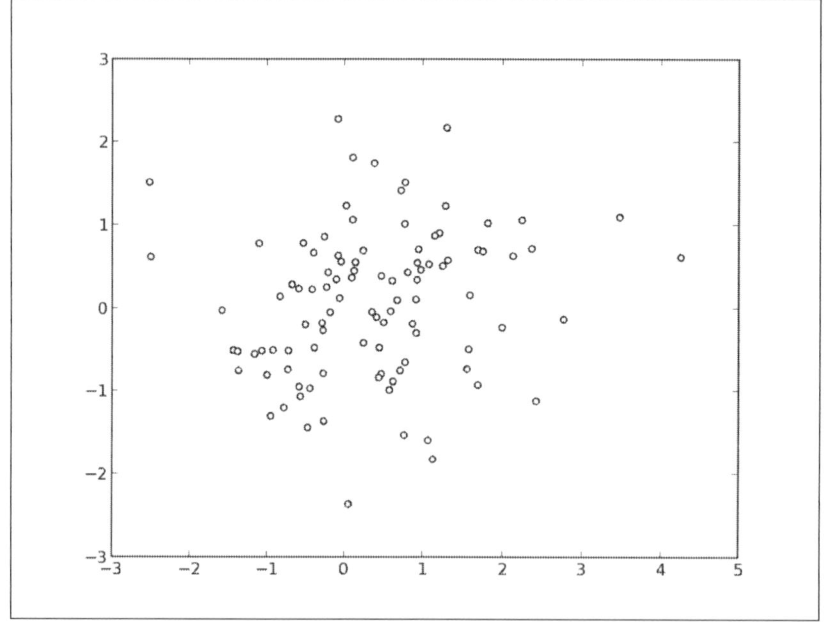

Using custom colors for bar charts

Bar charts are used a lot in web pages and presentations where one often has to follow an established color scheme. Thus, a good control on their colors is a must. In this recipe, we are going to see how to color a bar chart with our own colors.

How to do it...

In *Chapter 1, First Steps*, we have already seen how to make bar charts. Controlling which colors are used works the same as it does for curves plots and scatter plots, that is, through an optional parameter. In this example, we load the age pyramid of a country's population from a file as follows:

```
import numpy as np
import matplotlib.pyplot as plt

women_pop = np.array([5., 30., 45., 22.])
men_pop     = np.array([5., 25., 50., 20.])

X = np.arange(4)
plt.barh(X, women_pop, color = '.25')
plt.barh(X, -men_pop, color = '.75')

plt.show()
```

The preceding script shows one bar chart with the age repartition for men and another bar chart for women. Women appear in dark gray, while men appear in light gray, as shown in the following graph:

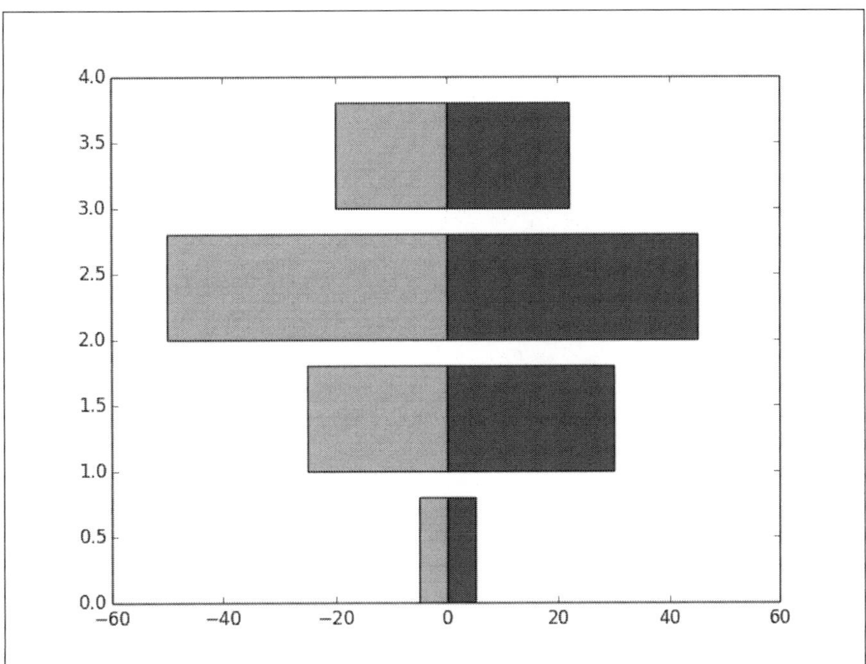

How it works...

The `pyplot.bar()` and `pyplot.barh()` functions work strictly like `pyplot.scatter()`. We simply have to set the optional parameter `color`. The parameter `edgecolor` is also available.

There's more...

In this example, we display a bar chart and color the bars depending on the values they represent. A value in the [0, 24], [25, 49], [50, 74], [75, 100] range will appear in a different shade of gray for each bar. The list of colors is built using a list comprehension as follows:

```
import numpy as np
import matplotlib.pyplot as plt

values = np.random.random_integers(99, size = 50)

color_set = ('.00', '.25', '.50', '.75')
color_list = [color_set[(len(color_set) * val) // 100] for val in
  values]
plt.bar(np.arange(len(values)), values, color = color_list)
plt.show()
```

The bars of the bar chart are colored according to their heights, as shown in the following graph:

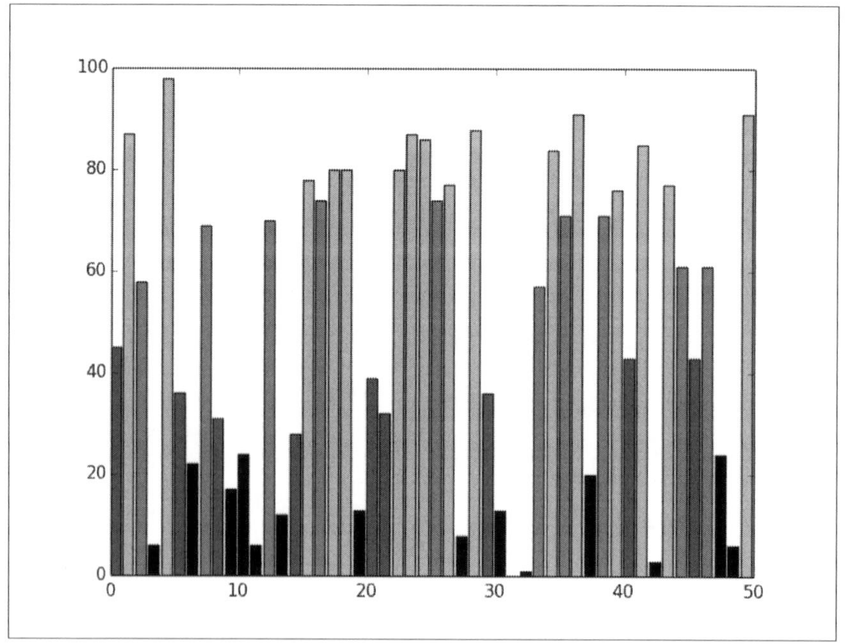

If we sort the values, the bars will form four distinct bands, as shown in the following graph:

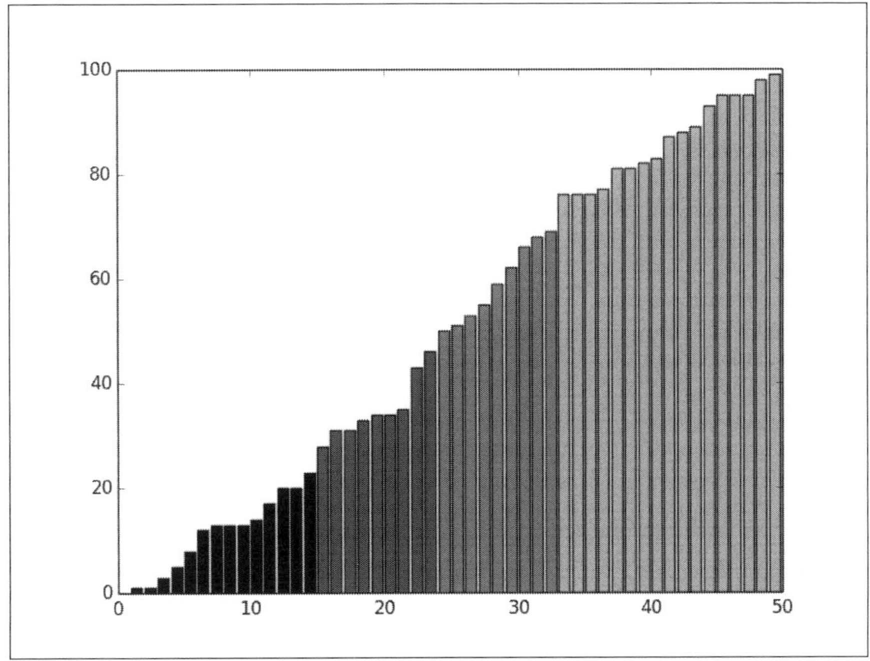

Using custom colors for pie charts

Like bar charts, pie charts are also used in contexts where the color scheme might matter a lot. Pie chart coloring works mostly like in bar charts. In this recipe, we are going to see how to color pie charts with our own colors.

How to do it...

The function `pyplot.pie()` accepts a list of colors as an optional parameter, as shown in the following script:

```
import numpy as np
import matplotlib.pyplot as plt

values = np.random.rand(8)
color_set = ('.00', '.25', '.50', '.75')

plt.pie(values, colors = color_set)
plt.show()
```

The preceding script will produce the following pie chart:

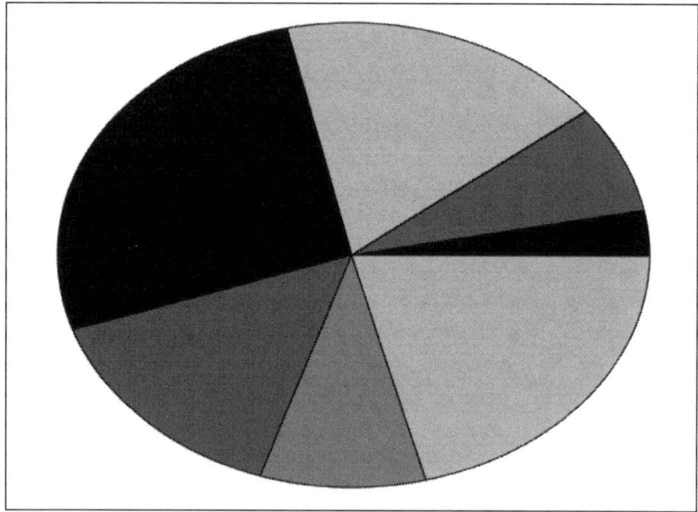

How it works...

Pie charts accept a list of colors using the `colors` parameter (beware, it is `colors`, not `color`). However, the color list does not have as many elements as the input list of values. If there are less colors than values, then `pyplot.pie()` will simply cycle through the color list. In the preceding example, we gave a list of four colors to color a pie chart that consisted of eight values. Thus, each color will be used twice.

Using custom colors for boxplots

Boxplots are common staple features of scientific publications. Colored boxplots are no trouble; however, you may need to use black and white only. In this recipe, we are going to see how to use custom colors with boxplots.

How to do it...

Every function that creates a specific figure returns some values—they are the low-level drawing primitives that constitute the figure. Most of the time, we don't bother to get those return values. However, manipulating those low-level drawing primitives allows some fine-tuning, such as custom color schemes for a box plot.

Making a boxplot appear totally black is a little bit trickier than it should be, as shown in the following script:

```
import numpy as np
import matplotlib.pyplot as plt
values = np.random.randn(100)

b = plt.boxplot(values)
for name, line_list in b.iteritems():
  for line in line_list:
    line.set_color('k')

plt.show()
```

The preceding script produces the following graph:

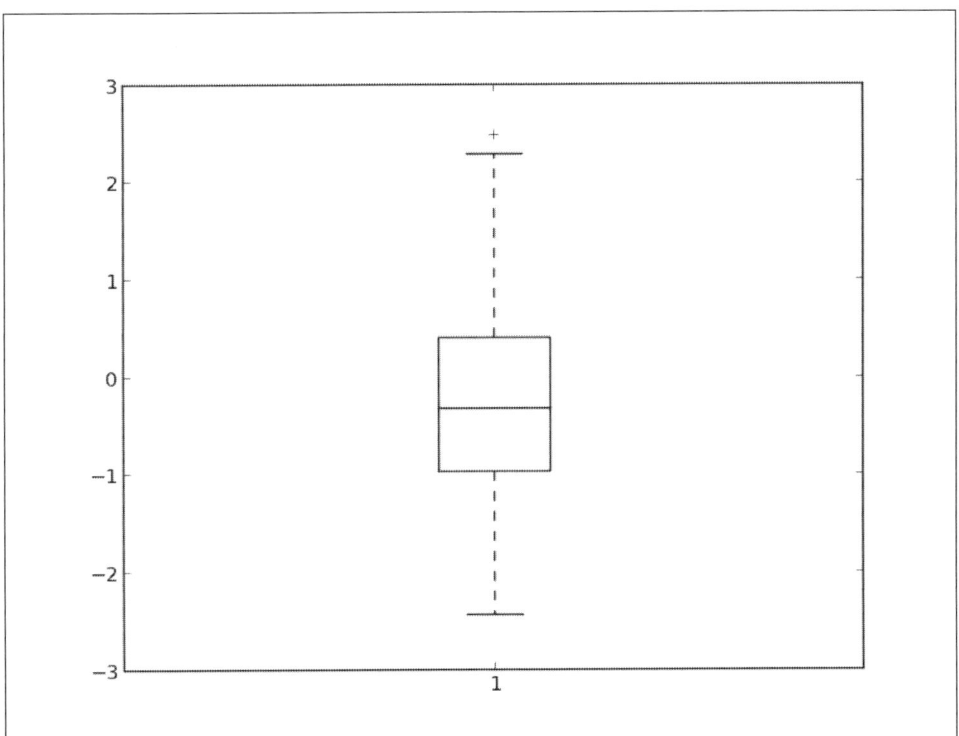

How it works...

Plotting functions returns a dictionary. The key of the dictionary is the name of the graphical elements. In the case of a boxplot, such elements will be medians, fliers, whiskers, boxes, and caps. The value associated with each of those keys is a list of low-level graphic primitives—lines, shapes, and so on. In the script, we iterate every graphic primitive that is a part of the boxplot and set its color to black. The same method allows you to render boxplots with your own color schemes.

Using colormaps for scatter plots

When using a lot of colors, defining each color one by one is tedious. Moreover, building a good set of colors is a problem in itself. In some cases, **colormaps** can address those issues. Colormaps define colors with a continuous function of one variable to one value, corresponding to one color. matplotlib provides several common colormaps; most of them are continuous color ramps. In this recipe, we are going to see how to color scatter plots with a colormap.

How to do it...

Colormaps are defined in the `matplotlib.cm` module. This module provides functions to create and use colormaps. It also provides an exhaustive choice of predefined color maps.

The function `pyplot.scatter()` accepts a list of values for the `color` parameter. When providing a colormap (with the `cmap` parameter), those values will be interpreted as a colormap index as follows:

```
import numpy as np
import matplotlib.cm as cm
import matplotlib.pyplot as plt

N = 256
angle  = np.linspace(0, 8 * 2 * np.pi, N)
radius = np.linspace(.5, 1., N)

X = radius * np.cos(angle)
Y = radius * np.sin(angle)

plt.scatter(X, Y, c = angle, cmap = cm.hsv)
plt.show()
```

The preceding script will generate a colorful spiral of dots as shown in the following graph:

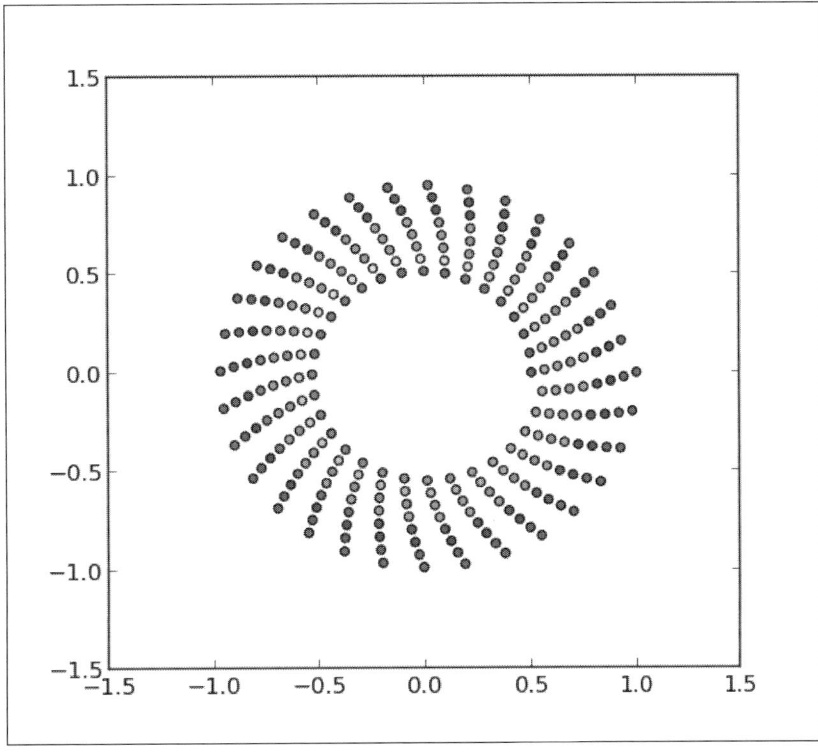

How it works...

In this script, we plot a spiral of dots. The dots are colored as a function of the angle variable, taking the color from a colormap. A large set of colormaps are available in the `matplotlib.cm` module. The `hsv` map contains the full spectrum of colors, which makes for a fancy rainbow theme. For scientific visualization, other colormaps are more appropriate, taking into account the perceived color intensity, such as the `PuOr` map. The same script with the `PuOr` map will give us the following result:

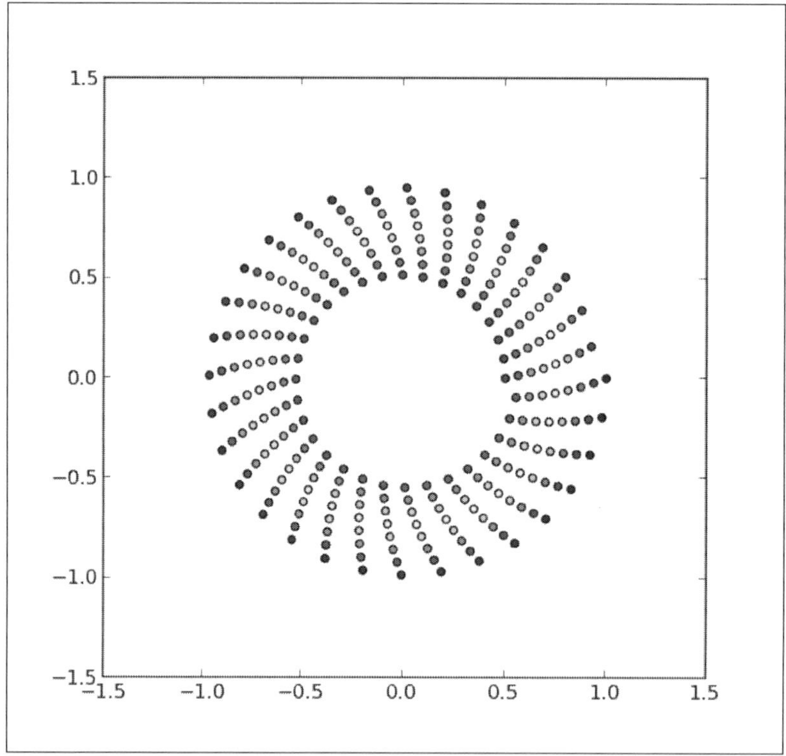

Using colormaps for bar charts

The `pyplot.scatter()` function has a built-in support for colormaps; some other plotting functions that we will discover later also have such support. However, some functions, such as `pyplot.bar()`, do not take colormaps as inputs to plot bar charts. In this recipe, we are going to see how to color a bar chart with a colormap.

matplotlib has helper functions to explicitly generate colors from a colormap. For instance, we can color the bars of a bar chart with the functions of the values they represent.

How to do it...

We will use the `matplotlib.cm` module in this recipe just as we did in the previous recipe. This time, we will directly use a colormap object rather than letting a rendering function use it automatically. We will also need the `matplotlib.colors` module, which contains the utility functions related to colors as shown in the following script:

```
import numpy as np
import matplotlib.cm as cm
import matplotlib.colors as col
import matplotlib.pyplot as plt

values = np.random.random_integers(99, size = 50)

cmap = cm.ScalarMappable(col.Normalize(0, 99), cm.binary)

plt.bar(np.arange(len(values)), values, color = cmap.to_rgba(values))
plt.show()
```

The preceding script will produce a bar chart where the color of a bar depends on its height, as shown in the following graph:

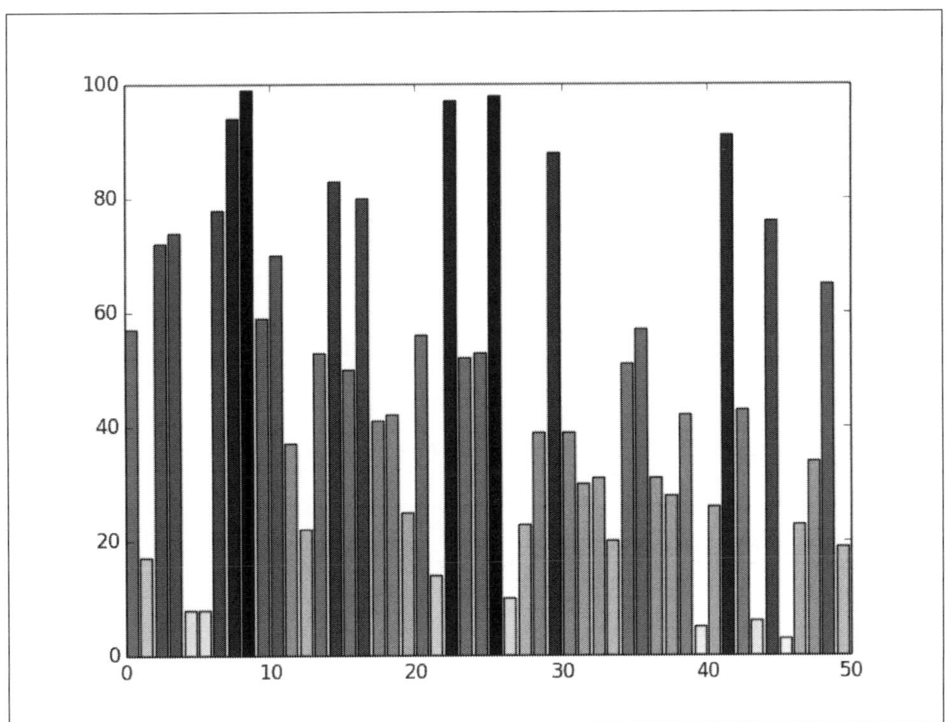

How it works...

We first create the colormap `cmap` so that it maps values from the [0, 99] range to the colors of the `matplotlib.cm.binary` colormap. Then, the function `cmap.to_rgba` converts the list of values to a list of colors. Thus, although `pyplot.bar` does not support colormaps, using colormaps does not involve complex code; there are functions to make this easy.

Note that if the list of values is sorted, the continuous aspect of the colormap used here becomes obvious, as shown in the follow graph:

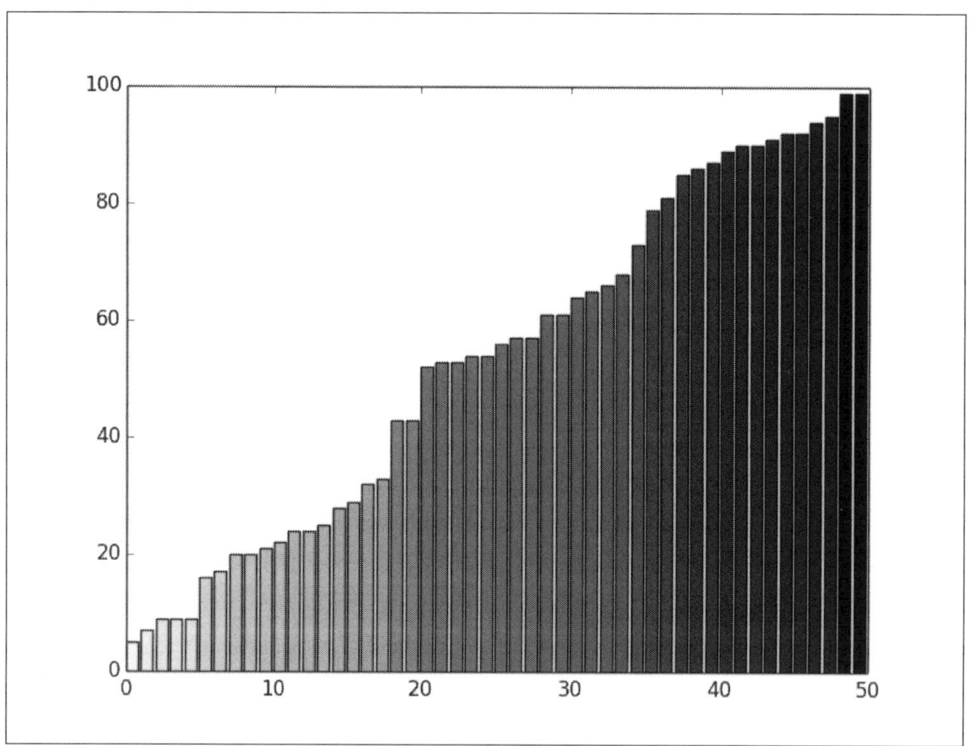

Controlling a line pattern and thickness

When creating figures for black and white documents, we are limited to gray levels. In practice, three levels of gray are usually the most we can reasonably use. However, using different line patterns allows some diversity. In this recipe, we are going to see how to control line pattern and thickness.

How to do it...

As in the case of colors, the line style is controlled by an optional parameter of `pyplot.plot()` as shown in the following script:

```
import numpy as np
import matplotlib.pyplot as plt

def pdf(X, mu, sigma):
  a = 1. / (sigma * np.sqrt(2. * np.pi))
  b = -1. / (2. * sigma ** 2)
  return a * np.exp(b * (X - mu) ** 2)

X = np.linspace(-6, 6, 1024)

plt.plot(X, pdf(X, 0., 1.),   color = 'k', linestyle = 'solid')
plt.plot(X, pdf(X, 0.,  .5),  color = 'k', linestyle = 'dashed')
plt.plot(X, pdf(X, 0.,  .25), color = 'k', linestyle = 'dashdot')

plt.show()
```

The preceding script will produce the following graph:

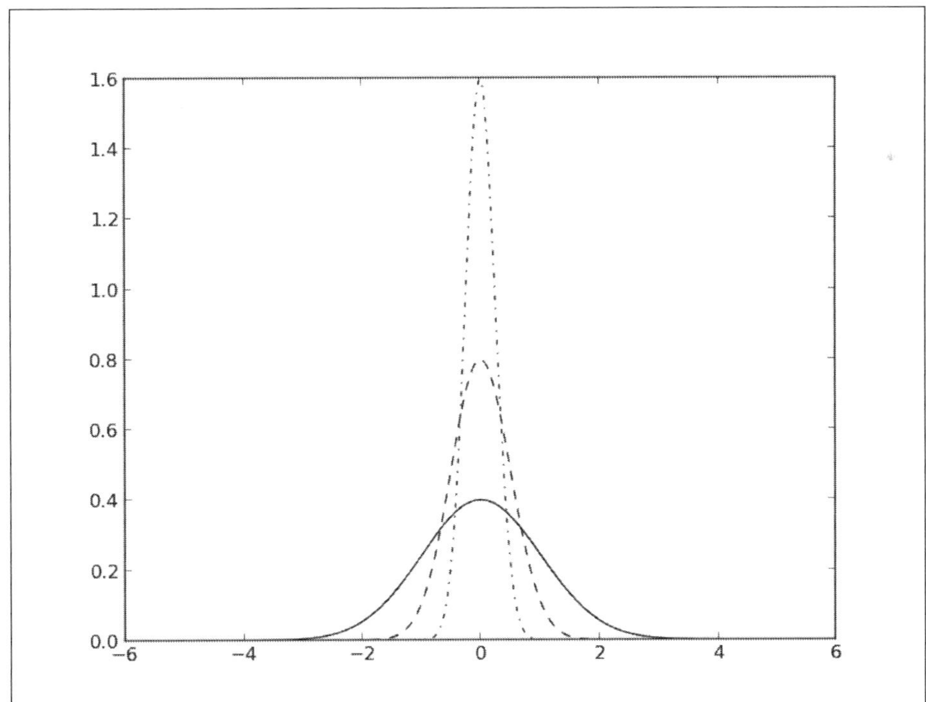

How it works...

In this example, we use the `linestyle` parameter of `pyplot.plot()` to control the line pattern of three different curves. The following line styles are available:

- Solid
- Dashed
- Dotted
- Dashdot

There's more...

Line style settings are not limited to `pyplot.plot()`; in fact, any graphics made of lines allows such settings. Moreover, you can also control line thickness.

The line style with other plot types

The `linestyle` parameter is available for all the commands that involve line rendering. For instance, we can modify the line pattern used for a bar chart as follows:

```
import numpy as np
import matplotlib.pyplot as plt

N = 8
A = np.random.random(N)
B = np.random.random(N)
X = np.arange(N)

plt.bar(X, A, color = '.75')
plt.bar(X, A + B, bottom = A, color = 'w', linestyle = 'dashed')

plt.show()
```

The preceding script will produce the following graph:

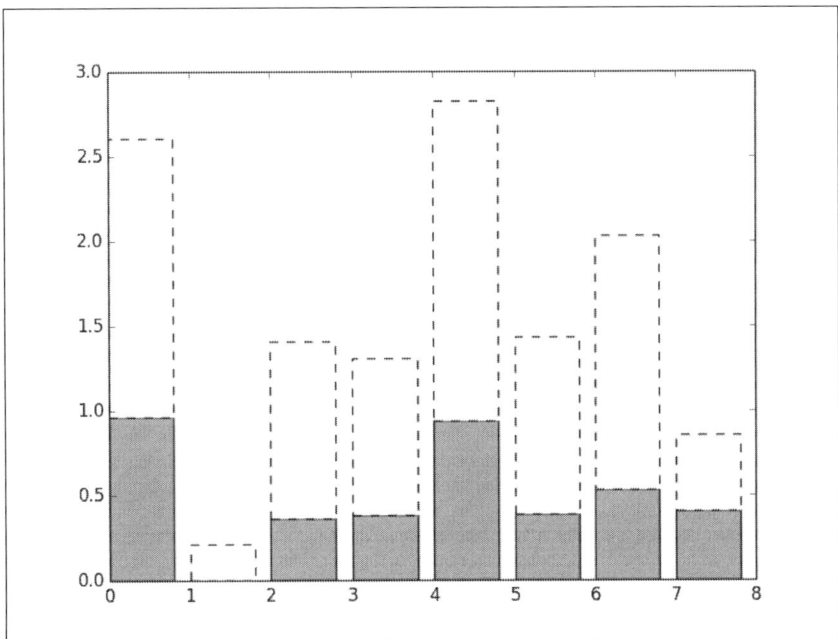

The line width

Likewise, the `linewidth` parameter will change the thickness of lines. By default, the thickness is set to 1 unit. Playing with the thickness of lines can help to put emphasis on one particular curve. The following is the script to set the thickness of lines using the `linewidth` parameter:

```
import numpy as np
import matplotlib.pyplot as plt

def pdf(X, mu, sigma):
  a = 1. / (sigma * np.sqrt(2. * np.pi))
  b = -1. / (2. * sigma ** 2)
  return a * np.exp(b * (X - mu) ** 2)

X = np.linspace(-6, 6, 1024)
for i in range(64):
  samples = np.random.standard_normal(50)
  mu, sigma = np.mean(samples), np.std(samples)
  plt.plot(X, pdf(X, mu, sigma), color = '.75', linewidth = .5)

plt.plot(X, pdf(X, 0., 1.), color = 'y', linewidth = 3.)
plt.show()
```

In the following graph, which is a result of the preceding script, 64 estimated Gaussians **PDF** (**Probability Density Functions**) are estimated from 50 samples and are shown as thin gray curves. The Gaussian distribution used to draw the samples is shown as a thick black curve.

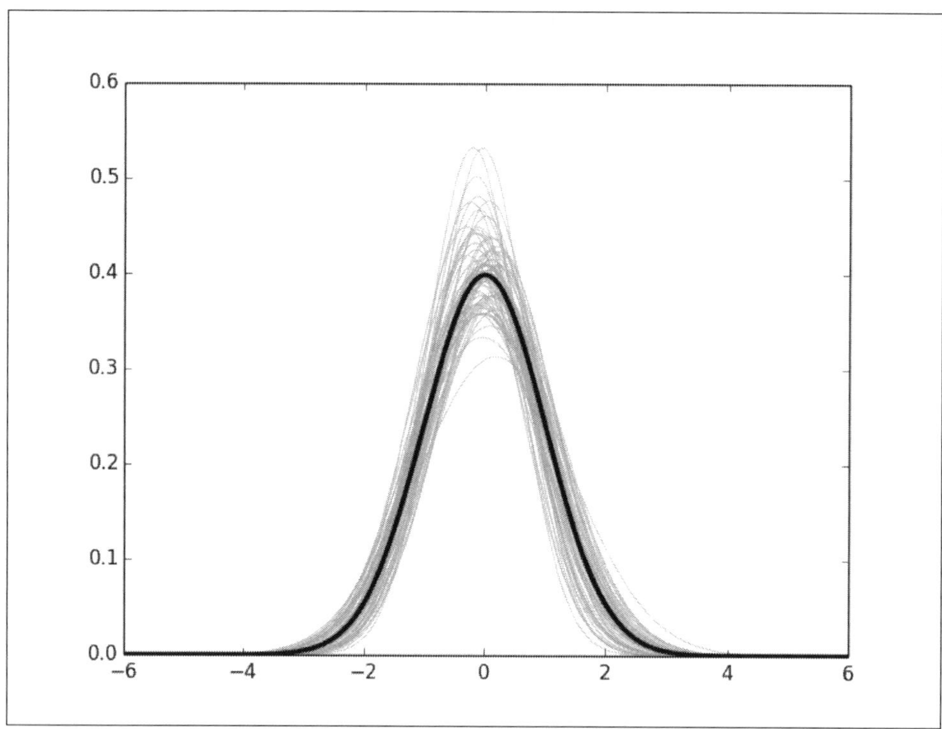

Controlling a fill pattern

matplotlib offers fairly limited support to fill surfaces with a pattern. For line patterns, it can be helpful when preparing figures for black-and-white prints. In this recipe, we are going to look at how we can fill surfaces with a pattern.

How to do it...

Let's demonstrate the use of fill patterns with a bar chart as follows:

```
import numpy as np
import matplotlib.pyplot as plt

N = 8
A = np.random.random(N)
```

```
B = np.random.random(N)
X = np.arange(N)

plt.bar(X, A, color = 'w', hatch = 'x')
plt.bar(X, A + B, bottom = A, color = 'w', hatch = '/')

plt.show()
```

The preceding script produces the following graph:

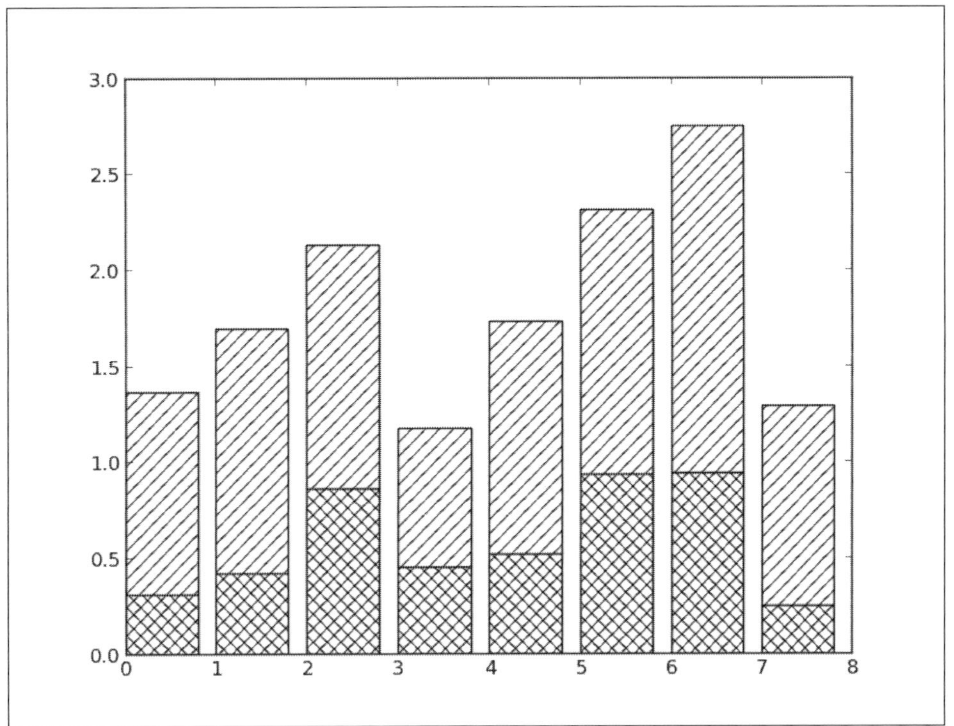

How it works...

Rendering function filling volumes, such as `pyplot.bar()`, accept an optional parameter, `hatch`. This parameter can take the following values:

- /
- \
- |
- -

- +
- x
- o
- O
- .
- *

Each value corresponds to a different hatching pattern. The `color` parameter will control the background color of the pattern, while the `edgecolor` parameter will control the color of the hatching.

Controlling a marker's style

In *Chapter 1, First Steps*, we have seen how we can display the points of a curve as dots. Also, scatter plots represent each point of a dataset. As it turns out, matplotlib offers a variety of shapes to replace dots with other kinds of markers. In this recipe, we are going to see how to set a marker's style.

Getting ready

Markers can be specified in various ways as follows:

- **Predefined markers**: They can be predefined shapes, represented as a number in the [0, 8] range, or some strings
- **Vertices list**: This is a list of value pairs, used as coordinates for the path of a shape
- **Regular polygon**: It represents a triplet (N, 0, angle) for an *N* sided regular polygon, with a rotation of angle degrees
- **Start polygon**: It represents a triplet (N, 1, angle) for an *N* sided regular star, with a rotation of angle degrees

How to do it...

Let's take a script that shows two sets of points with two different colors. Now we will display all the points in black, but with different markers as follows:

```
import numpy as np
import matplotlib.pyplot as plt

A = np.random.standard_normal((100, 2))
A += np.array((-1, -1))
```

```
B = np.random.standard_normal((100, 2))
B += np.array((1, 1))

plt.scatter(A[:,0], A[:,1], color = 'k', marker = 'x')
plt.scatter(B[:,0], B[:,1], color = 'k', marker = '^')

plt.show()
```

Two Gaussian clouds of dots will appear, each using a different marker, as shown in the following graph:

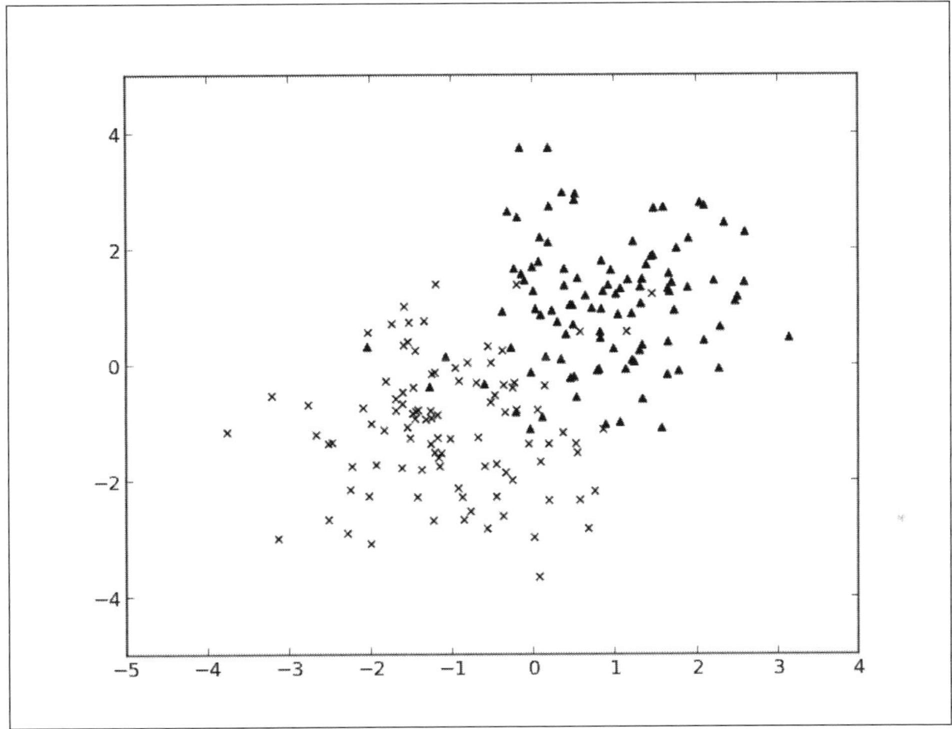

How it works...

In this script, we set the color of both scatter plots to black. Using the `marker` parameter, we specify a different marker for each set.

Unlike the `color` parameter, the `marker` parameter does not accept a list of marker specifications as inputs. Thus, we cannot use one single call to `pyplot.scatter()` to display several set of points with different markers. We need to segregate points per type of marker and use a separate call to `pyplot.scatter()` for each set as follows:

```
import numpy as np
import matplotlib.pyplot as plt

label_list = (
  b'Iris-setosa',
  b'Iris-versicolor',
  b'Iris-virginica',
)

def read_label(label):
  return label_list.index(label)

data = np.loadtxt('iris.data.txt',
  delimiter = ',',
  converters = { 4 : read_label })

marker_set = ('^', 'x', '.')
for i, marker in enumerate(marker_set):
  data_subset = numpy.asarray([x for x in data if x[4] == i])
  plt.scatter(data_subset[:,0], data_subset[:,1],
    color = 'k',
    marker = marker)

plt.show()
```

Each cluster from the dataset appears with its own marker as shown in the following graph:

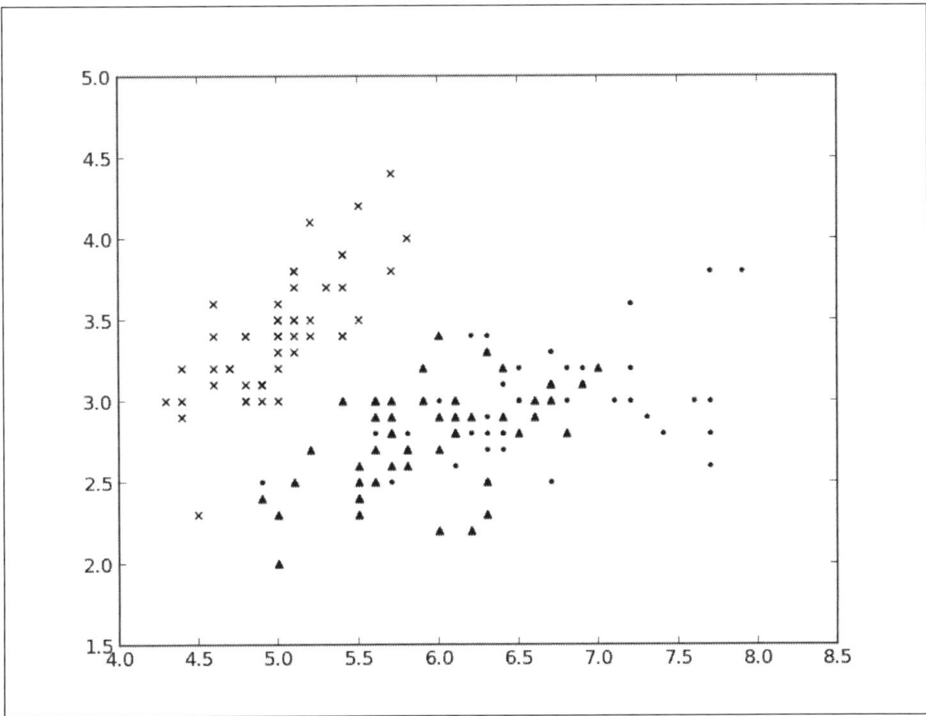

This example is similar to the previous example where we load a dataset and display each point according to the label. Here, however, we segregate points per label. Then, we iterate through each entry of the map and call `pyplot.scatter()` for each subset of points.

There's more...

The marker style is also accessible for `pyplot.plot()` using the same `marker` parameter. Using one marker for each data point can be a problem as it will display more points than we want to. The `markevery` parameter allows you to display only one marker for every *N* points as shown in the following script:

```
import numpy as np
import matplotlib.pyplot as plt

X = np.linspace(-6, 6, 1024)
Y1 = np.sinc(X)
Y2 = np.sinc(X) + 1
```

```
plt.plot(X, Y1, marker = 'o', color = '.75')
plt.plot(X, Y2, marker = 'o', color = 'k', markevery = 32)

plt.show()
```

The preceding script produces the following graph:

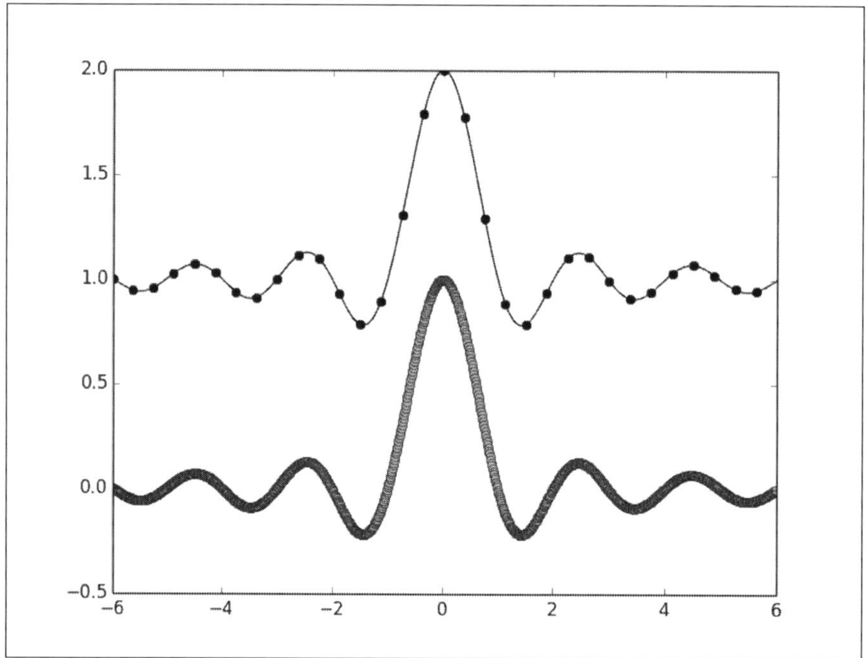

Controlling a marker's size

As seen in the previous recipe, we can control the style of markers; controlling their size also works along the same lines. In this recipe, we are going to see how to control marker sizes.

How to do it...

A marker's size is controlled in the same way as other marker attributes, with a dedicated optional parameter as shown in the following script:

```
import numpy as np
import matplotlib.pyplot as plt
A = np.random.standard_normal((100, 2))
A += np.array((-1, -1))
```

```
B = np.random.standard_normal((100, 2))
B += np.array((1, 1))

plt.scatter(B[:,0], B[:,1], c = 'k', s = 100.)
plt.scatter(A[:,0], A[:,1], c = 'w', s = 25.)

plt.show()
```

The preceding script produces the following graph:

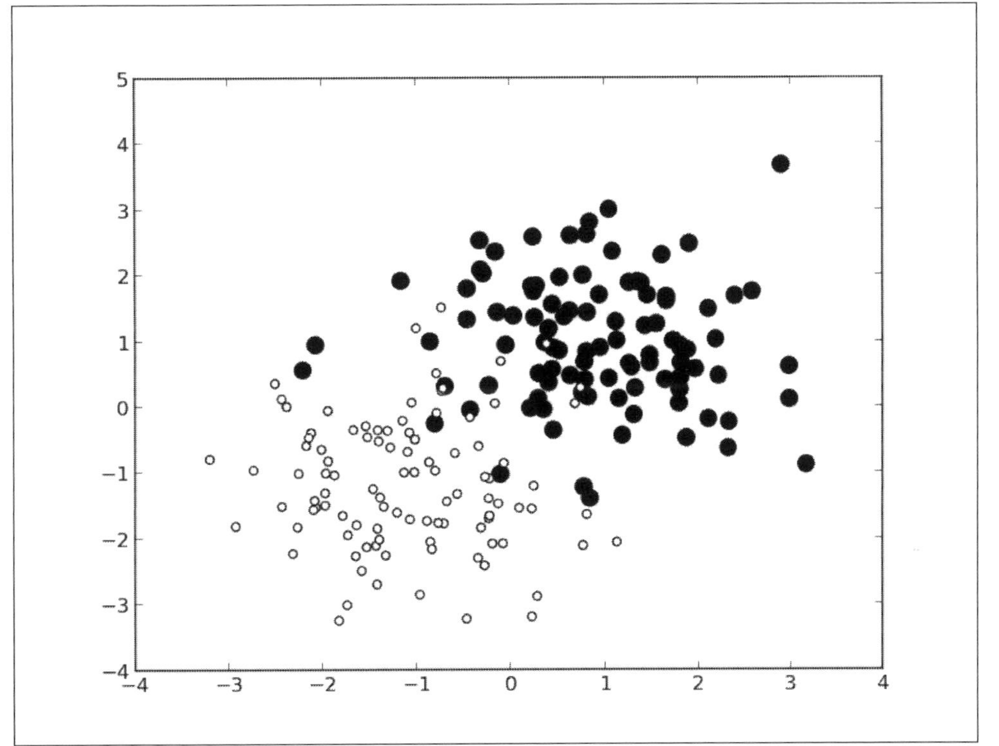

In this example, we display two sets of points of different sizes. The marker's size is set by the parameter `s` for `pyplot.scatter()`. Oddly enough, it sets the surface area of a marker and not its radius.

Because the sizes are the actual surface areas and not the radii, they follow a quadratic progression—the markers that are four times larger will have radii that are two times larger.

There's more...

The `pyplot.scatter()` function also takes a list as an input for the `s` parameter—one size for each point as shown in the following script:

```
import numpy as np
import matplotlib.pyplot as plt

M = np.random.standard_normal((1000, 2))
R = np.sum(M ** 2, axis = 1)

plt.scatter(M[:, 0], M[:, 1], c = 'w', marker = 's', s = 32. * R)
plt.show()
```

The preceding script produces the following graph:

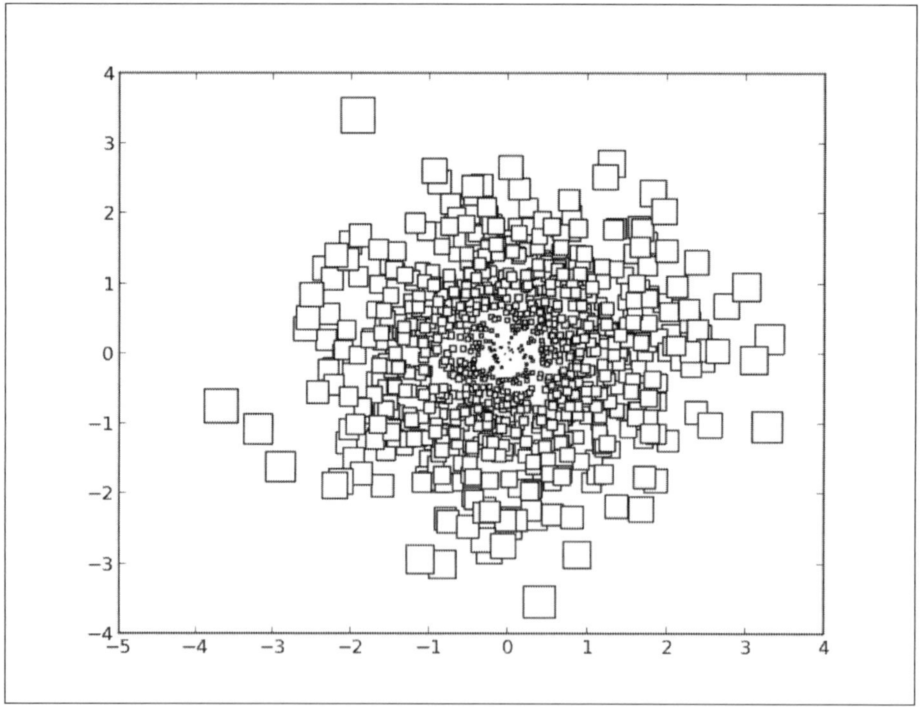

In this script, we drew random points according to a bivariate Gaussian distribution. The radius of a point depends on its distance from the origin.

The `pyplot.plot()` function also allows to change the size of the markers with the help of the `markersize` (or its shortcut `ms`) parameter. This parameter does not accept a list of values as an input.

Creating your own markers

matplotlib offers a large variety of marker shapes. But you might not find something that suits your specific need. For instance, you might wish to use an animal silhouette, a company's logo, and so on. In this recipe, we are going to see how to define our own marker shapes.

How to do it...

matplotlib describes shapes as a path—a sequence of points linked together. Thus, to define our own marker shapes, we have to provide a sequence of points. In the following script example, we will define a cross-like shape:

```
import numpy as np
import matplotlib.path as mpath
from matplotlib import pyplot as plt

shape_description = [
  ( 1.,  2., mpath.Path.MOVETO),
  ( 1.,  1., mpath.Path.LINETO),
  ( 2.,  1., mpath.Path.LINETO),
  ( 2., -1., mpath.Path.LINETO),
  ( 1., -1., mpath.Path.LINETO),
  ( 1., -2., mpath.Path.LINETO),
  (-1., -2., mpath.Path.LINETO),
  (-1., -1., mpath.Path.LINETO),
  (-2., -1., mpath.Path.LINETO),
  (-2.,  1., mpath.Path.LINETO),
  (-1.,  1., mpath.Path.LINETO),
  (-1.,  2., mpath.Path.LINETO),
  ( 0.,  0., mpath.Path.CLOSEPOLY),
]

u, v, codes = zip(*shape_description)
my_marker = mpath.Path(np.asarray((u, v)).T, codes)
data = np.random.rand(8, 8)
plt.scatter(data[:,0], data[:, 1], c = '.75', marker = my_marker,
  s = 64)
plt.show()
```

The preceding script produces the following graph:

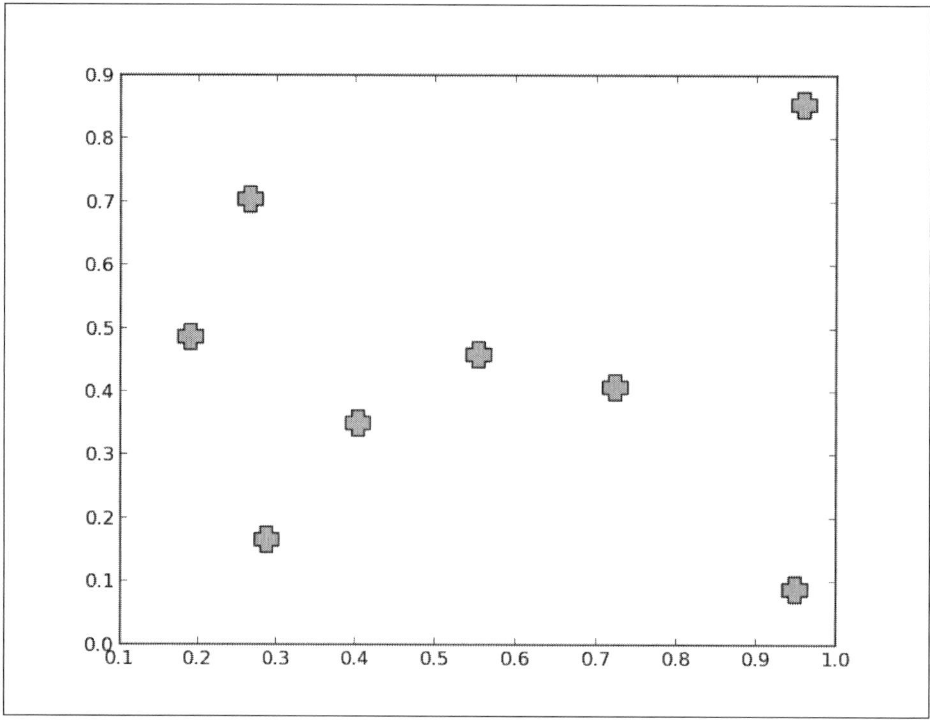

How it works...

All the `pyplot` functions that render figures with markers have an optional argument, that is, `marker`. We have seen in the previous recipe that an argument can be a string to pick one of the predefined matplotlib markers. But the `marker` argument can be an instance of `Path` as well. The `Path` object is defined in the `matplotlib.path` module.

The constructor for the `Path` object takes a list of coordinates and a list of instructions as inputs; one instruction per coordinate. Rather than having two separate lists for coordinates and instructions, we use a single list `shape_description`, fusing together coordinates and instructions. A bit of code is used to manipulate `shape_description` and feed separate lists of coordinates and instructions to the `Path` constructor as follows:

```
u, v, codes = zip(*shape_description)
my_marker = mpath.Path(np.asarray((u, v)).T, codes)
```

Shapes are described by the movements of a cursor. We use the following three types of instructions:

- `MOVETO`: This instruction will move the cursor to the specified coordinates; no line is drawn.
- `LINETO`: This will move the cursor to the specified coordinates, while drawing a line.
- `CLOSEPOLY`: It won't do anything, it will close the path. Your path will be concluded by this instruction.

In theory, any shape is possible, you simply need to describe its path. In practice, if you wish to use a complex shape (for instance, the logo of a company), you will have to do some conversion work. matplotlib does not provide conversion routines from popular vector file formats (such as SVG) to `Path` objects.

Getting more control over markers

Fine controls, such as edge color, interior color, and so on, are possible on markers. It is, for instance, possible to draw a curve with markers of a different color than the color of the curve. In this recipe, we will look at how to have a fine control on a marker's aspect.

How to do it...

We have learned about the optional parameters to set the shape, color, and size of markers. There are plenty of others to play with, as demonstrated in the following script:

```
import numpy as np
import matplotlib.pyplot as plt

X = np.linspace(-6, 6, 1024)
Y = np.sinc(X)

plt.plot(X, Y,
  linewidth = 3.,
  color = 'k',
  markersize = 9,
  markeredgewidth = 1.5,
  markerfacecolor = '.75',
  markeredgecolor = 'k',
  marker = 'o',
  markevery = 32)
plt.show()
```

The call to `pyplot.plot()` is broken over several lines for the readability purpose—one line per optional parameter. The preceding script will produce the following graph:

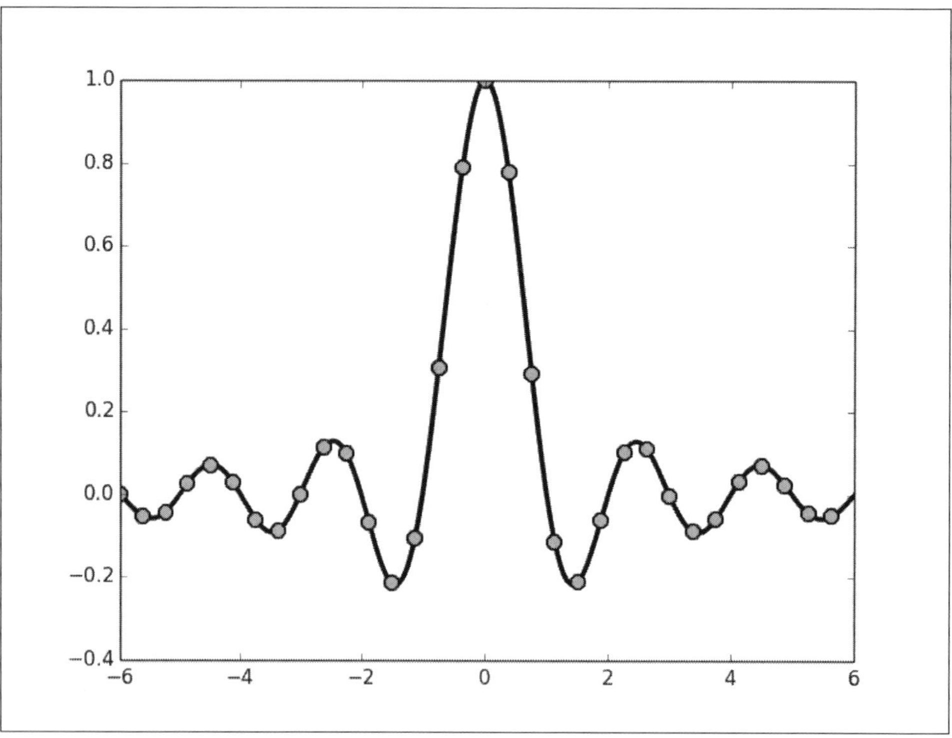

How it works...

This example demonstrates the use of the `markeredgecolor`, `markerfacecolor`, and `markeredgewidth` parameters, which controls the edge color, the inside color, and the line width of a marker, respectively. All rendering functions that can use markers, such as `pyplot.plot`, accept those optional parameters.

Creating your own color scheme

The default colors used by matplotlib are meant to be reasonably publication-ready for printed documents. Thus, the background is white by default, while the labels, axes, and other annotations appear in black. In a different usage context, you might prefer a different color scheme; for instance, having the figure's background turned to black with the annotation in white. In this recipe, we will show how to change matplotlib's default settings.

How to do it...

In matplotlib, various objects, such as axes, figures, and labels can be addressed individually. Changing the color settings of all those objects, one by one, would be very cumbersome. Fortunately, all matplotlib objects choose their default colors from a centralized configuration object.

In the following script, we use matplotlib's centralized configuration to have a black background and white annotations:

```
import numpy as np
import matplotlib as mpl
from matplotlib import pyplot as plt


mpl.rc('lines', linewidth = 2.)
mpl.rc('axes', facecolor = 'k', edgecolor = 'w')
mpl.rc('xtick', color = 'w')
mpl.rc('ytick', color = 'w')
mpl.rc('text', color = 'w')
mpl.rc('figure', facecolor = 'k', edgecolor ='w')
mpl.rc('axes', color_cycle = ('w', '.5', '.75'))

X = np.linspace(0, 7, 1024)

plt.plot(X, np.sin(X))
plt.plot(X, np.cos(X))
plt.show()
```

The preceding script produces the following graph:

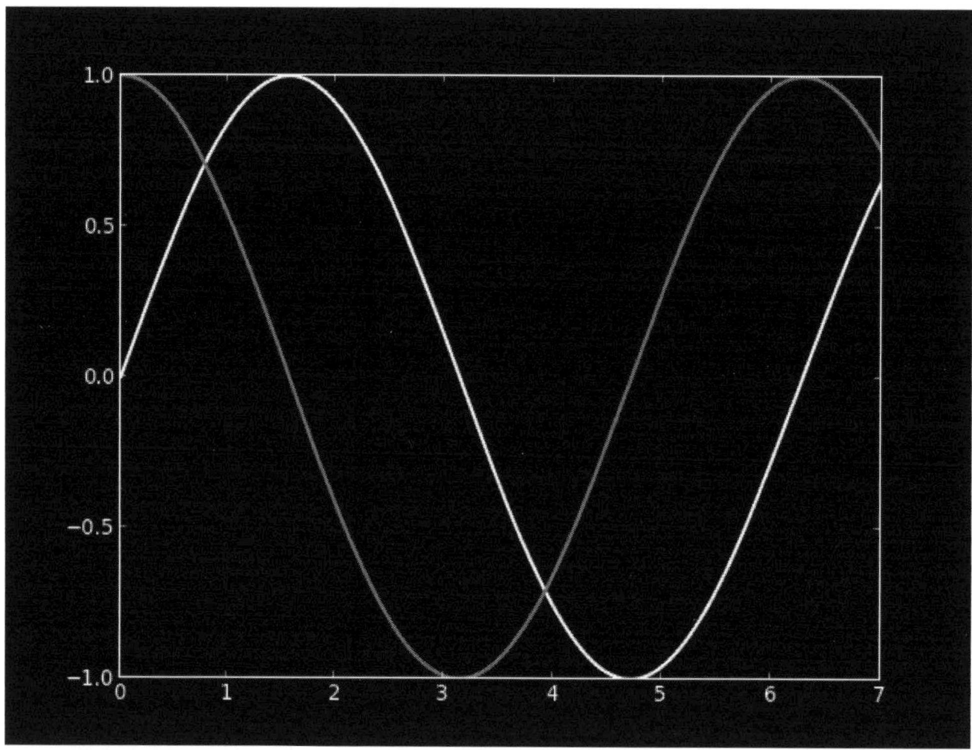

How it works...

The `matplotlib` module has an `rc` object that acts as a centralized configuration. Every matplotlib object will pick its default settings from that `rc` object. The `rc` object holds a set of properties and associated values. For instance, `mpl.rc('lines', linewidth = 2.)` will set the property `lines.linewidth` to 2; by default, lines will have now a width of two. Here, we set the background of the figure to black (using the `figure.facecolor` and `axes.facecolor` properties), while we set all the annotations to white (using the `figure.edgecolor`, `axes.edgecolor`, `text.color`, `xtick.color`, `ytick.color` properties). We also redefine the colors automatically picked by matplotlib with the `axes.color_cycle` property. A good reference for matplotlib's properties is available at `http://matplotlib.org/_static/matplotlibrc`.

There's more...

We now know how to change matplotlib's default settings to suit our tastes. However, if we want all our scripts to use those settings, we have to copy and paste them. This is very inconvenient. Fortunately, default settings can be saved in a `matplotlibrc` file. A `maptplotlibrc` file is a plain text file that contains properties and their corresponding values; one property per line. The following is the settings of this recipe in the `matplotlibrc` format:

```
lines.linewidth : 2
axes.facecolor : black
axes.edgecolor : white
xtick.color : white
ytick.color : white
text.color : white
figure.facecolor : black
figure.edgecolor : white
axes.color_cycle : white, #808080, #b0b0b0
```

If a `matplotlibrc` file is found in your current directory (that is, the directory from where you launched your script from), it will override matplotlib's default settings.

You can also save your `matplotlibrc` file in a specific location to make your own default settings. In the interactive Python shell, run the following command:

```
import matplotlib
mpl.get_configdir()
```

This command will display the location where you can place your `matplotlibrc` file so that those settings will be your own default settings.

3
Working with Annotations

In this chapter, we will cover the following topics:

- Adding a title
- Using LaTeX-style notations
- Adding a label to each axis
- Adding text
- Adding arrows
- Adding a legend
- Adding a grid
- Adding lines
- Adding shapes
- Controlling tick spacing
- Controlling tick labeling

Introduction

It is considered a good practice to make your figures self-explanatory. However, it can be hard to make some curves and dots self-explanatory without any annotations. How should one read the vertical and horizontal axes? Which quantity is represented by that box and this curve? matplotlib offers a great number of possibilities to annotate a figure, which we are going to explore in this chapter.

Adding a title

Let's start with something simple: adding a title to a graphic.

How to do it...

The following code will add a title to the figure:

```
import numpy as np
import matplotlib.pyplot as plt

X = np.linspace(-4, 4, 1024)
Y = .25 * (X + 4.) * (X + 1.) * (X - 2.)

plt.title('A polynomial')
plt.plot(X, Y, c = 'k')
plt.show()
```

Here, we render a simple curve and add a title to the figure, which appears at the top of the figure:

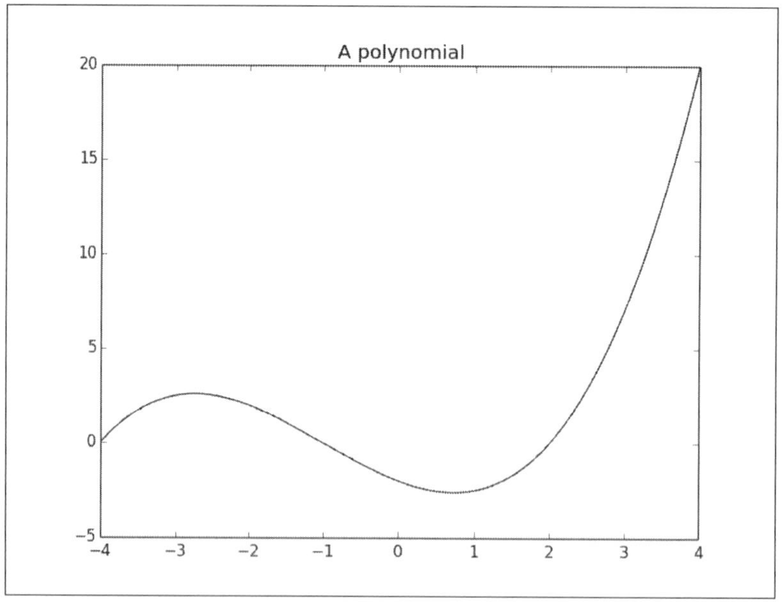

How it works...

It's simply done with the `pyplot.title()` function, which takes one string as a parameter and sets the title for the whole figure.

Using LaTeX-style notations

We can now annotate figures. However, in a scientific and engineering context, the solution demonstrated previously suffers from one annoying limitation. We cannot use mathematical notations! Or, can we? In this recipe, we are going to see how to use LaTeX to display mathematical scripts in a figure.

Getting ready

You need a working LaTeX setup installed on your computer so that matplotlib can interpret a LaTeX-style notation to render mathematical text. Fall short of this, and you will not be able to try this recipe. You can find useful explanations on installing LaTeX on the LaTeX Wikibook (`http://en.wikibooks.org/wiki/LaTeX/Installation`).

LaTeX

LaTeX is a document preparation system widely used in academia. Unlike document editors such as Microsoft Word or LibreOffice Writer, a LaTeX user cannot see how the final document will look while editing it. Documents are described as a mix of text and commands stored in a plain text file. Then, LaTeX will interpret the document description to render a document. LaTeX is a fairly large environment. LaTeX has a specific language to describe mathematical text. This language is so popular that it became a de facto standard to simply write formulae rather than render them. For instance, in the science and engineering community, LaTeX's formula language is commonly used to write mathematical text in e-mails and forums.

How to do it...

Rendering some text with LaTeX is surprisingly simple:

```
import numpy as np
import matplotlib.pyplot as plt

X = np.linspace(-4, 4, 1024)
Y = .25 * (X + 4.) * (X + 1.) * (X - 2.)

plt.title('$f(x)=\\frac{1}{4}(x+4)(x+1)(x-2)$')
plt.plot(X, Y, c = 'k')
plt.show()
```

This script does exactly what we did in the previous recipe: it shows a figure with a title at the top. However, as the title of the recipe might hint it, the title is rendered with LaTeX, allowing us to use mathematical notations.

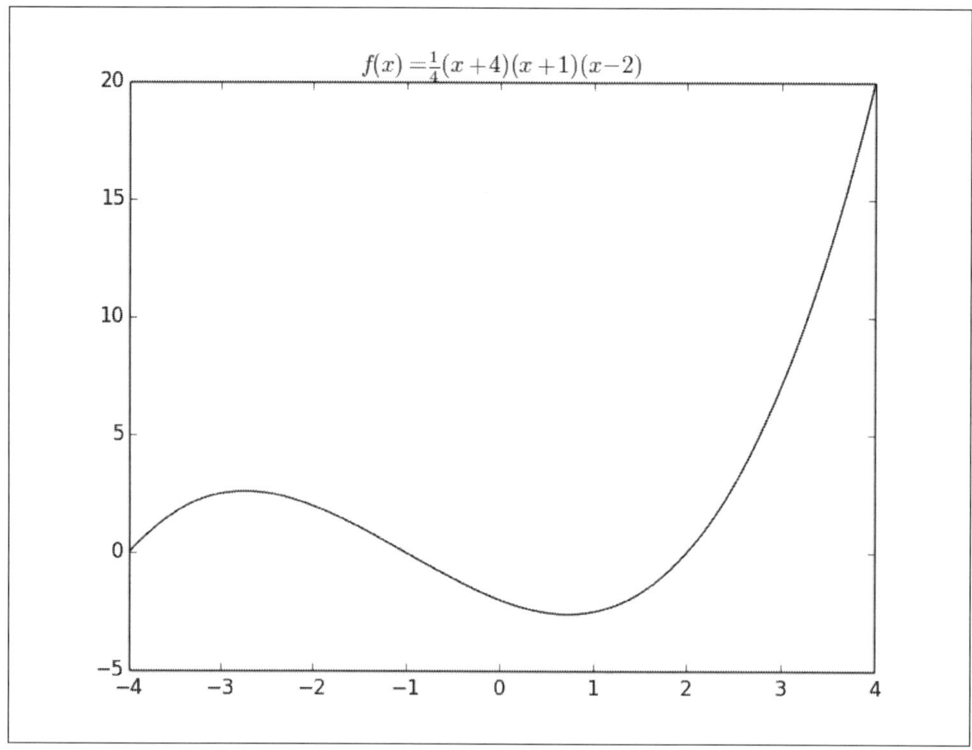

How it works...

The only difference with the usual way to set a title is the string given to `pyplot.title()`. The string starts and ends with the `$` character; this is to signal matplotlib to interpret and render the text as a LaTeX-style mathematical text. Then, the string content is just the standard LaTeX language for the mathematical text.

The LaTeX language relies heavily on the escape character, `\`, which also happens to be the string escape character for Python. Thus, where you would use one `\` character in a LaTeX text, put two in your Python string. To avoid fumbling with escape characters, you can prefix your string with `r` and you won't need any escape characters. Thus, `'$f(x)=\\frac{1}{4}(x+4)(x+1)(x-2)$'` and `r'$f(x)=\frac{1}{4}(x+4)(x+1)(x-2)$'` are equivalent.

You don't know the LaTeX language for mathematical text? No worries, you can learn it quickly! In the matplotlib context, you can find the definitive guide at http://matplotlib.org/users/mathtext.html. A fairly complete tutorial can be found at http://en.wikibooks.org/wiki/LaTeX/Mathematics.

This LaTeX-notation feature is not limited to titles; it can be used for any annotation. Here, we simply demonstrate this on the title text.

Adding a label to each axis

After a title, a proper description of the figure's axis helps a great deal for users understand a graphic. In this recipe, we will show you how to get a label next to each axis of a figure.

How to do it...

Adding such annotations is very simple, as demonstrated in the following example:

```
import numpy as np
import matplotlib.pyplot as plt

X = np.linspace(-4, 4, 1024)
Y = .25 * (X + 4.) * (X + 1.) * (X - 2.)

plt.title('Power curve for airfoil KV873')
plt.xlabel('Air speed')
plt.ylabel('Total drag')

plt.plot(X, Y, c = 'k')
plt.show()
```

The figure will be the same as the one obtained in the first recipe of this chapter. However, both the axes will feature a legend.

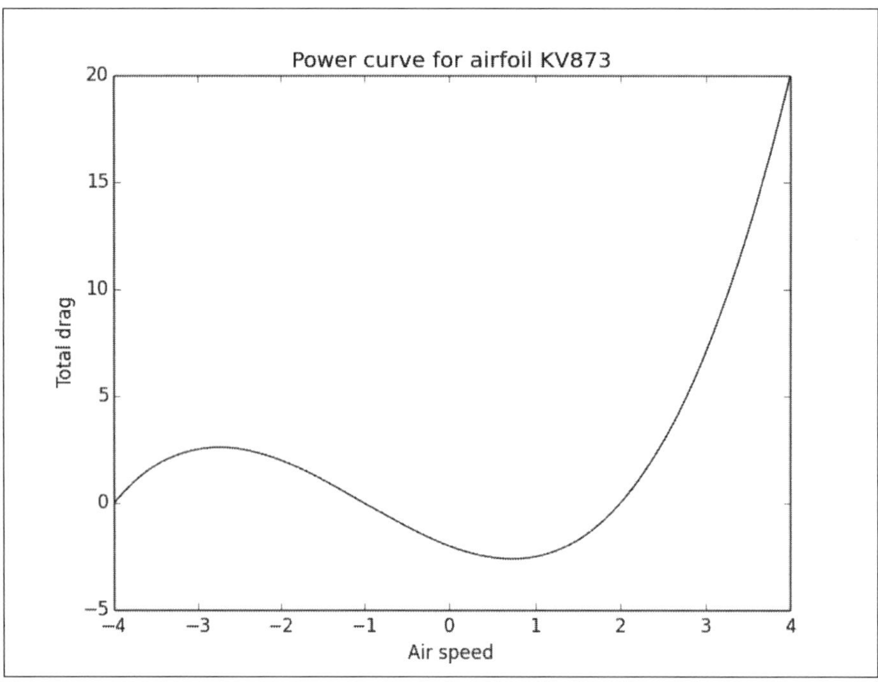

How it works...

We use the `pyplot.xlabel()` and `pyplot.ylabel()` functions to add a description of the horizontal axis and the vertical axis, respectively. As for the `pyplot.title()` function, this function accepts the LaTeX notation. These functions are available for any kind of graphic; you would use the same functions to annotate a scatter plot, a histogram, and so on.

Adding text

So far, we have seen how to set text at preset locations, such as title and axes. In this recipe, we are going to see how to add text at any location using text boxes.

How to do it...

matplotlib has a very flexible function called `pyplot.text()`, that displays text:

```
import numpy as np
import matplotlib.pyplot as plt
```

```
X = np.linspace(-4, 4, 1024)
Y = .25 * (X + 4.) * (X + 1.) * (X - 2.)

plt.text(-0.5, -0.25, 'Brackmard minimum')

plt.plot(X, Y, c = 'k')
plt.show()
```

This script displays text next to a curve:

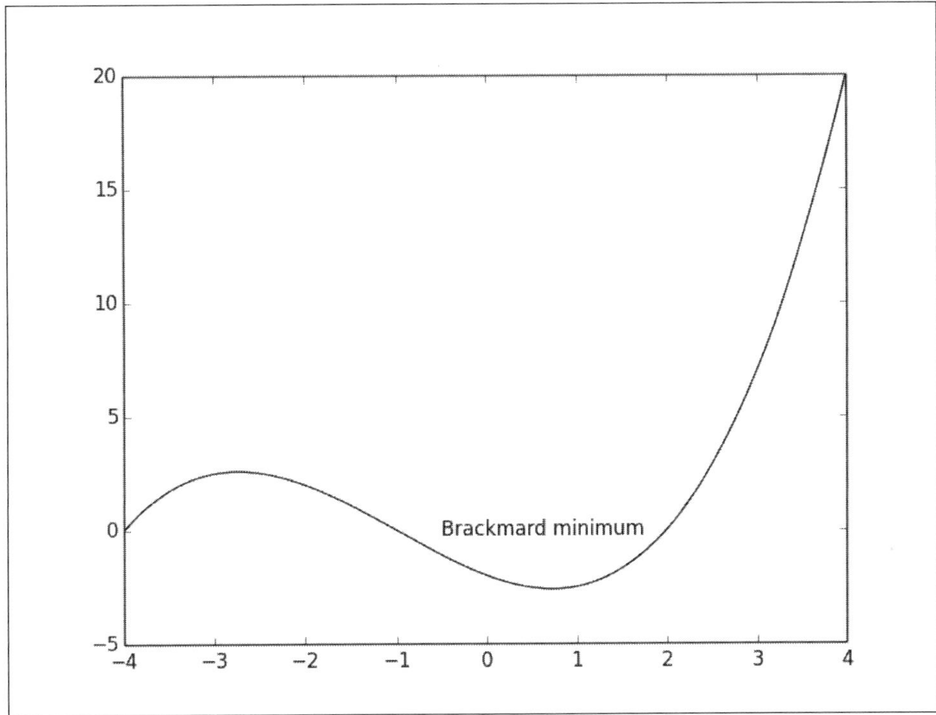

How it works...

We use the `pyplot.text()` function that takes a position and the text to display. The position is given in the graphic coordinates, specifying the position of the left border and the vertical baseline of the text.

There's more...

matplotlib's text rendering is very flexible. Let's explore the important options available.

Alignment control

The text is bound by a box. This box is used to relatively align the text to the coordinates passed to `pyplot.text()`. Using the `verticalalignment` and `horizontalalignment` parameters (respective shortcut equivalents are `va` and `ha`), we can control how the alignment is done.

The vertical alignment options are as follows:

- `'center'`: This is relative to the center of the textbox
- `'top'`: This is relative to the upper side of the textbox
- `'bottom'`: This is relative to the lower side of the textbox
- `'baseline'`: This is relative to the text's baseline

The horizontal alignment options are as follows:

- `'center'`: This is relative to the center of the textbox
- `'left'`: This is relative to the left side of the textbox
- `'right'`: This is relative to the right-hand side of the textbox

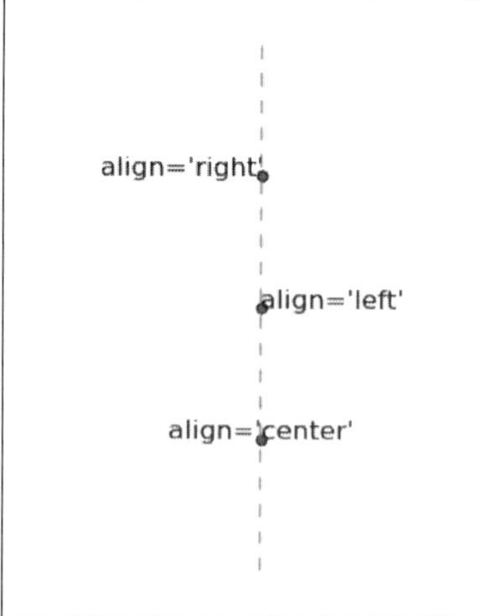

Bounding box control

The `pyplot.text()` function supports a `bbox` parameter that takes a dictionary as the input. This dictionary defines the various settings for the text box. Here's an illustration:

```
import numpy as np
import matplotlib.pyplot as plt

X = np.linspace(-4, 4, 1024)
Y = .25 * (X + 4.) * (X + 1.) * (X - 2.)

box = {
  'facecolor'  : '.75',
  'edgecolor' : 'k',
  'boxstyle'    : 'round'
}

plt.text(-0.5, -0.20, 'Brackmard minimum', bbox = box)

plt.plot(X, Y, c='k')
plt.show()
```

The preceding code will give the following output:

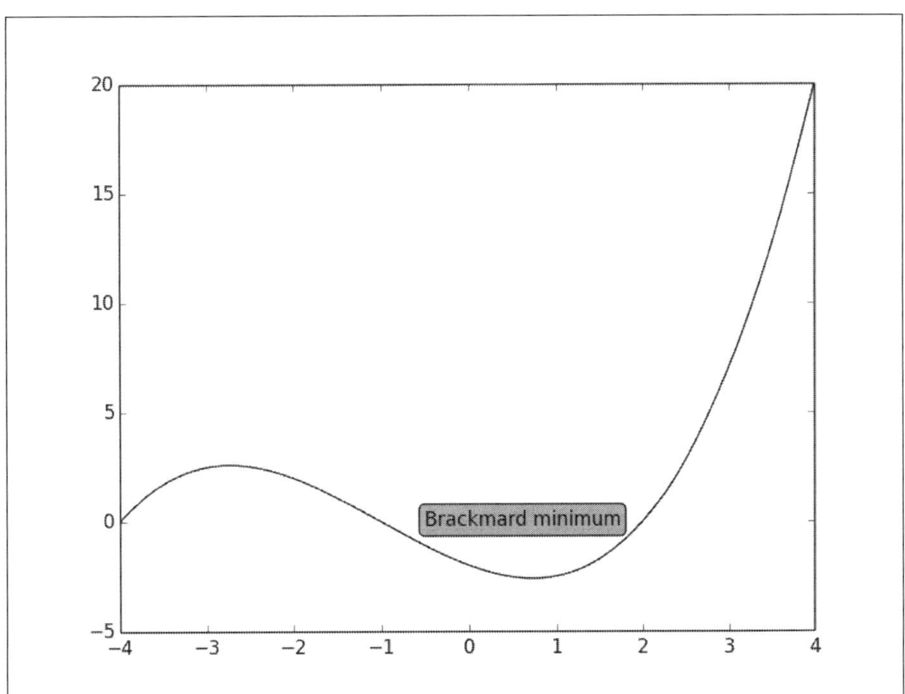

The dictionary passed to the `bbox` parameter defines the following key-value pairs:

- `'facecolor'`: This is the color used for the box. It will be used to set the background and the edge color
- `'edgecolor'`: This is the color used for the edges of the box's shape
- `'alpha'`: This is used to set the transparency level so that the box blends with the background
- `'boxstyle'`: This sets the style of the box, which can either be `'round'` or `'square'`
- `'pad'`: If `'boxstyle'` is set to `'square'`, it defines the amount of padding between the text and the box's sides

Adding arrows

Adding text boxes can help you to annotate a figure. However, to show a specific part of a picture, nothing beats the use of an arrow. In this recipe, we will show you how to add arrows on a figure.

How to do it...

matplotlib have a function to draw arrows with the `pyplot.annotate()` function as shown in the following code snippet:

```
import numpy as np
import matplotlib.pyplot as plt

X = np.linspace(-4, 4, 1024)
Y = .25 * (X + 4.) * (X + 1.) * (X - 2.)

plt.annotate('Brackmard minimum',
ha = 'center', va = 'bottom',
xytext = (-1.5, 3.),
xy = (0.75, -2.7),
arrowprops = { 'facecolor' : 'black', 'shrink' : 0.05 })

plt.plot(X, Y)
plt.show()
```

This script annotates a curve with text and an arrow, as shown in the following graph:

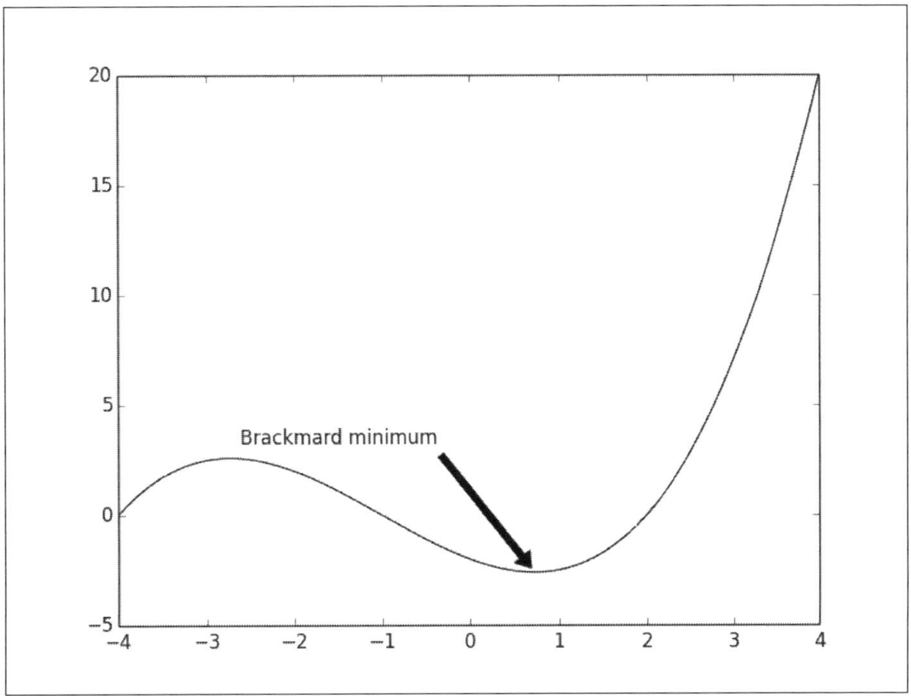

How it works...

The `pyplot.annotate()` function shows text working on the same lines as `pyplot.text()`. However, an arrow is also rendered. The text to be displayed is the first parameter. The `xy` parameter specifies the arrow's destination. The `xytext` parameter specifies the text position. Similar to `pyplot.text()`, one can play with the text alignment through the `horizontalalignment` and `verticalalignment` parameters. The `shrink` parameter controls the gap between the arrow's endpoints and the arrow itself.

The aspect of the arrow is controlled by a dictionary passed to the `arrowprops` parameter:

- `'arrowstyle'`: The parameters `''<-''`, `''<''`, `''-''`, `''wedge''`, `''simple''`, and `"fancy"` control the style of the arrow
- `'facecolor'`: This is the color used for the arrow. It will be used to set the background and the edge color
- `'edgecolor'`: This is the color used for the edges of the arrow's shape

- `'alpha'`: This is used to set the transparency level so that the arrow blends with the background

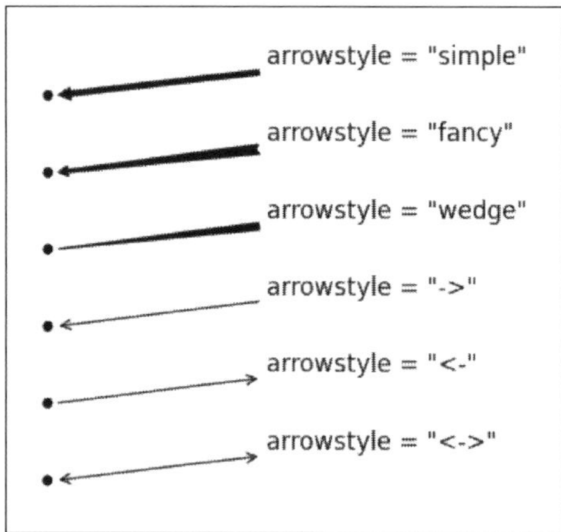

Adding a legend

A proper figure is not complete without its own legend. matplotlib provides a way to generate a legend with the minimal amount of effort. In this recipe, we will see how to add a legend to a graph.

How to do it...

For this recipe, we use the `pyplot.legend()` function as well as the `label` optional parameter:

```
import numpy as np
import matplotlib.pyplot as plt

X = np.linspace(0, 6, 1024)
Y1 = np.sin(X)
Y2 = np.cos(X)

plt.xlabel('X')
plt.ylabel('Y')

plt.plot(X, Y1, c = 'k',  lw = 3.,              label = 'sin(X)')
plt.plot(X, Y2, c = '.5', lw = 3., ls = '--', label = 'cos(X)')

plt.legend()
plt.show()
```

The preceding code gives the following output:

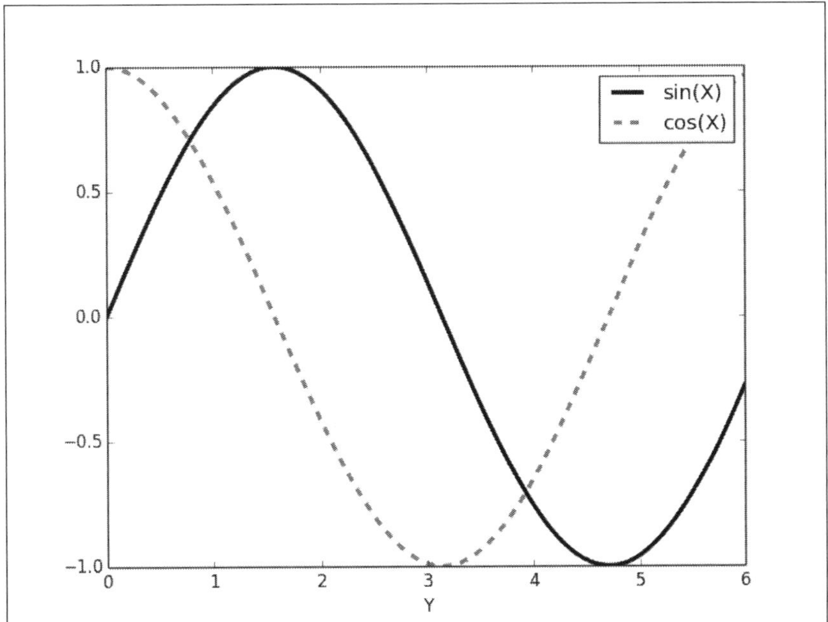

How it works...

Each `pyplot` function has an optional `label` parameter to name an element, such as curve, histogram, and so on, of a figure. matplotlib keeps a track of these labels. The `pyplot.legend()` function will render a legend. The legend is automatically generated from the labels.

There's more...

The `pyplot.legend` function has a couple of interesting parameters to control the legend aspects:

- `'loc'`: This is the location of the legend. The default value is `'best'`, which will place it automatically. Other valid values are `'upper left'`, `'lower left'`, `'lower right'`, `'right'`, `'center left'`, `'center right'`, `'lower center'`, `'upper center'`, and `'center'`.
- `'shadow'`: This can be either `True` or `False`, and it renders the legend with a shadow effect.
- `'fancybox'`: This can be either `True` or `False` and renders the legend with a rounded box.

- `'title'`: This renders the legend with the title passed as a parameter.
- `'ncol'`: This forces the passed value to be the number of columns for the legend.

Adding a grid

When preparing graphics, we might need to have a quick guess of the coordinates of any part of a figure. Adding a grid to the figure is a natural way to improve the readability of a figure. In this recipe, we are going to see how to add a grid to a figure.

How to do it...

matplotlib's grid functionality is controlled with the `pyplot.grid()` function.

```
import numpy as np
import matplotlib.pyplot as plt

X = np.linspace(-4, 4, 1024)
Y = .25 * (X + 4.) * (X + 1.) * (X - 2.)

plt.plot(X, Y, c = 'k')
plt.grid(True, lw = 2, ls = '--', c = '.75')
plt.show()
```

This script will show a curve with a grid in the background. The grid is aligned to the ticks of the axes' legend as shown in the following graph:

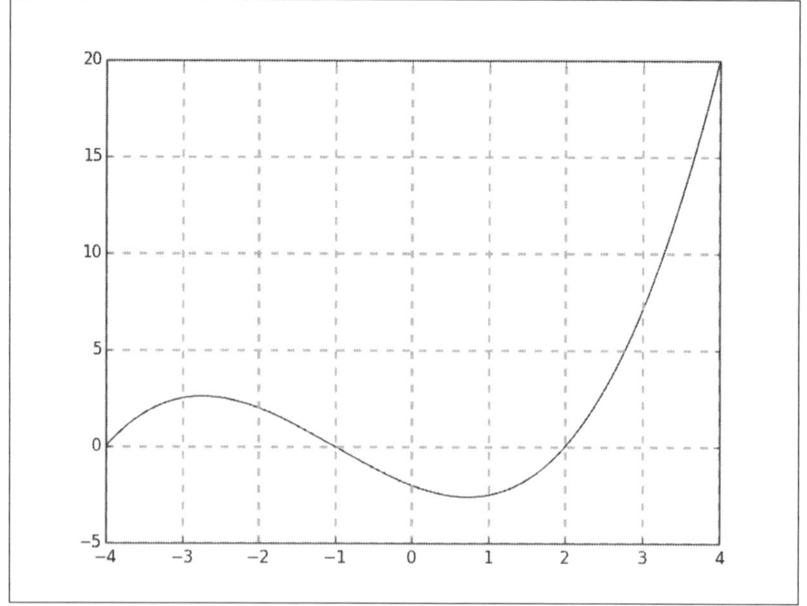

How it works...

Adding a grid is as simple as calling the `pyplot.grid()` function with `True` as the argument. A grid is comprised of lines and as such, `pyplot.grid()` accepts line style parameters, such as `linewidth`, `linestyle`, or `color`. These parameters will apply to the lines used to draw the grid.

Adding lines

When you have a very specific need in mind, the figures offered by matplotlib might not be of much help to you. All the graphics made by matplotlib consist of basic primitives. When demonstrating how to change the color of a boxplot, we mention that most matplotlib plotting functions return collections of lines and shapes. Now, we are going to demonstrate how to directly use a fundamental primitive: lines.

How to do it...

The following script will show a simple but aesthetic pattern made of independent lines:

```
import matplotlib.pyplot as plt

N = 16
for i in range(N):
  plt.gca().add_line(plt.Line2D((0, i), (N - i, 0), color = '.75'))

plt.grid(True)
plt.axis('scaled')
plt.show()
```

The preceding code gives the following output:

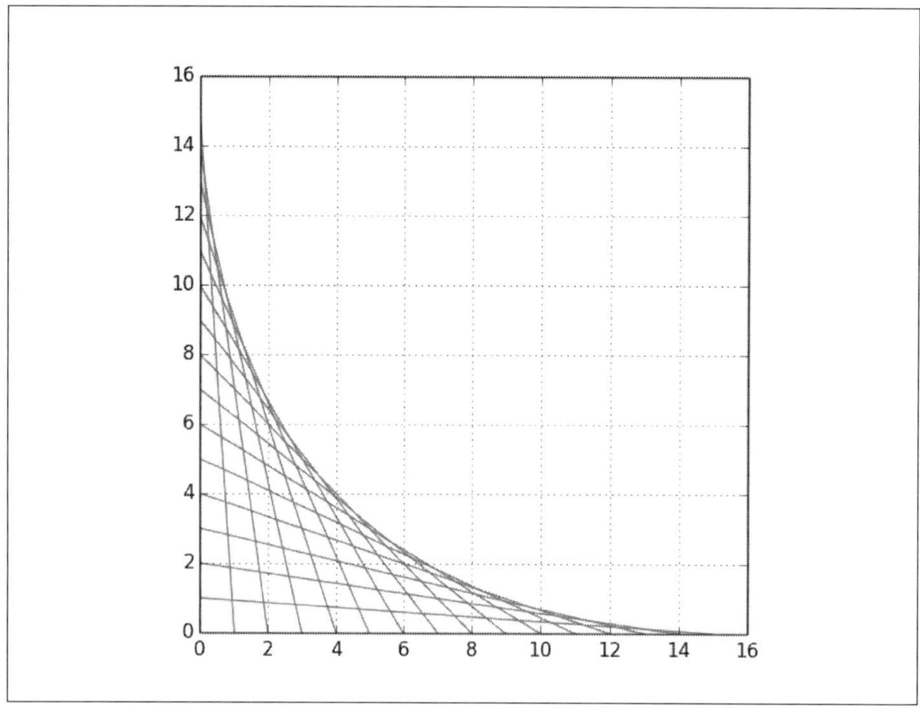

How it works...

In this script, we plot 16 independent lines. The `pyplot.Line2D()` function creates a new `Line2D` object. The mandatory parameters are the endpoints of the line. The optional parameters are all the parameters we have seen before for line-based figures. Thus, you can use `linestyle`, `linewidth`, `marker`, `markersize`, `color`, and so on.

The `pyplot.Line2D()` function creates the line, but the line will not be rendered unless you explicitly ask for it; this is done using `pyplot.gca().add_line()`. The `pyplot.gca()` function returns the object that is in charge of keeping track of what to render. Calling `gca().add_line()` simply signals that we want to render a line.

The `pyplot.axis('scaled')` function is required to ensure that the figure uses a uniform scale: the same scale as the one used on the *x* and *y* axes. This to be contrasted with the default behavior, `'tight'`, where matplotlib will give a different scale to the *x* and *y* axes to fit the figure as tightly as possible into the display surface. This feature will be introduced in *Chapter 4, Working with Figures*.

Adding shapes

To make your own figures out of basic primitives, lines are a good way to start, but you will most likely need more shapes. Rendering shapes works along the same lines as rendering lines. In this recipe, we will show you how to add shapes in a figure.

How to do it...

In the following script, we create and render several shapes. The comments indicate which part renders which shape:

```
import matplotlib.patches as patches
import matplotlib.pyplot as plt

# Circle
shape = patches.Circle((0, 0), radius = 1., color = '.75')
plt.gca().add_patch(shape)

# Rectangle
shape = patches.Rectangle((2.5, -.5), 2., 1., color = '.75')
plt.gca().add_patch(shape)

# Ellipse
shape = patches.Ellipse((0, -2.), 2., 1., angle = 45., color =
  '.75')
plt.gca().add_patch(shape)

# Fancy box
shape = patches.FancyBboxPatch((2.5, -2.5), 2., 1., boxstyle =
  'sawtooth', color = '.75')
plt.gca().add_patch(shape)

# Display all
plt.grid(True)
plt.axis('scaled')
plt.show()
```

Four different shapes are shown:

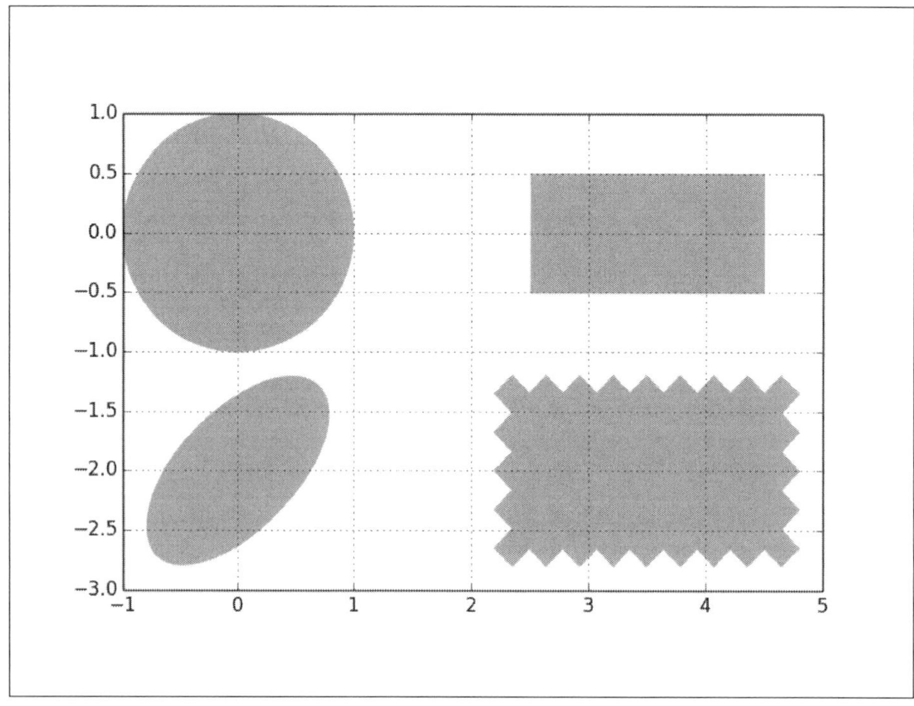

How it works...

No matter which shapes are displayed, the principle is the same. Internally, a shape is described as a path called patch in matplotlib API. Paths for several kinds of shapes are available in the `matplotlib.patches` module. Indeed, this module contains patches used for all the figures. As is the case for lines, creating a path won't be enough to render it; you will have to signal that you want to render it. This is done by `pyplot.gca().add_patch()`.

A lot of path constructors are available. Let's review those used in the example:

- **Circle**: This takes the coordinates of its center and the radius as the parameters
- **Rectangle**: This takes the coordinates of its lower-left corner and its size as the parameters
- **Ellipse**: This takes the coordinates of its center and the half-length of its two axes as the parameters
- **FancyBox**: This is like a rectangle but takes an additional `boxstyle` parameter (either `'larrow'`, `'rarrow'`, `'round'`, `'round4'`, `'roundtooth'`, `'sawtooth'`, or `'square'`)

There's more...

Apart from the predefined shapes, we can define arbitrary shapes using polygons.

Working with polygons

Polygons are barely more complex than paths and are defined by a list of points:

```
import numpy as np
import matplotlib.patches as patches
import matplotlib.pyplot as plt

theta = np.linspace(0, 2 * np.pi, 8)
points = np.vstack((np.cos(theta), np.sin(theta))).transpose()

plt.gca().add_patch(patches.Polygon(points, color = '.75'))

plt.grid(True)
plt.axis('scaled')
plt.show()
```

The preceding code gives the following polygon as the output:

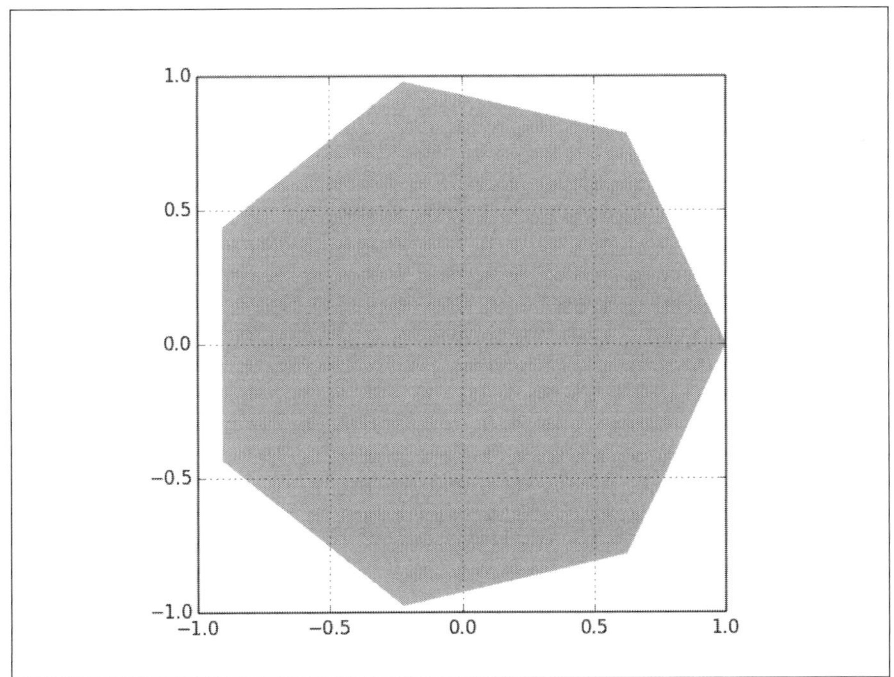

The `matplotlib.patches.Polygon()` constructor takes a list of coordinates as the inputs, that is, the vertices of the polygon.

Working with path attributes

All paths have several attributes that we already explored before: `linewidth`, `linestyle`, `edgecolor`, `facecolor`, `hatch`, and so on, as follows:

```
import numpy as np
import matplotlib.patches as patches
import matplotlib.pyplot as plt

theta = np.linspace(0, 2 * np.pi, 6)
points = np.vstack((np.cos(theta), np.sin(theta))).transpose()

plt.gca().add_patch(plt.Circle((0, 0), radius = 1., color =
  '.75'))
plt.gca().add_patch(plt.Polygon(points, closed=None, fill=None,
  lw = 3., ls = 'dashed', edgecolor = 'k'))

plt.grid(True)
plt.axis('scaled')
plt.show()
```

The following graph is the output of the preceding code:

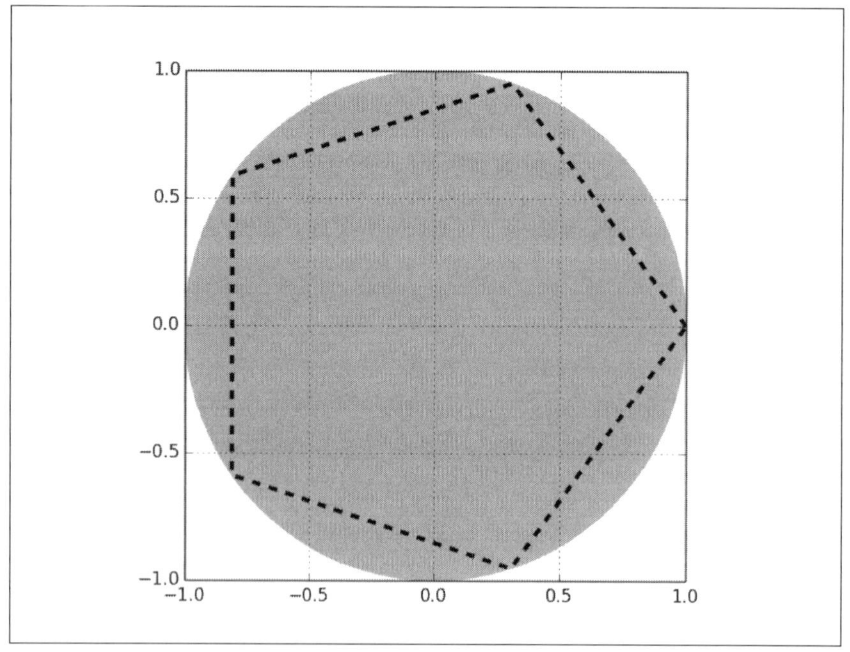

Here, we use a nonfilled (`fill = None`) polygon with dashed edges (`ls = 'dashed'`) to draw a polygon outline without having to create several line objects. Numerous effects can be achieved by just playing with the attributes of a path.

Controlling tick spacing

In matplotlib, ticks are small marks on both the axes of a figure. So far, we let matplotlib handle the position of the ticks on the axes legend. As we will see in this recipe, we can manually override this mechanism.

How to do it...

In this script, we will manipulate the gap between the ticks on the *x* axis:

```
import numpy as np
import matplotlib.pyplot as plt
import matplotlib.ticker as ticker

X = np.linspace(-15, 15, 1024)
Y = np.sinc(X)

ax = plt.axes()
ax.xaxis.set_major_locator(ticker.MultipleLocator(5))
ax.xaxis.set_minor_locator(ticker.MultipleLocator(1))

plt.plot(X, Y, c = 'k')
plt.show()
```

Now, smaller ticks are seen between the usual ticks:

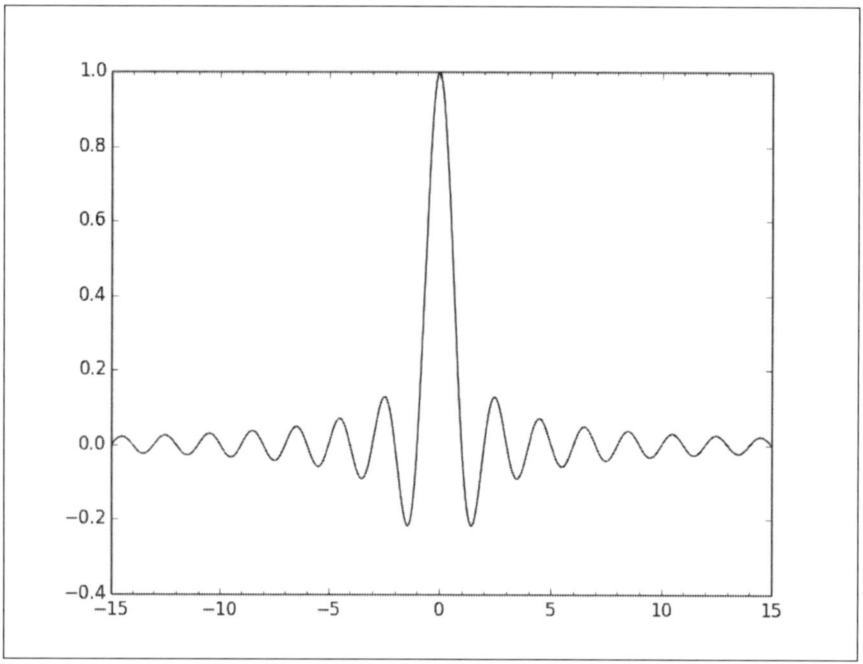

How it works...

We forced the horizontal ticks to appear by steps of 5 units. Moreover, we also added small ticks, appearing by steps of 1 unit. To do so, we perform the following steps:

1. We get an instance of the `Axes` object: the object that manages the axes of a figure. This is the purpose of `ax = plot.axes()`.
2. For the *x* axis (`ax.xaxis`), we set a `Locator` instance for both the major and minor ticks.

There's more...

If we wish to add a grid, we can take into account the minor ticks, as follows:

```
import numpy as np
import matplotlib.pyplot as plt
import matplotlib.ticker as ticker

X = np.linspace(-15, 15, 1024)
Y = np.sinc(X)
```

```
ax = plt.axes()
ax.xaxis.set_major_locator(ticker.MultipleLocator(5))
ax.xaxis.set_minor_locator(ticker.MultipleLocator(1))

plt.grid(True, which='both')
plt.plot(X, Y)
plt.show()
```

The preceding code snippet gives the following output:

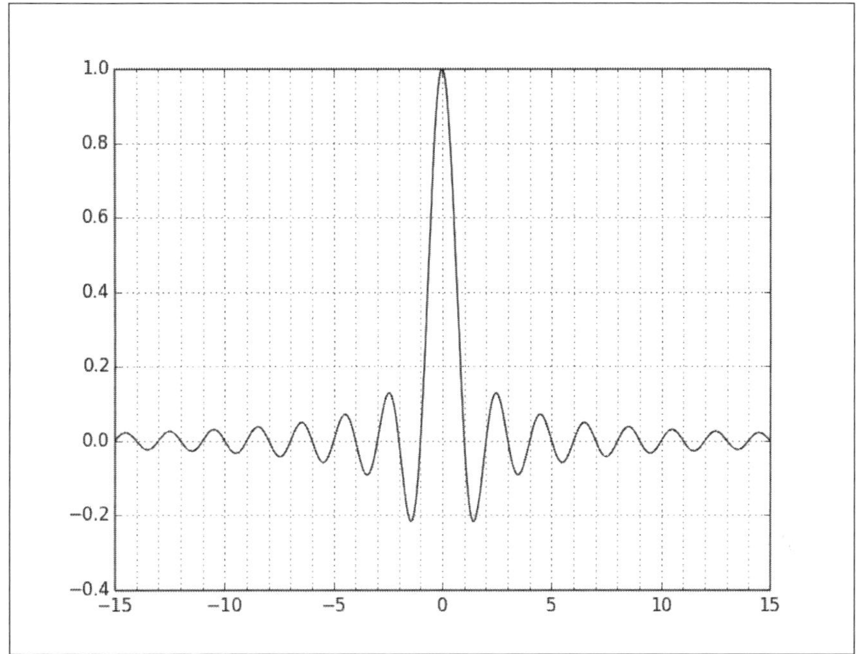

As shown previously, we can add a grid with `pyplot.grid()`. This function takes an optional parameter, `which`. It can accept three values: `'minor'`, `'major'`, and `'both'`. It determines at which ticks the grid should be displayed.

Controlling tick labeling

Tick labels are coordinates in the figure space. Although it makes sense for a fair number of cases, it is not always adequate. For instance, let's imagine a bar chart that shows the median income of 10 countries. We would like to see the names of the countries under each bar, rather than the coordinates of the bars. For a time series, we would like to see dates rather than some abstract coordinate. matplotlib provides a comprehensive API precisely for this. In this recipe, we will see how to control tick labeling.

How to do it...

Using the standard matplotlib ticks API, setting ticks for a bar chart (or any other kind of graphics) is done as follows:

```
import numpy as np
import matplotlib.ticker as ticker
import matplotlib.pyplot as plt

name_list = ('Omar', 'Serguey', 'Max', 'Zhou', 'Abidin')
value_list = np.random.randint(0, 99, size = len(name_list))
pos_list = np.arange(len(name_list))

ax = plt.axes()
ax.xaxis.set_major_locator(ticker.FixedLocator((pos_list)))
ax.xaxis.set_major_formatter(ticker.FixedFormatter((name_list)))

plt.bar(pos_list, value_list, color = '.75', align = 'center')
plt.show()
```

Each bar of the bar chart has its own tick and its own legend:

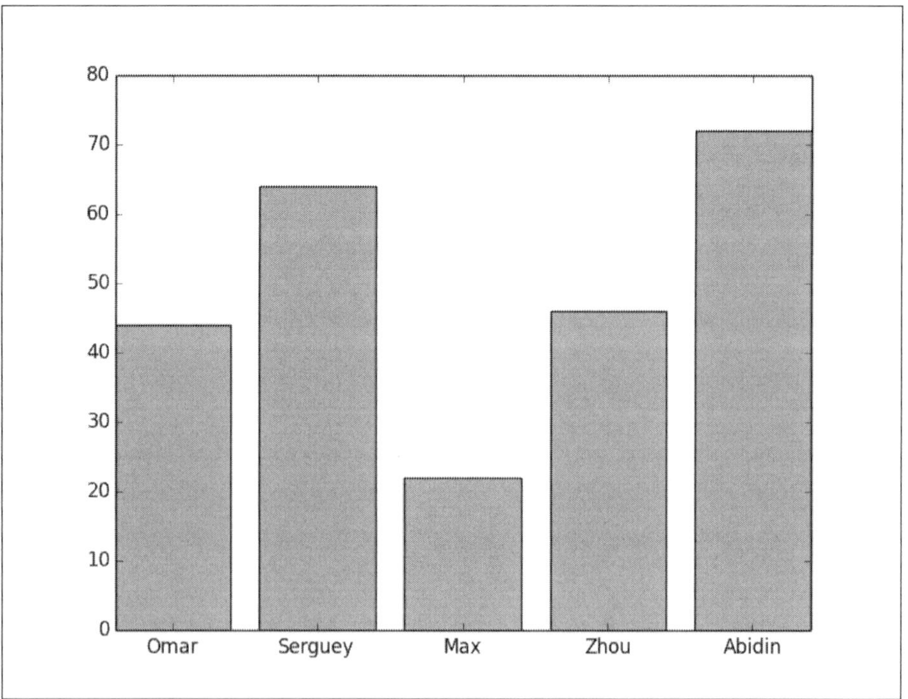

How it works...

We have seen the `ticker.Locator` to generate the location of ticks. A `ticker.Formatter` object instance will generate labels for the ticks. The `Formatter` instance we have used here is a `FixedFormatter`, which will take the labels from a list of strings. We then set the *x* axis with our `Formatter` instance. For this particular example, we also use a `FixedLocator` to ensure that each bar is right at the middle of one tick.

There's more...

We have barely touched the surface of the topic; there's more, much more, about ticks.

A simpler way to create bar charts with fixed labels

For the particular case of fixed labels for a bar chart, we can take the advantage of a shortcut:

```
import numpy as np
import matplotlib.pyplot as plt

name_list = ('Omar', 'Serguey', 'Max', 'Zhou', 'Abidin')
value_list = np.random.randint(0, 99, size = len(name_list))
pos_list = np.arange(len(name_list))

plt.bar(pos_list, value_list, color = '.75', align = 'center')
plt.xticks(pos_list, name_list)
plt.show()
```

The preceding code snippet gives the following bar chart:

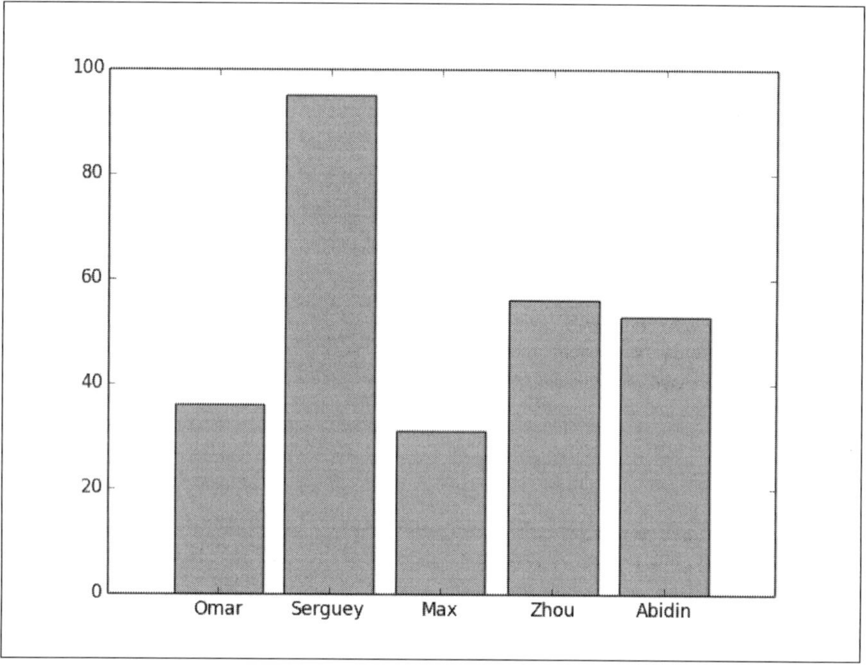

Rather than using the ticker API, we use the `pyplot.xticks()` function to give a fix label to a fixed set of ticks. This function takes a list of positions and a list of names as the parameters. The result is the same as the previous example; it's just shorter and easier to remember.

Advanced label generation

What if the point of the ticker API is that we have shortcuts around it? The ticker API can do better than show fixed labels for each tick, as follows:

```
import numpy as np
import matplotlib.pyplot as plt
import matplotlib.ticker as ticker

def make_label(value, pos):
  return '%0.1f%%' % (100. * value)

ax = plt.axes()
ax.xaxis.set_major_formatter(ticker.FuncFormatter(make_label))

X = np.linspace(0, 1, 256)
```

```
plt.plot(X, np.exp(-10 * X), c ='k')
plt.plot(X, np.exp(-5 * X), c= 'k', ls = '--')

plt.show()
```

The preceding code gives the following output:

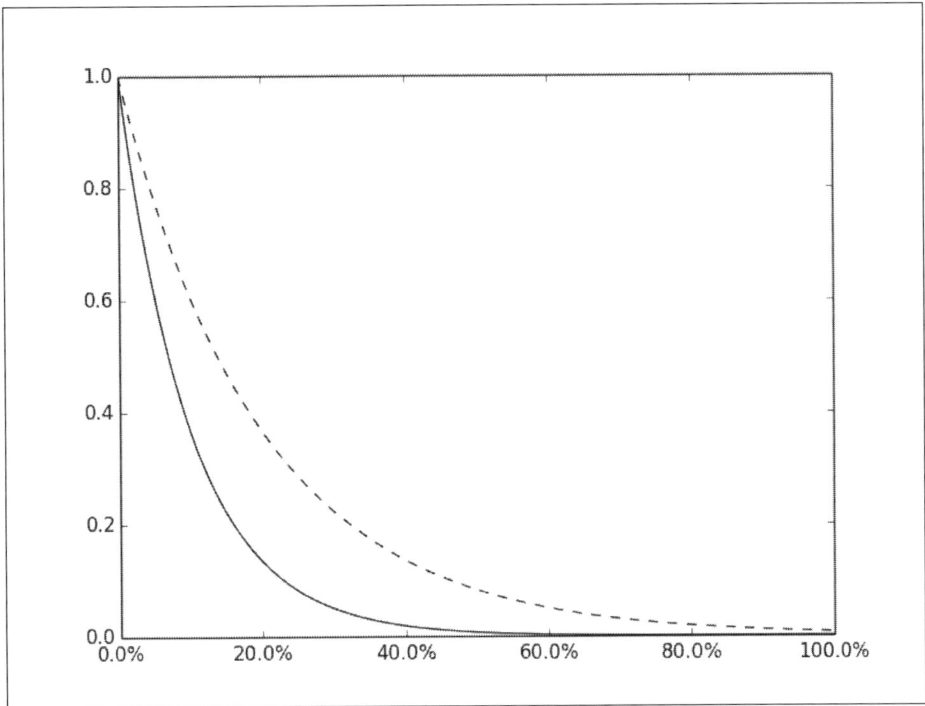

In this example, the ticks are generated by a custom function, `make_label`. This function takes the coordinates of a tick as the input and generates a string; here, a percentage. No matter how many ticks matplotlib decides to show, we can generate the right label for it. This is more flexible than giving a fixed list of strings. The only new thing here is `FuncFormatter`, a formatter that takes a function as a parameter.

This approach of delegating the actual task of generating labels to a function is called **delegation**. Our delegate is `make_label`. It is a beautiful programming technique. Let's say, we want to display dates for each tick. This can be done using the standard Python time and date functions:

```
import numpy as np
import datetime
import matplotlib.pyplot as plt
import matplotlib.ticker as ticker
```

```
start_date = datetime.datetime(1998, 1, 1)

def make_label(value, pos):
  time = start_date + datetime.timedelta(days = 365 * value)
  return time.strftime('%b %y')

ax = plt.axes()
ax.xaxis.set_major_formatter(ticker.FuncFormatter(make_label))

X = np.linspace(0, 1, 256)
plt.plot(X, np.exp(-10 * X), c = 'k')
plt.plot(X, np.exp(-5 * X), c = 'k', ls = '--')

labels = ax.get_xticklabels()
plt.setp(labels, rotation = 30.)
plt.show()
```

The preceding code gives the following output:

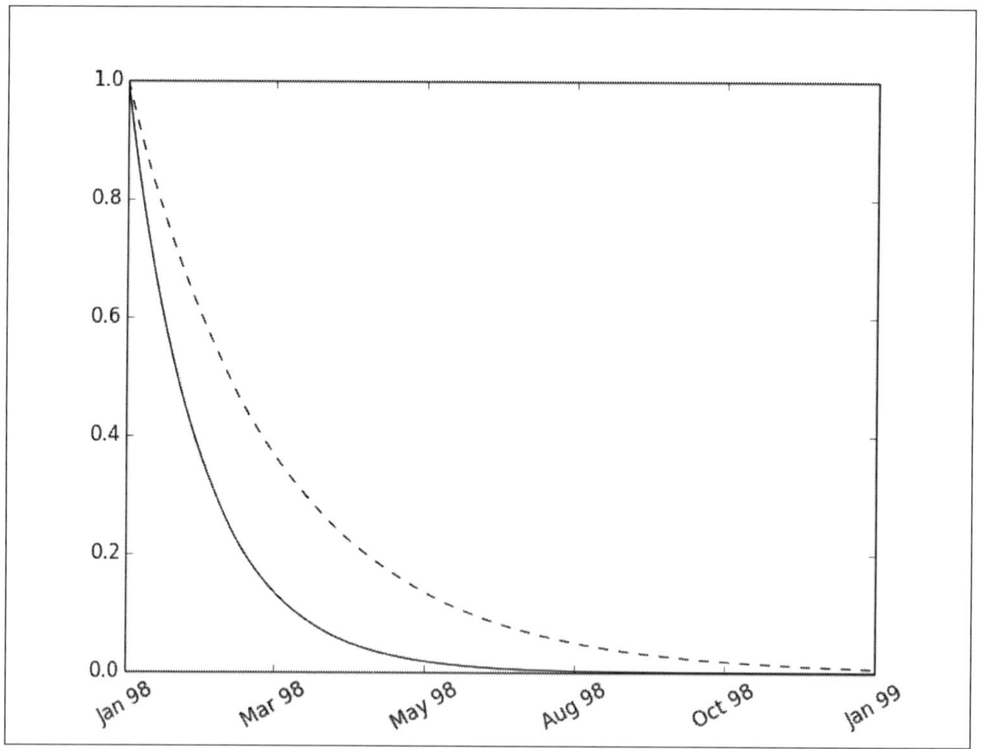

Now, each tick appears as a date formatted in a human-readable fashion. The approach is the same as we used previously: we use a `FuncFormatter`. In the label generation function, we convert the position of the tick to a date, thanks to the `datetime` standard module. Here, we map values in the `[0, 1]` range to the year 1998. The `datetime` module also offers a powerful formatting function `strftime`, which we use to produce the label itself.

4

Working with Figures

In this chapter, we will cover:

- Compositing multiple figures
- Scaling both the axes equally
- Setting an axis range
- Setting the aspect ratio
- Inserting subfigures
- Using a logarithmic scale
- Using polar coordinates

Introduction

Designing a scientific plotting package is a daunting task—the needs to cover are extremely diverse. On one hand, ideally, creating any kind of figure should be possible with a minimal amount of coding and fiddling around. On the other, we want to be able to customize any aspect of a graphic. Those two goals are diametrically opposed. matplotlib offers a rare balance between the two goals. In this chapter, we will explore ways to modify fundamental aspects of the stock figures, such as changing the coordinate system used.

Compositing multiple figures

When examining some data, we might want to see several aspects of it at once. For instance, with population statistics data from one country, we would like to see the male/female age pyramid, the wealth repartition, and the population size per year as three distinct graphics. matplotlib offers the possibility to composite several figures together. Since Version 1.2, the API for this is really convenient. In this recipe, we are going to see how to compose several figures together.

How to do it...

We are going to use the `pyplot.subplot2grid()` function as follows:

```
import numpy as np
from matplotlib import pyplot as plt

T = np.linspace(-np.pi, np.pi, 1024)

grid_size = (4, 2)

plt.subplot2grid(grid_size, (0, 0), rowspan = 3, colspan = 1)
plt.plot(np.sin(2 * T), np.cos(0.5 * T), c = 'k')

plt.subplot2grid(grid_size, (0, 1), rowspan = 3, colspan = 1)
plt.plot(np.cos(3 * T), np.sin(T), c = 'k')

plt.subplot2grid(grid_size, (3, 0), rowspan=1, colspan=3)

plt.plot(np.cos(5 * T), np.sin(7 * T), c= 'k')

plt.tight_layout()
plt.show()
```

Three figures are drawn, dividing the graphic in three areas, as follows:

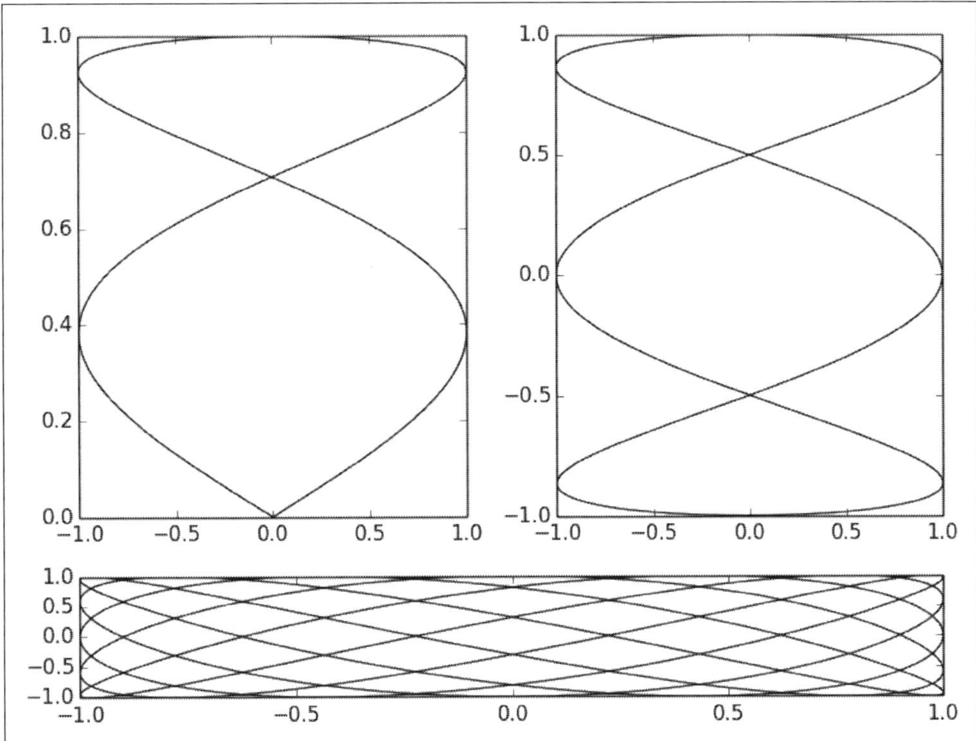

How it works...

The idea behind `pyplot.subplot2grid()` is to define a grid of R rows and C columns. Then, we can render a figure to a rectangular patch of that grid.

The `pyplot.subplot2grid()` function has four parameters:

- The first parameter is the number of rows and columns of the grid, passed as a tuple. If we want a grid of R rows and C columns, we would pass (R, C).
- The second parameter is a coordinate in the grid, in rows and columns, also passed as a tuple.
- The optional parameter `rowspan` defines how many rows the figure will span.
- The optional parameter `colspan` defines how many columns the figure will span.

Once `pyplot.subplot2grid()` is called, further calls to `pyplot` will define a figure within the specified rectangular area. To render another figure in another area, we call `pyplot.subplot2grid()` again.

In the example script, we define a 2 x 4 grid. The two top figures span over 1 column and 3 rows, thus filling almost one full column each. The third figure spans over 2 columns but only 1 row, filling the bottom row. Once all the figures are described, we then call `pyplot.tight_layout()`. This command asks matplotlib to pack all the figures so that none of them overlap each other.

There's more...

We have seen `pyplot.title()` add a title to a figure. In the following example, we are using `pyplot.title()` to give a title to each subfigure:

```
import numpy as np
from matplotlib import pyplot as plt

def get_radius(T, params):
  m, n_1, n_2, n_3 = params
  U = (m * T) / 4

  return (np.fabs(np.cos(U)) ** n_2 + np.fabs(np.sin(U)) ** n_3) **
(-1. / n_1)

grid_size = (3, 4)
T = np.linspace(0, 2 * np.pi, 1024)

for i in range(grid_size[0]):
  for j in range(grid_size[1]):
    params = np.random.random_integers(1, 20, size = 4)
    R = get_radius(T, params)

    axes = plt.subplot2grid(grid_size, (i, j), rowspan=1, colspan=1)
    axes.get_xaxis().set_visible(False)
    axes.get_yaxis().set_visible(False)

    plt.plot(R * np.cos(T), R * np.sin(T), c = 'k')
    plt.title('%d, %d, %d, %d' % tuple(params), fontsize = 'small')

plt.tight_layout()
plt.show()
```

The following graphic contains 12 figures, each with its own title:

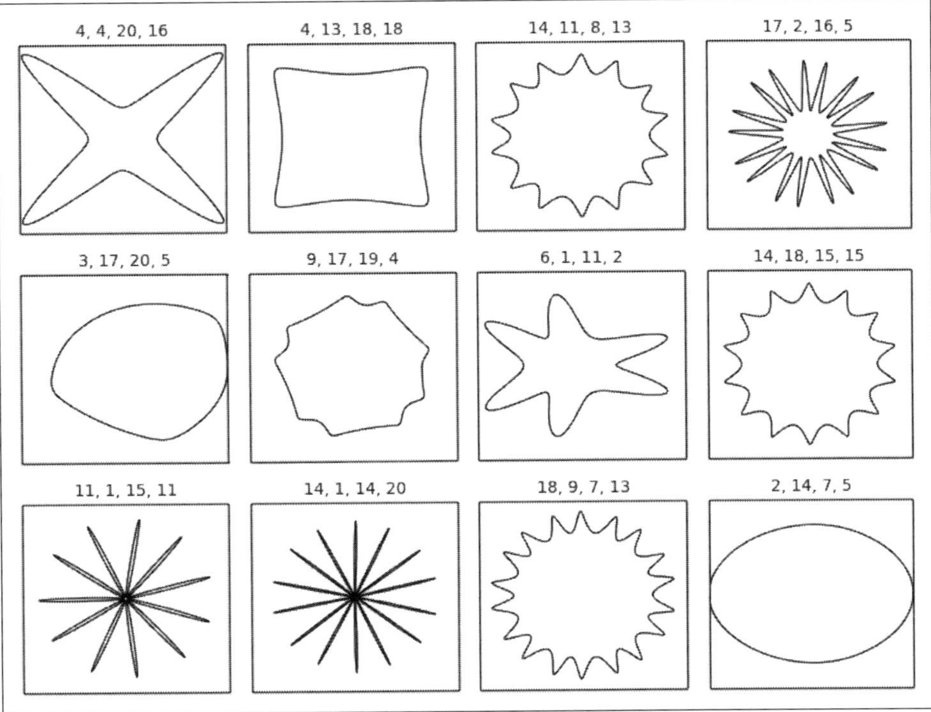

The `pyplot.title()` function gives a title for one subfigure. If we need one title for the whole graphic, we should use `pyplot.suptitle()`, where `suptitle` stands for SUPerior TITLE.

An alternative way to composite figures

The subplot mechanism introduced here is fairly general; it allows us to create complex layouts. If we just need to have a couple of figures in one row or one column, we can use simpler code, as follows:

```
import numpy as np
from matplotlib import pyplot as plt

T = np.linspace(-np.pi, np.pi, 1024)

fig, (ax0, ax1) = plt.subplots(ncols =2)
ax0.plot(np.sin(2 * T), np.cos(0.5 * T), c = 'k')
ax1.plot(np.cos(3 * T), np.sin(T), c = 'k')

plt.show()
```

With just one call to `pyplot.subplots()`, we created two subfigures next to each other, as shown in the following figure:

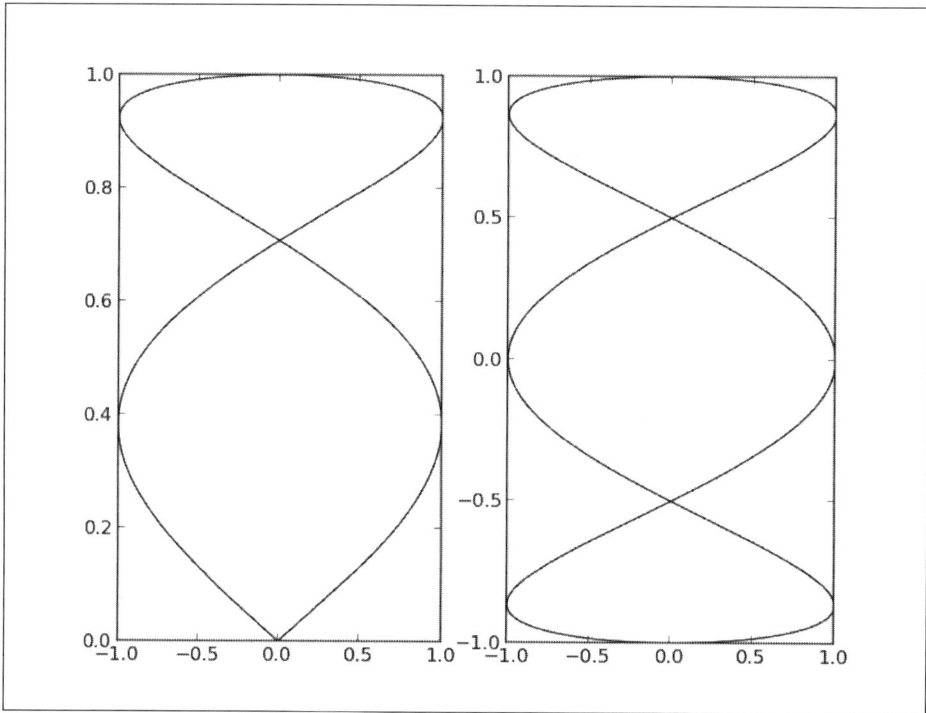

The `pyplot.subplot()` function takes two optional parameters, `ncols` and `nrows`, and will return a `Figure` object with `ncols * nrows` instances of `Axes`. The `Axes` instances are laid out in a grid of `ncols` columns by `nrows` rows. This makes grid layouts very easy to create.

Scaling both the axes equally

By default, matplotlib will use a different scale for both the axes of a figure. In this recipe, we are going to see how to use the same scale for the two axes of a figure.

How to do it...

To accomplish this, we will need to play with the `pyplot` API and the `Axes` object, as shown in the following code:

```
import numpy as np
import matplotlib.pyplot as plt
```

```
T = np.linspace(0, 2 * np.pi, 1024)

plt.plot(2. * np.cos(T), np.sin(T), c = 'k', lw = 3.)
plt.axes().set_aspect('equal')

plt.show()
```

The preceding script draws an ellipse with its real aspect ratio, as follows:

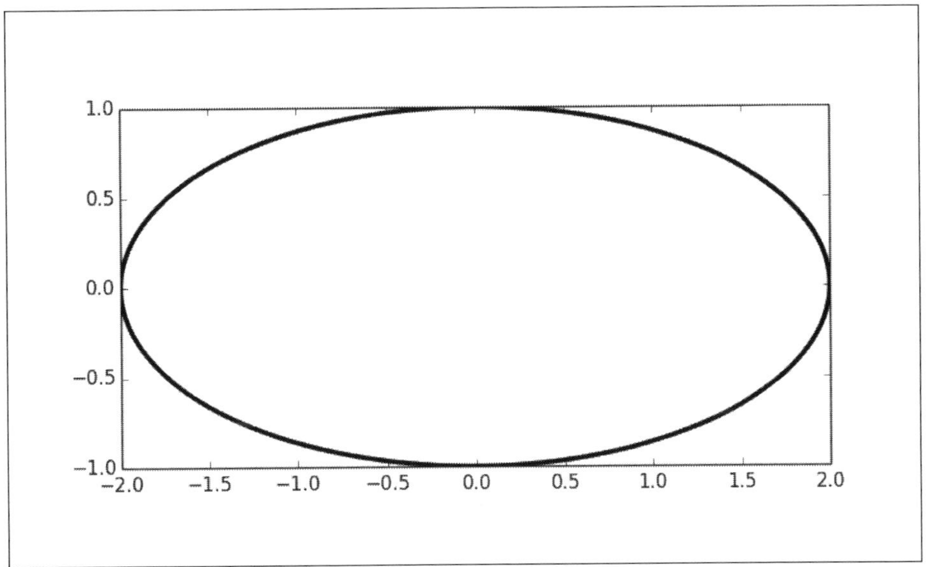

How it works...

In this example, we display an ellipse where the major axis is twice the length of the minor axis. Indeed, the rendered ellipse follows those proportions.

The `pyplot.axes()` function returns an instance of the `Axes` object, the object in charge of the axes. The `Axes` instance have a `set_aspect` method, which we set to `'equal'`. Now, both axes use the same scale. If we did not set the same aspect, the figure would look different.

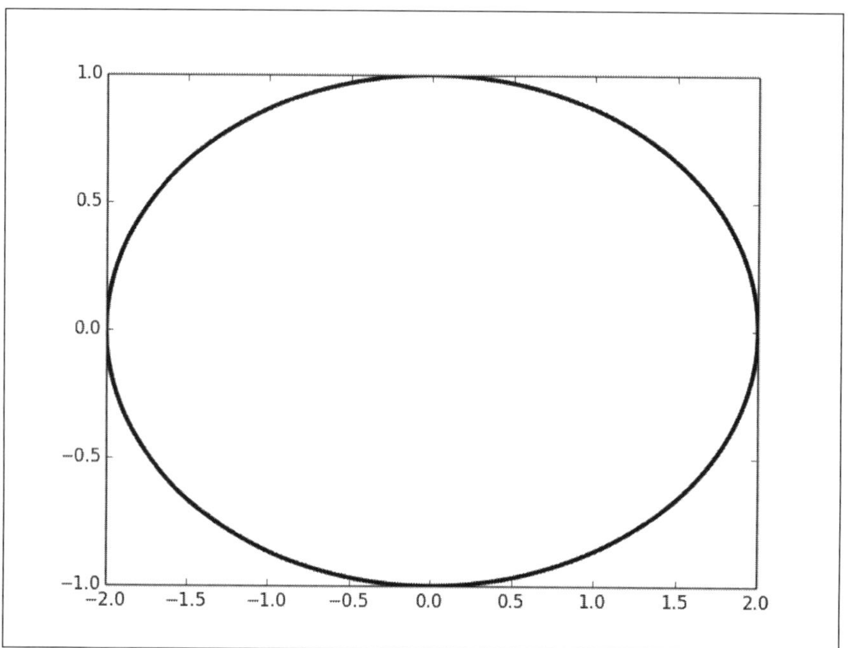

The preceding figure is still an ellipse, but with a deformed aspect ratio.

Setting an axis range

By default, matplotlib will find the minimum and maximum of your data on both axes and use this as the range to plot your data. However, it is sometimes preferable to manually set this range, to get a better view of the data's extrema. In this recipe, we are going to see how to set an axis range.

How to do it...

The `pyplot` API provides a function to directly set the range of one axis, as follows:

```
import numpy as np
import matplotlib.pyplot as plt
```

```
X = np.linspace(-6, 6, 1024)

plt.ylim(-.5, 1.5)
plt.plot(X, np.sinc(X), c = 'k')
plt.show()
```

The preceding script draws a curve. In contrast with the default settings, the graphic does not fit the curve perfectly; we have some room at the upper part of the curve, as shown in the following figure:

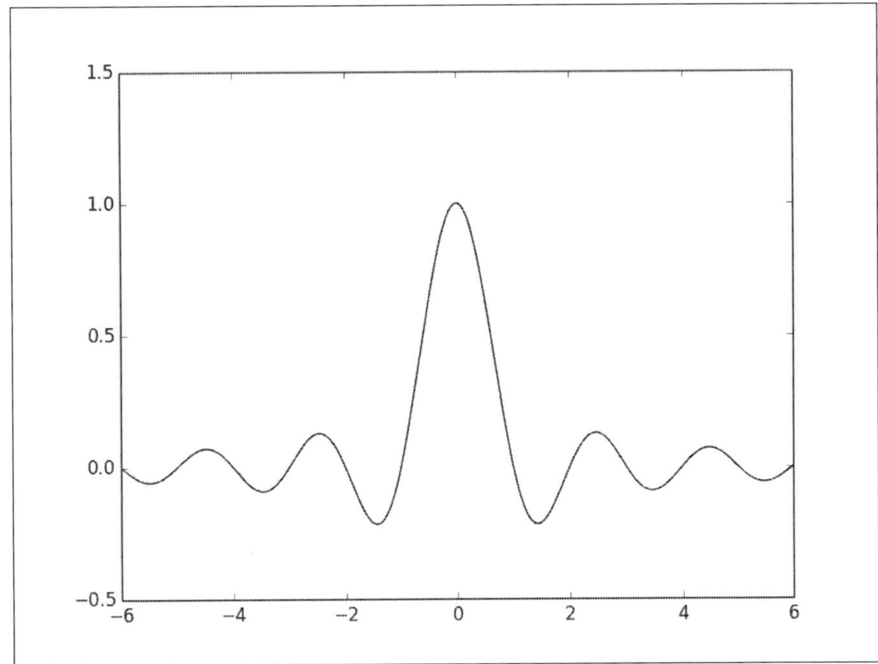

How it works...

The `pyplot.xlim()` and `pyplot.ylim()` parameters allow us to control the range of the *x* axis and *y* axis respectively. These parameters are the maximum and minimum values.

Setting the aspect ratio

When preparing figures for a journal publication or a website, one might need a figure that has one specific aspect ratio. In this recipe, we are going to see how to control the aspect ratio of a figure.

How to do it...

The `pyplot` API provides a simple way to set up a custom aspect ratio, as follows:

```
import numpy as np
import matplotlib.pyplot as plt

X = np.linspace(-6, 6, 1024)
Y1, Y2 = np.sinc(X), np.cos(X)

plt.figure(figsize=(10.24, 2.56))
plt.plot(X, Y1, c='k', lw = 3.)
plt.plot(X, Y2, c='.75', lw = 3.)

plt.show()
```

The aspect ratio of the following figure is much different from what we would get by default:

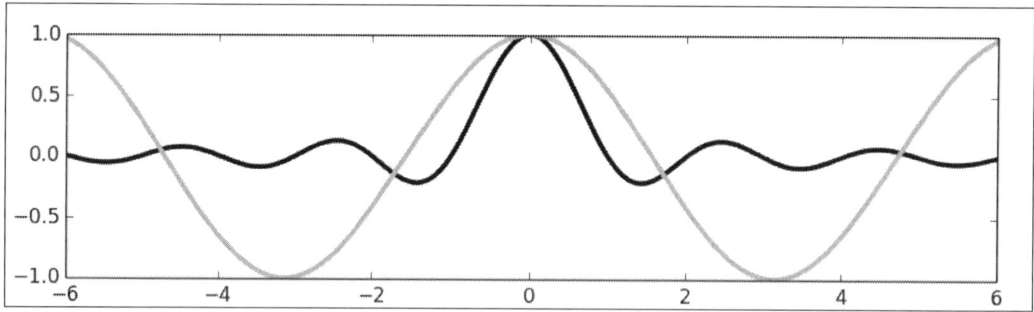

How it works...

We use the `pyplot.figure()` function, which creates a new `Figure` instance. A `Figure` object represents a figure as a whole. Usually, this object is created implicitly, behind the scenes. However, by creating the object explicitly, we can control various aspects of a figure, including its aspect ratio. The `figsize` parameter allows us to specify its size. In this example, we set the horizontal size as four times the vertical size, giving it a 4:1 aspect ratio.

Inserting subfigures

Inserting a small, embedded figure can be helpful in showing a detail of a figure, or more generally, to emphasize a particular part of a graphic. In this recipe, we are going to see how to insert a subfigure into a figure.

How to do it...

matplotlib allows us to create subregions in any part of a figure, and assign a figure to that subregion. In the following example, a subregion is created to show a detail of the curve:

```
import numpy as np
from matplotlib import pyplot as plt

X = np.linspace(-6, 6, 1024)
Y = np.sinc(X)

X_detail = np.linspace(-3, 3, 1024)
Y_detail = np.sinc(X_detail)

plt.plot(X, Y, c = 'k')

sub_axes = plt.axes([.6, .6, .25, .25])
sub_axes.plot(X_detail, Y_detail, c = 'k')
plt.setp(sub_axes)

plt.show()
```

The subregion is shown on the upper-right part of the figure.

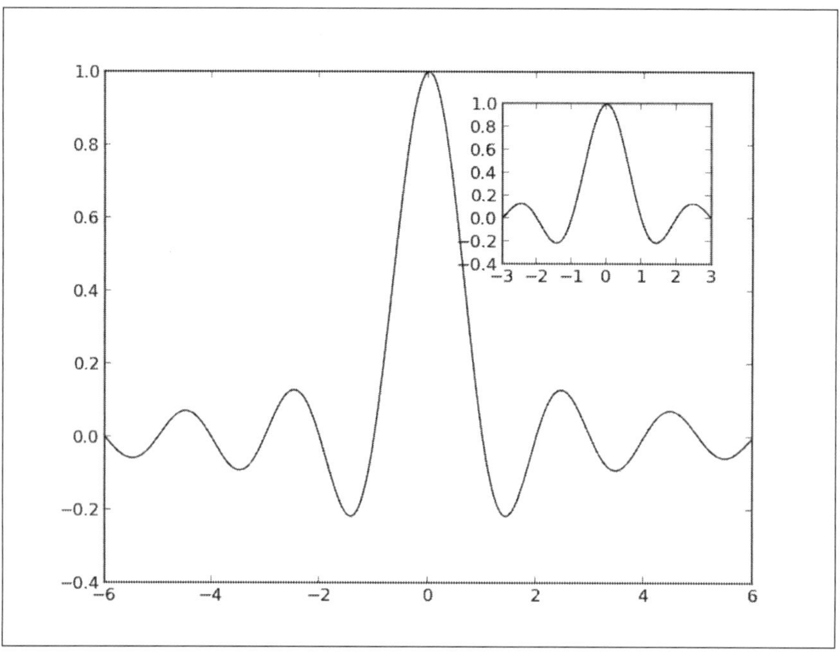

How it works...

We start by creating a subregion on the figure as follows:

```
sub_axes = plt.axes([.6, .6, .25, .25])
```

The region is in figure-wise coordinates; that is, (0, 0) is the bottom-left corner and (1, 1) is the top-right corner of the overall figure. The subregion is defined by four values: the coordinates of the bottom-left corner of the region and its dimensions.

Once the subregion is defined, we have an `Axes` instance in which we create a figure. Then, we need to call `pyplot.setp()` on our `Axes` instance as follows:

```
plt.setp(sub_axes)
```

Note that there is no limit on how many subregions you can create.

Using a logarithmic scale

When visualizing data that varies across a very wide range, a logarithmic scale allows us to visualize variations that would otherwise be barely visible. In this recipe, we are going to show you how to manipulate the scaling system of a figure.

How to do it...

There are several ways to set up a logarithmic scale. The way it is done here works for any kind of figure and not only curve plots. In the following example, we set up a logarithmic scale that will apply to all plot elements:

```
import numpy as np
import matplotlib.pyplot as plt

X = np.linspace(1, 10, 1024)

plt.yscale('log')
plt.plot(X, X, c = 'k', lw = 2., label = r'$f(x)=x$')
plt.plot(X, 10 ** X, c = '.75', ls = '--', lw = 2., label =
r'$f(x)=e^x$')
plt.plot(X, np.log(X), c = '.75', lw = 2., label = r'$f(x)=\log(x)$')

plt.legend()
plt.show()
```

Several curves are shown in the following figure, with the vertical axis using a logarithmic scale:

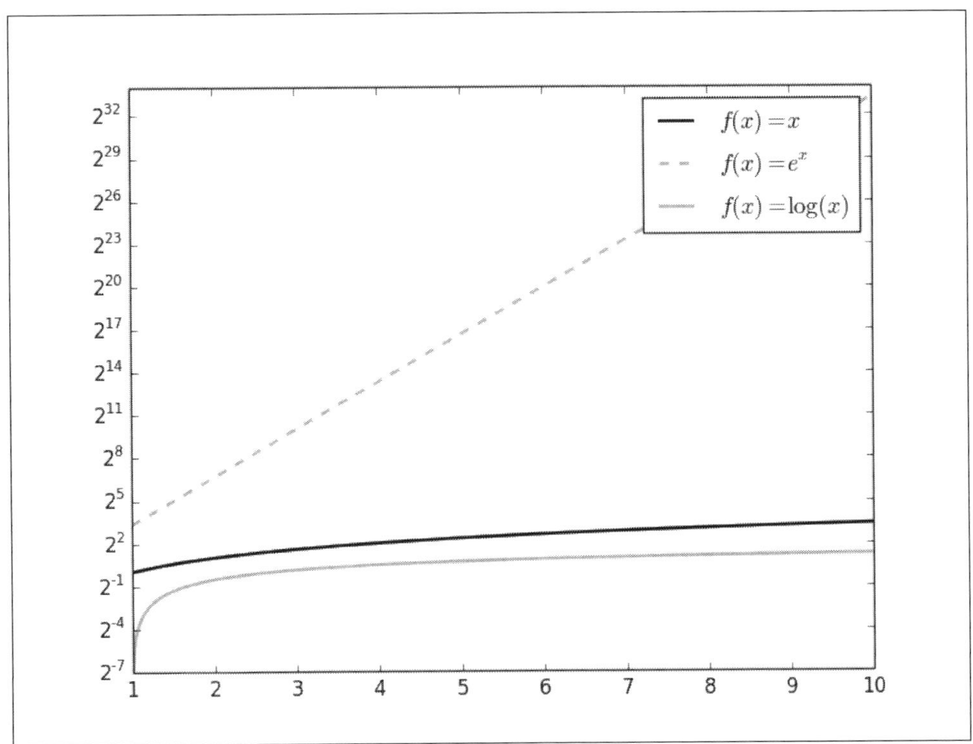

How it works...

In this example, we display three functions, with the *y* axis following a logarithmic scale. All the work is done by `pyplot.yscale()`, where we pass `'log'` to specify the type of scale we wish to have. Likewise, we would use `plot.xscale()` to achieve the same result on the *x* axis. A log-log plot can be created quite simply, as follows:

```
plt.xscale('log')
plt.yscale('log')
```

The logarithm base is 10 by default, but it can be changed with the optional parameters `basex` and `basey`.

There's more...

Using a logarithmic scale can also be useful to zoom in on one small range over data with a very large range, as demonstrated in the following example:

```
import numpy as np
import matplotlib.pyplot as plt

X = np.linspace(-100, 100, 4096)

plt.xscale('symlog', linthreshx=6.)
plt.plot(X, np.sinc(X), c = 'k')

plt.show()
```

The central part of the curve (the `[-6, 6]` range) is shown with a linear scale, while the other parts are shown with a logarithmic scale in the following figure:

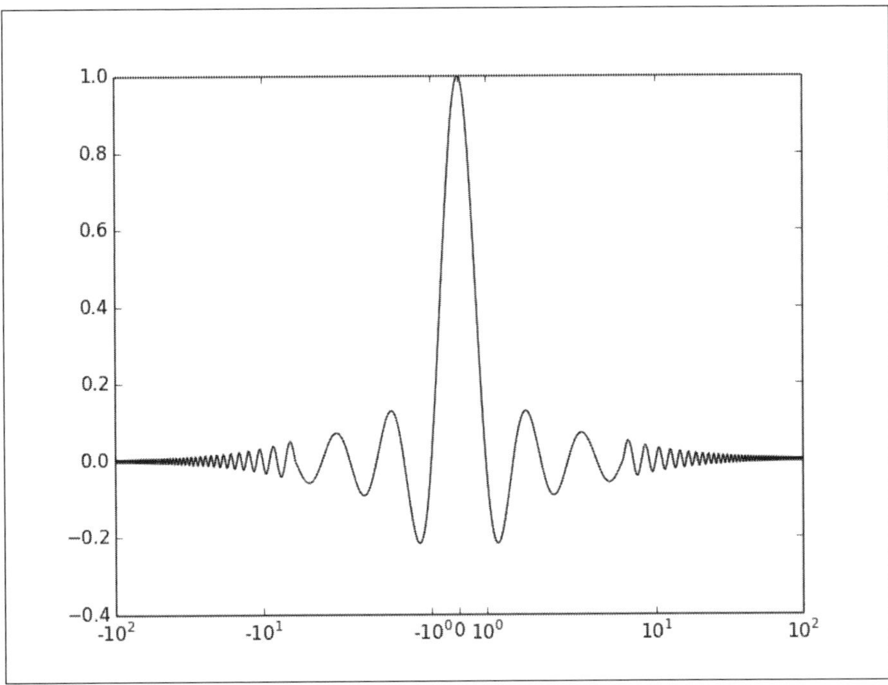

Here, we pass `'symlog'` as a parameter for `pyplot.xscale()`, a symmetric logarithmic scale centered on 0. By setting `'linthreshx=6.'`, we specify that in the [-6, 6] range, we want a linear and logarithmic scale outside that range. This way, we have a detailed view on one range, while still having a view on a large range of the remaining data.

Using polar coordinates

Some phenomenon are of an angular nature. An example would be the power of a loudspeaker depending on the angle we measure it from. Polar coordinates are a natural choice to represent such data. Also, cyclic data such as annual or daily statistics can be conveniently plotted in polar coordinates. In this recipe, we are going to see how to work with polar coordinates.

How to do it...

Let's render a simple polar curve as follows:

```
import numpy as np
import matplotlib.pyplot as plt

T = np.linspace(0 , 2 * np.pi, 1024)
```

```
plt.axes(polar = True)
plt.plot(T, 1. + .25 * np.sin(16 * T), c= 'k')

plt.show()
```

The following figure shows a specialized layout for polar plots:

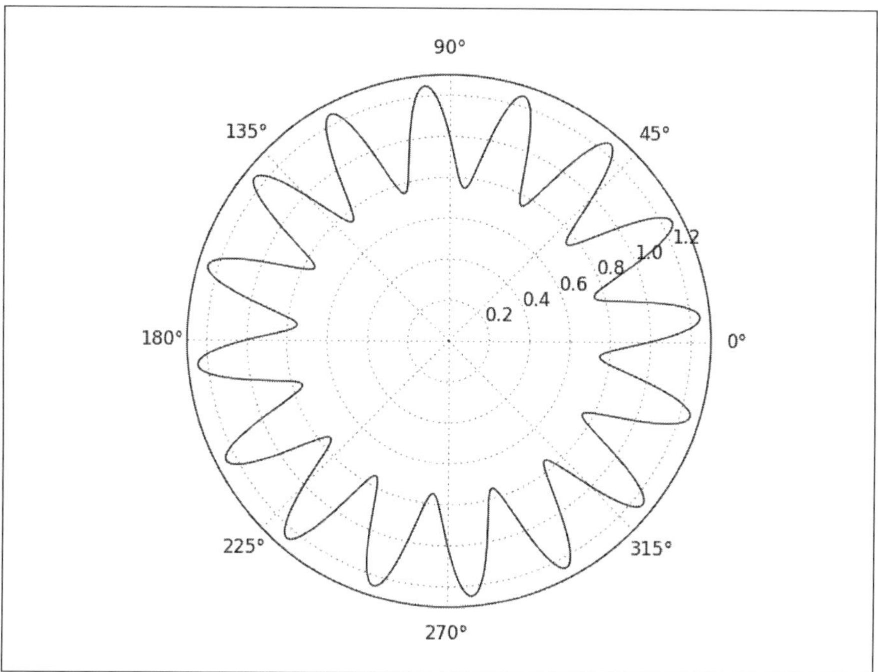

How it works...

As we have seen before, `pyplot.axes()` explicitly creates an `Axes` instance, which allows some custom settings. Simply using the optional polar parameter will set up a polar projection. Note how the legend adapts to the projection.

There's more...

Plotting curves is maybe the most common usage for polar projections. However, we can use any other kinds of plots, such as bar charts, and display shapes. For instance, using polar projections and polygons, you can make a radar plot. Use the following code to do so:

```
import numpy as np
import matplotlib.patches as patches
import matplotlib.pyplot as plt
```

```
ax = plt.axes(polar = True)

theta = np.linspace(0, 2 * np.pi, 8, endpoint = False)
radius = .25 + .75 * np.random.random(size = len(theta))
points = np.vstack((theta, radius)).transpose()

plt.gca().add_patch(patches.Polygon(points, color = '.75'))
plt.show()
```

The following figure shows the polygon we have defined with polar coordinates:

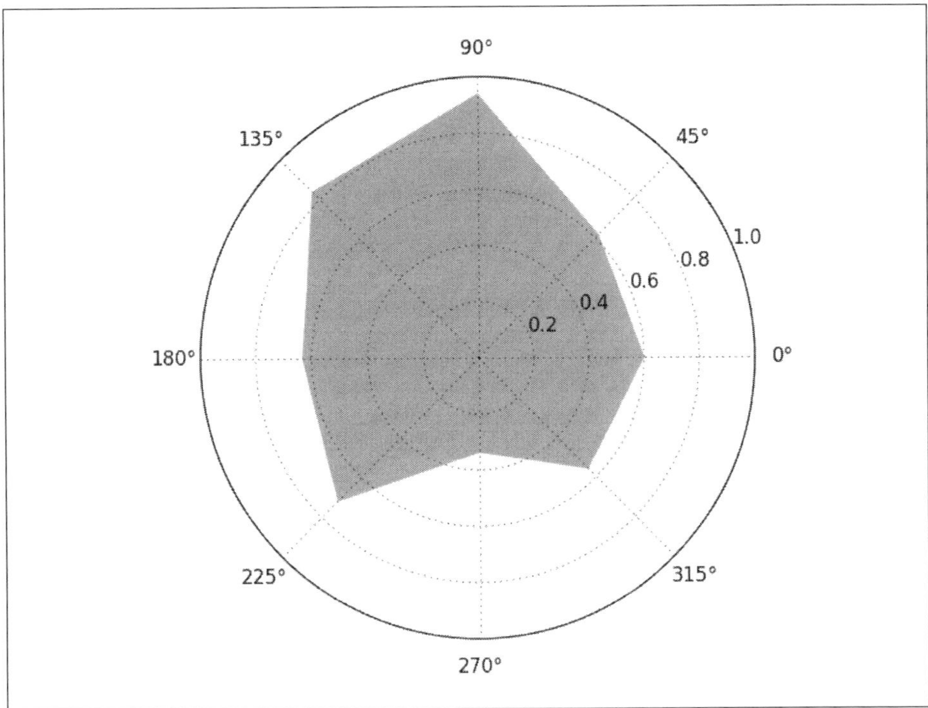

Note that the coordinates for the polygon are angles and distances to the origin. We do not need to perform explicit conversions from polar to Cartesian coordinates.

5
Working with a File Output

In this chapter, we will cover:

- Generating a PNG picture file
- Handling transparency
- Controlling the output resolution
- Generating PDF or SVG documents
- Handling multiple-page PDF documents

Introduction

Like other kinds of technical figures, scientific figures are rarely standalone documents—they are meant to be part of a document. matplotlib can render any figure to various common file formats such as PNG, EPS, SVG, and PDF. By default, a figure is shown with a minimalistic user interface, which allows you to save a figure to a file. However, this approach is not convenient if you have to generate a large batch of figures. Also, you might want to be able to generate a new figure every time some data is updated. In this chapter, we explore the file output capabilities of matplotlib. Apart from programmatically generating the file output, we are going to learn how to control important factors such as the resolution and size of the output, and dealing with transparency.

Generating a PNG picture file

By default, matplotlib shows a figure in a window with a rudimentary user interface. This interface allows you to save the figure to a file. Although it is a reasonable approach for prototyping, it is not convenient in several common usage cases. For instance, you might want to generate a dozen pictures to be included on an automatically generated report. You might want to generate one picture per input file as a batch processor. matplotlib allows you to directly save the figure to a picture file with great flexibility.

To get started, we are going to see how to output a figure to a PNG file. A PNG file is ideal for a bitmap output, and it is also the de-facto standard for bitmap pictures. It's a well-supported standard; it relies on a lossless compression algorithm (thus avoiding unsightly compression artifacts), and handles transparency.

How to do it...

We are going to use the `pyplot.savefig()` call instead of the usual `pyplot.show()` call when asking matplotlib to render the figure as follows:

```
import numpy as np
from matplotlib import pyplot as plt

X = np.linspace(-10, 10, 1024)
Y = np.sinc(X)

plt.plot(X, Y)
plt.savefig('sinc.png', c = 'k')
```

This script, rather than showing a figure in a window with a user interface, will simply create a file named `sinc.png`. Its resolution will be 800 x 600 pixels, in 8-bit colors (24-bits per pixel). This file is a representation of the following graph:

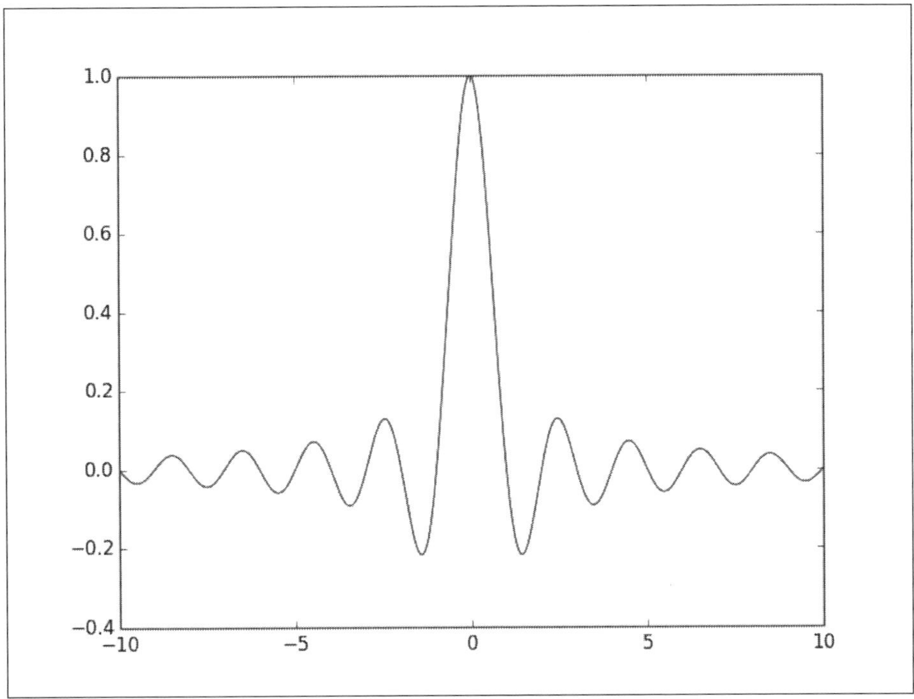

How it works...

The function `pyplot.savefig()` works exactly like `pyplot.show()`—it interprets all the commands issued to `pyplot` and produces a figure. The only difference is what is done at the end of the processing. The `pyplot.show()` function sends the picture data to whatever user interface library it can use, while the `pyplot.savefig()` function writes that data to a file. Thus, all the commands work exactly the same way, no matter what the nature of the final output is.

The `pyplot.savefig()` function offers a variety of optional parameters, which we will explore in the following sections.

Handling transparency

When creating figures, they are rarely meant to be used as alone. For instance, figures can be part of a website or a presentation. In such cases, the figures will have to be integrated with other graphics. Transparency is important for such integration—figures will blend in an aesthetically pleasing and consistent manner with their background. In this recipe, we are going to see how to output figures with transparency.

How to do it...

To demonstrate transparency, we are going to create a figure and embed it in a webpage. The figure is going to blend with the webpage background. All the files that are created in this recipe should be in the same directory. We are going to do the following in this section:

- Render a figure to a PNG file, with a transparent background
- Make a HTML page that includes a figure

Rendering a figure to a PNG file with a transparent background

To render a figure to a PNG file, we will again use `pyplot.savefig()`. However, the optional parameter `transparent` is set to `True` as shown in the following script:

```
import numpy as np
import matplotlib.pyplot as plt

X = np.linspace(-10, 10, 1024)
Y = np.sinc(X)

plt.plot(X, Y, c = 'k')
plt.savefig('sinc.png', transparent = True)
```

Making a HTML page that includes the figure

Let's use the PNG file on a webpage with a background. A minimal HTML code to show `sinc.png` with a `background.png` picture tiled in the background is shown as follows :

```
<html>
  <head>
    <style>
      body {
        background: white url(background.png);
      }
    </style>
  </head>
  <body>
    <img src='sinc.png' width='800 height='600'></img>
  </body>
</html>
```

When viewing the webpage with a browser, the figure blends in with the tiled background as shown in the following graph. The same thing would happen in other contexts, such as when using the figure in a presentation.

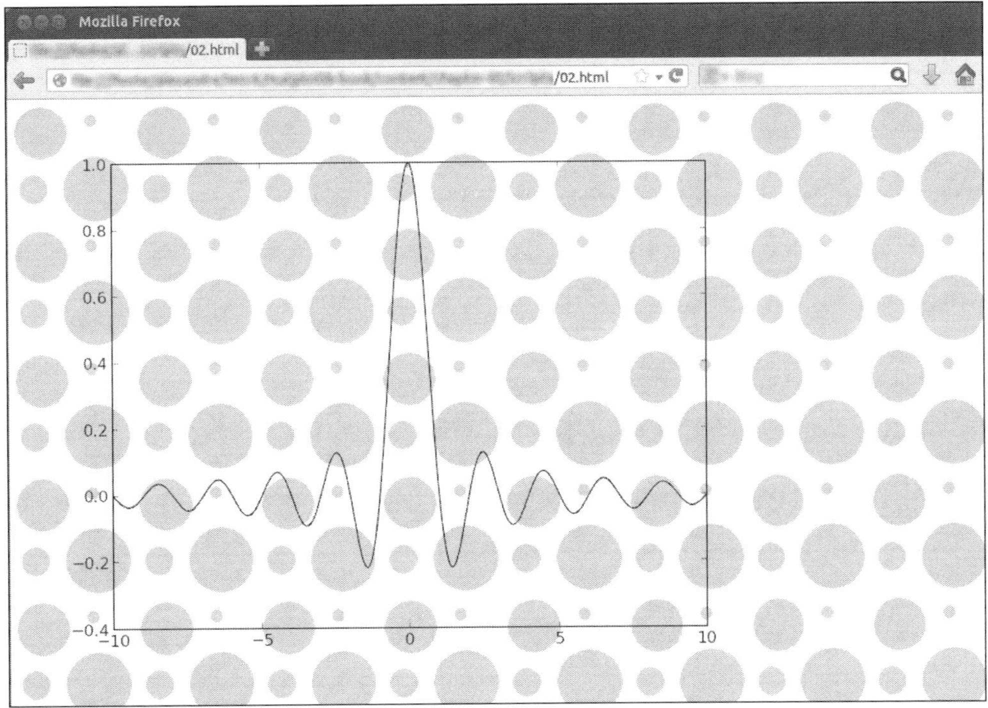

How it works...

By default, `pyplot.savefig()` will not include transparency information in the output. For instance, when we output PNG pictures, the PNG file will use 24-bits per pixels by default, storing only the red, green, and blue components of a pixel on 8-bits. However, when enabling the `transparent` output, `pyplot.savefig()` will use 32-bits per pixel—an additional channel, the alpha channel, stores the transparency information.

There's more...

So far, the only transparency information that concerns the background of the figure is that the elements of the figure are either background (fully transparent) or foreground (fully opaque). However, we can control the level of transparency of any graphics generated with matplotlib.

matplotlib allows you to define the level of transparency of a figure as an optional parameter, `alpha`. If `alpha` is equal to `1`, the figure will be completely opaque, which is the default setting. If `alpha` is equal to `0`, the figure will be completely invisible. An intermediary value of `alpha` will give partial transparency. The optional parameter `alpha` is available for most figure-drawing functions.

The following script demonstrates this:

```
import numpy as np
import matplotlib.pyplot as plt

name_list = ('Omar', 'Serguey', 'Max', 'Zhou', 'Abidin')
value_list = np.random.randint(99, size=len(name_list))
pos_list = np.arange(len(name_list))

plt.bar(pos_list, value_list, alpha = .75, color = '.75', align =
  'center')
plt.xticks(pos_list, name_list)

plt.savefig('bar.png', transparent = True)
```

The preceding script will create a bar graph and save the figure to a PNG file. When using this PNG file in a web page, we can see that not only does the background of the figure blend in, but the content of the figure also blends in, as shown in the following screenshot:

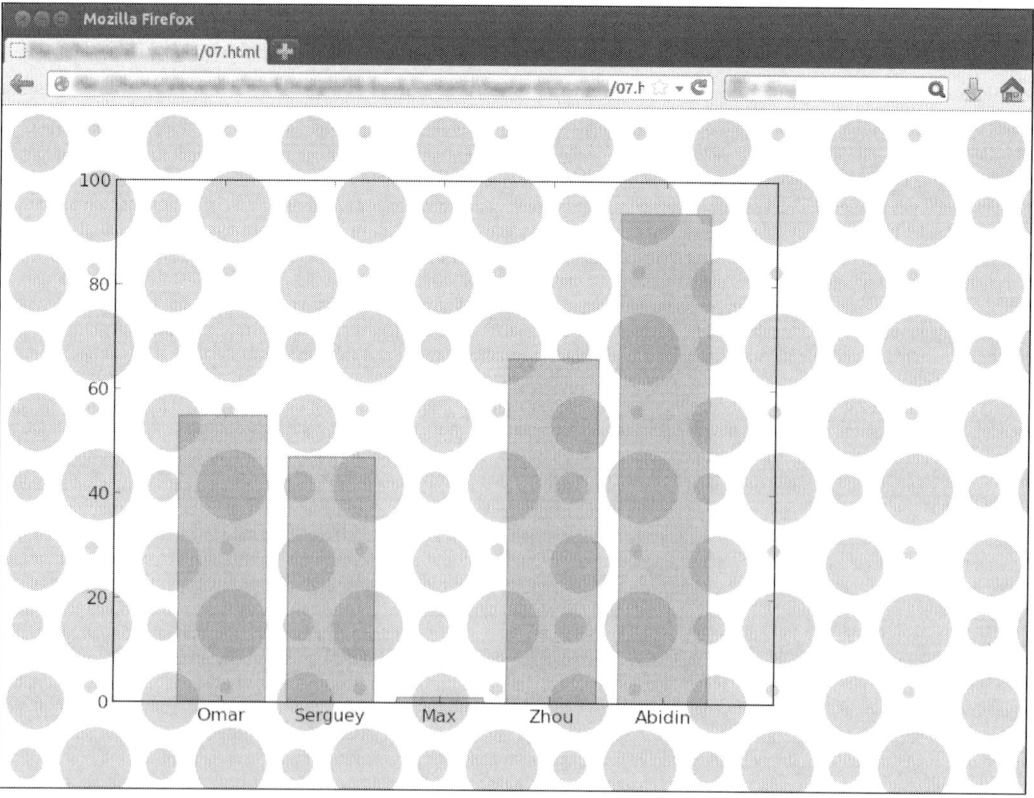

Controlling the output resolution

By default, when using the output to a bitmap picture, matplotlib chooses the size and the resolution of the output for us. Depending on what the bitmap picture will be used for, we might want to choose the resolution ourselves. For instance, if a picture is to be part of a large poster, we might prefer a high resolution, or, if we want to generate a thumbnail, then the resolution would be very low. In this recipe, we will learn how to control the output resolution.

How to do it...

The `pyplot.savefig()` function provides an optional parameter to control the output resolution, as shown in the following script:

```
import numpy as np
from matplotlib import pyplot as plt

X = np.linspace(-10, 10, 1024)
Y = np.sinc(X)

plt.plot(X, Y)
plt.savefig('sinc.png', dpi = 300)
```

The preceding script draws a curve and outputs the result to a file. Instead of the usual 800 x 600 pixels output, it will be 2400 x 1800 pixels.

How it works...

The `pyplot.savefig()` function has an optional parameter called `dpi`. This parameter controls the resolution of the picture expressed in **DPI** (**Dots Per Inches**). For those more familiar with metric units, 1 inch equals 2.54 centimeters. This unit expresses how many dots are found in 1 inch of the actual document. A good inkjet printer will print a document with a resolution of 300 dpi. A high quality laser printer can easily print at 600 dpi.

By default, matplotlib will output a figure of 8 x 6 spatial units—a 4/3 aspect ratio. In matplotlib, 1 spatial unit equals to 100 pixels. Thus, by default, matplotlib will give a picture file of 800 x 600 pixels. If we use dpi = 300, the picture size will be 8 * 300 x 6 * 300, that is, 2400 x 1800 pixels.

There's more...

In *Chapter 4, Working with Figures*, we saw how to control the aspect ratio. If we combine the aspect ratio and DPI, we have full control on the general proportions of a picture. Let's say we want to display a hexagon in a 512 x 512 pixels picture. We would do this as follows:

```
import numpy as np
import matplotlib.pyplot as plt

theta = np.linspace(0, 2 * np.pi, 8)
points = np.vstack((np.cos(theta), np.sin(theta))).transpose()

plt.figure(figsize=(4., 4.))
plt.gca().add_patch(plt.Polygon(points, color = '.75'))

plt.grid(True)
plt.axis('scaled')

plt.savefig('polygon.png', dpi = 128)
```

The result of the preceding script would be the following graph:

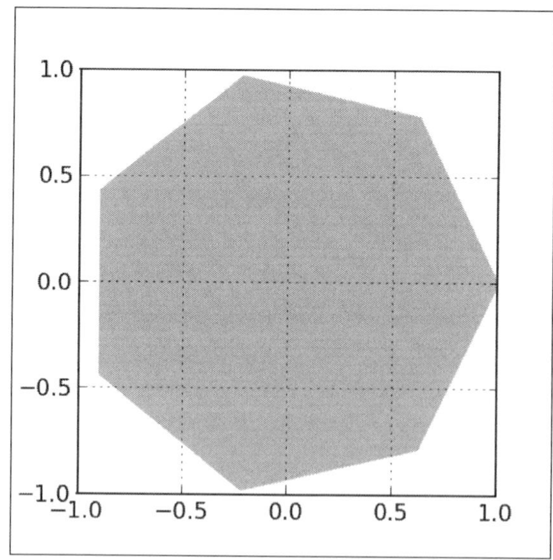

We display the figure on a 4 x 4 unit area, and output this at 128 dpi—the output will be 512 x 512 pixels. We can also display 512 pixels with a 8 x 8 unit area and output it at 64 dpi. This will give us the following result:

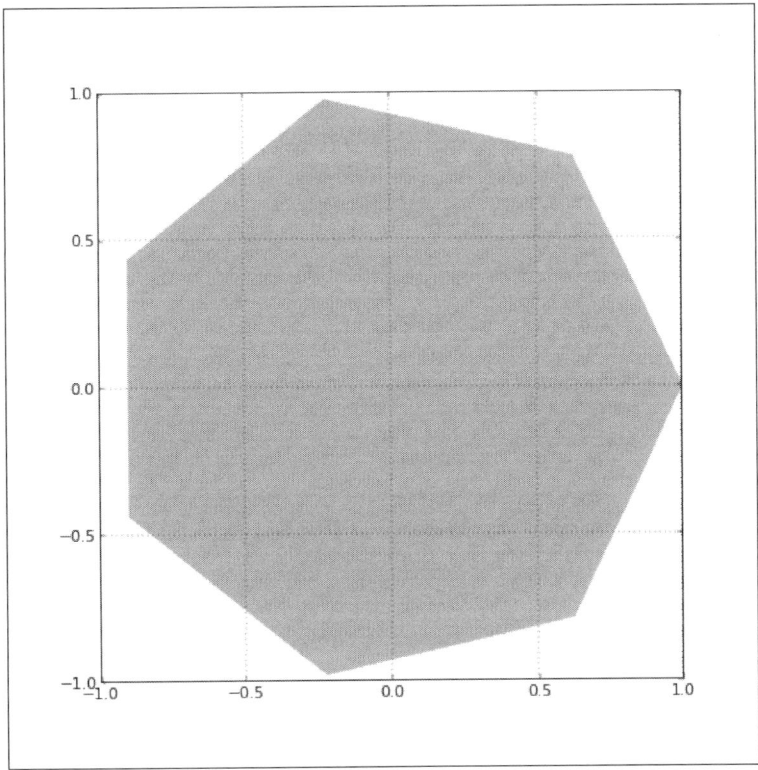

The annotations are smaller and the grid has thinner lines. The annotations and the thickness of the lines have their own default values expressed in spatial units. Thus, dividing the output resolution by two will make the annotations two times smaller. If you start manipulating the spatial resolution and each individual element size, it can become confusing very quickly. As a rule, it would be better for you to change the size of individual elements (annotations and thickness) only relative to each other. If you want to make all annotations appear uniformly larger, then you may play with the resolution settings.

Generating PDF or SVG documents

An output to a bitmap picture is not always ideal. Bitmap pictures represent pictures as an array of pixels at one given scale. Zoom in and you will get some well-known artifacts (jaggies, staircases, blur, and so on), depending on the sampling algorithm employed. Vector pictures are scale invariant; no matter at which scale you observe them, no loss of details or artifacts will show up. As such, vector pictures are desirable when composing a larger document, such as a journal article. We do not need to generate new pictures when adjusting the scale of a figure. matplotlib can output vector pictures such as PDF and SVG pictures.

How to do it...

The output to a PDF document is a simple affair, as shown in the following script:

```
import numpy as np
from matplotlib import pyplot as plt

X = np.linspace(-10, 10, 1024)
Y = np.sinc(X)

plt.plot(X, Y)
plt.savefig('sinc.pdf')
```

The preceding script will draw a figure and save it to a file named `sinc.pdf`.

How it works...

We have already discussed the `pyplot.savefig()` function, which renders a figure to a file. The filename is enough to specify whether the file should be PNG, PDF, or SVG. matplotlib will look at the file extension of the filename and deduce the type of file.

There's more...

In some cases, you might want to save a file under a given format, say SVG, but you do not want the name to have the `.svg` extension. The `pyplot.savefig` parameter, as an optional parameter, allows you to do that. Setting `format = 'svg', pyplot.savefig` will not deduce the output file type from the file name passed to the function, it will use the name passed to the format instead.

Handling multiple-page PDF documents

In *Chapter 4, Working with Figures*, saw seen how to compose several figures in one matplotlib graph. This allows you to create very elaborate plots. When using the PDF output, we have to keep in mind that the graph has to fit on one page. However, with some additional work, we can output PDF documents of several pages. Be warned, matplotlib is a scientific plotting package, not a document composition system, such as LaTeX or ReportLab. Thus, support for multiple pages is fairly minimal. In this recipe, we will see how to generate multiple page PDF documents.

How to do it...

To demonstrate multiple page PDF outputs with matplotlib, let's generate 15 bar charts, with five charts per page. The following script will output a three-page document named `barcharts.pdf`:

```
import numpy as np
from matplotlib import pyplot as plt
from matplotlib.backends.backend_pdf import PdfPages

# Generate the data
data = np.random.randn(15, 1024)

# The PDF document
pdf_pages = PdfPages('barcharts.pdf')

# Generate the pages
plots_count = data.shape[0]
plots_per_page = 5
pages_count = int(np.ceil(plots_count / float(plots_per_page)))
grid_size = (plots_per_page, 1)

for i, samples in enumerate(data):
  # Create a figure instance (ie. a new page) if needed
  if i % plots_per_page == 0:
    fig = plt.figure(figsize=(8.27, 11.69), dpi=100)

  # Plot one bar chart
  plt.subplot2grid(grid_size, (i % plots_per_page, 0))
  plt.hist(samples, 32, normed=1, facecolor='.5', alpha=0.75)

  # Close the page if needed
  if (i + 1) % plots_per_page == 0 or (i + 1) == plots_count:
    plt.tight_layout()
    pdf_pages.savefig(fig)

# Write the PDF document to the disk
pdf_pages.close()
```

The bar charts are neatly laid out on the three pages, as shown in the following screenshot:

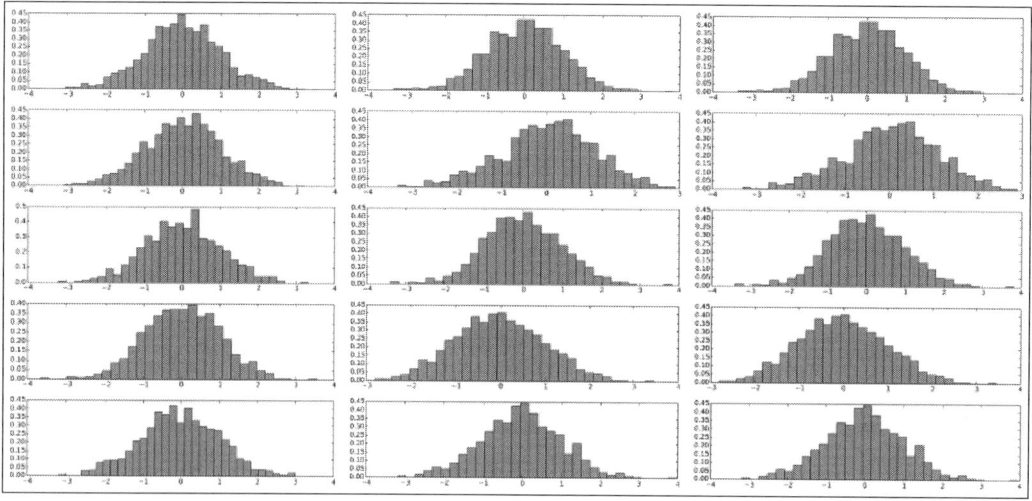

How it works...

Usually, a script using matplotlib does not depend on the type of the output. We always use `pyplot.savefig()` for all kinds of output. Here, however, we have to play with the specifics of the PDF output. Thus, this script does the following operations:

- Imports the matplotlib package that handles the PDF output, `matplotlib.backends.backend_pdf`. From this package, we just need the `PdfPages` object. This object represents a PDF document.
- Creates an instance of the PDF document, named `pdf_pages`. This is done by using the `pdf_pages = PdfPages('histograms.pdf')` function.
- To generate each page, it does the following:
    - Creates a new figure instance, with the dimensions of an A4 page. This is done by using the `fig = plot.figure(figsize=(8.27, 11.69), dpi=100)` function.
    - Populates the figure with plots. In this example, we use subplots to lay several plots in one figure.
    - Creates a new page in our PDF document, which will contain our figure. This is done by using the `pdf_pages.savefig(fig)` function.
- Once we have generated all the figures we want, we can output the document by using the `pdf_pages.close()` function.

Note that *page* is used here as a fairly general term. A page does not have to be of a specific size. Different pages can have different sizes. The script is written so that the number of pages is automatically computed from the total number of figures and the number of figures per page.

There's more...

Because matplotlib is not a full-fledged document-composition system, things like page numbers or page headers are not easily achieved without awful tricks. If you really need such features, you would be wise to generate each figure as a single PDF document. Then, those figures would be used by a document-composition system to automatically generate a PDF document. For instance, DocBook is a system that takes XML descriptions to generate documents in PDF or other common formats. This is, of course, a whole different scale of effort.

6
Working with Maps

In this chapter, we will cover the following topics:

- Visualizing the content of a 2D array
- Adding a colormap legend to a figure
- Visualizing nonuniform 2D data
- Visualizing a 2D scalar field
- Visualizing contour lines
- Visualizing a 2D vector field
- Visualizing the streamlines of a 2D vector field

Introduction

Up until now, we have covered plotting primitives for data of essentially unidimensional characters. By drawing a map of some kind, you can visualize the influence that two variables have on the third one. Imagine you have weather stations scattered over a country. A map visualization would show at a glance how rainfall and winds are distributed over the country. matplotlib offers powerful primitives driven by a simple API to create maps.

Visualizing the content of a 2D array

Let's start with the most basic scenario. We have a 2D array, and we want to visualize its content. As an example, we will visualize the Mandelbrot set. The Mandelbrot set, a famous fractal shape, associates a number of iterations to each point on the plane.

How to do it...

We will first fill a 2D square array with values and then call `pyplot.imshow()` to visualize it, as shown in the following code:

```
import numpy as np
import matplotlib.cm as cm
from matplotlib import pyplot as plt

def iter_count(C, max_iter):
  X = C
  for n in range(max_iter):
    if abs(X) > 2.:
      return n
    X = X ** 2 + C
  return max_iter

N = 512
max_iter = 64
xmin, xmax, ymin, ymax = -2.2, .8, -1.5, 1.5
X = np.linspace(xmin, xmax, N)
Y = np.linspace(ymin, ymax, N)
Z = np.empty((N, N))

for i, y in enumerate(Y):
  for j, x in enumerate(X):
    Z[i, j] = iter_count(complex(x, y), max_iter)

plt.imshow(Z, cmap = cm.gray)
plt.show()
```

This script might take a few seconds to a few minutes to produce the output, depending on your computer. Reducing `N`, the size of the square array we are filling, will reduce the amount of computations. The result will be a view of the Mandelbrot set in all of its fractal glory:

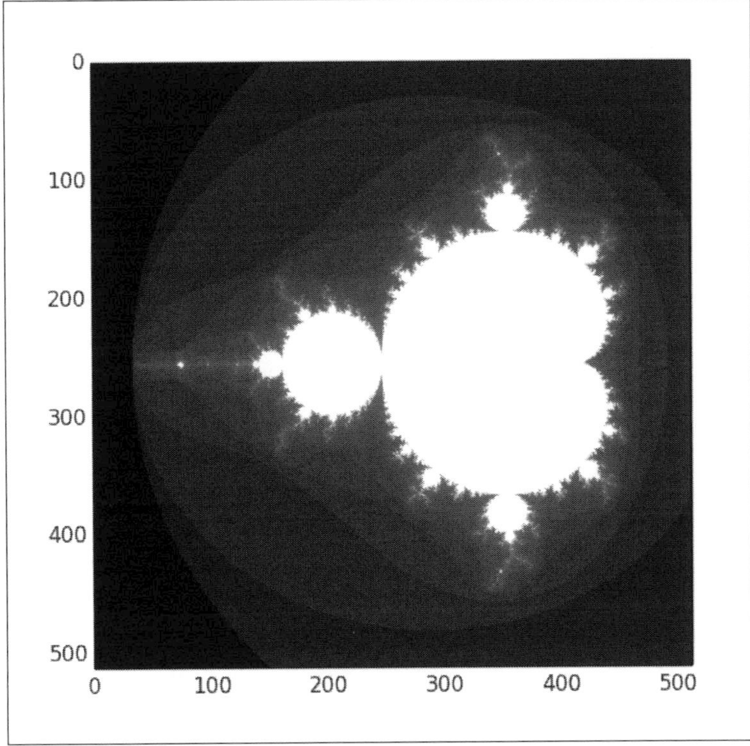

Note that the coordinates shown on the axes are the 2D array indexes.

How it works...

The `pyplot.imshow()` function is very simple; give it a 2D array and it will render a picture where each pixel represents one value taken from the 2D array. The color of the pixel is picked from a colormap—each value of the array is linearly normalized in the `[0, 1]` interval. The `pyplot.imshow()` function renders a figure, but it won't show it. As usual, we should call `pyplot.show()` to see the figure. However, having two functions with such similar names is arguably confusing.

The remaining parts of the script generate our example data. The 2D array `Z` is created and then filled with a double loop. This loop samples the `[-2.2, 0.8]*[-1.5, 1.5]` square. For each sample, the `iter_count` function computes the Mandelbrot set iterations. The data in the `Z` array could have come from a file or any other source.

There's more...

The result we got from `pyplot.imshow()` is a bit raw. The coordinates shown on the axes are the 2D array indexes. We might prefer different coordinates; in this case, the coordinates of the square we sampled. The colormap used here is less than ideal. This can be addressed using the optional parameters of `pyplot.imshow()`. Let's change the call to `pyplot.imshow()`:

```
plt.imshow(Z, cmap = cm.binary, extent=(xmin, xmax, ymin, ymax))
```

Since we use a colormap, we should import the colormap module of matplotlib. At the beginning of the script, add the following line:

```
import matplotlib.cm as cm
```

While the data is strictly the same, the output will change:

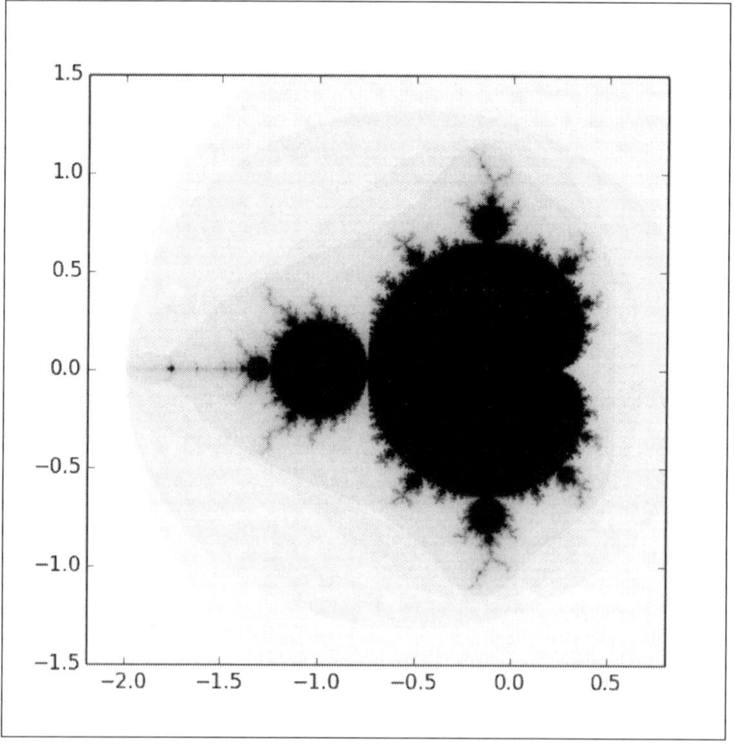

The `extent` optional parameter specifies the coordinate system for the data stored in the 2D array. The coordinate system is a tuple of four values; the minimum and maximum extent on the horizontal axis and then the vertical axis. Now, the axes show the coordinates of the square we sample to compute the Mandelbrot set. The parameter `cmap` specifies the colormap.

Now, let's reduce the size of our sample data from `512` to `32` in our script. The output will look like the following screenshot:

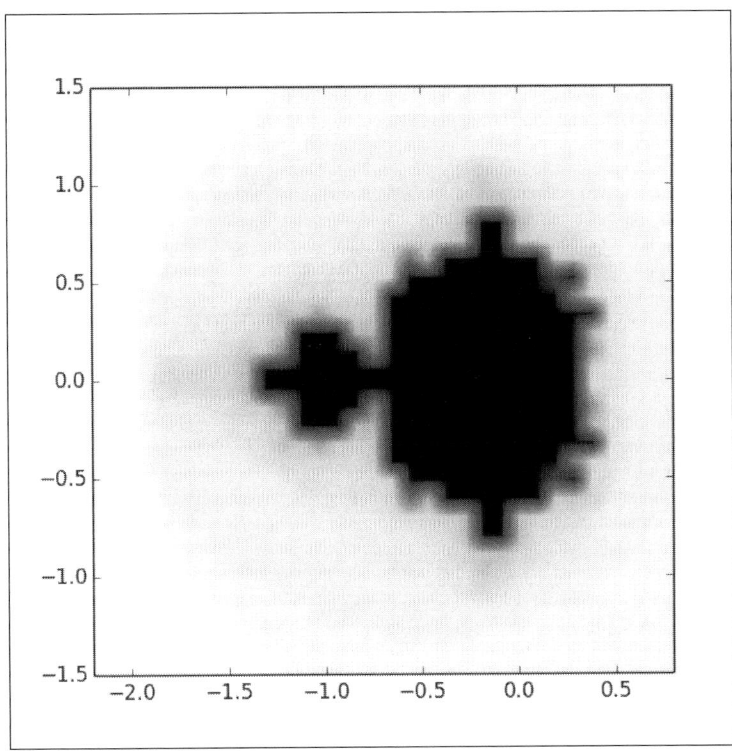

We use `32*32` samples rather than `512*512` samples to represent the Mandelbrot set. But the resulting figure is not smaller. Actually, `pyplot.imshow()` does more than coloring pixels to represent a 2D array. The `pyplot.imshow()` function will produce a picture of a given arbitrary size and perform an interpolation if the input data is smaller or bigger than the figure. In this example, we can see that the default interpolation is linear. This is not always ideal. The `pyplot.imshow()` function has an optional parameter, `interpolation`, that allows us to specify what kind of interpolation to use. matplotlib offers an impressive list of interpolation schemes. Let's look at the simplest interpolation scheme, nearest neighbor interpolation:

```
plt.imshow(Z, cmap = cm.binary, interpolation = 'nearest',
  extent=(xmin, xmax, ymin, ymax))
```

The raw data is now much more evident:

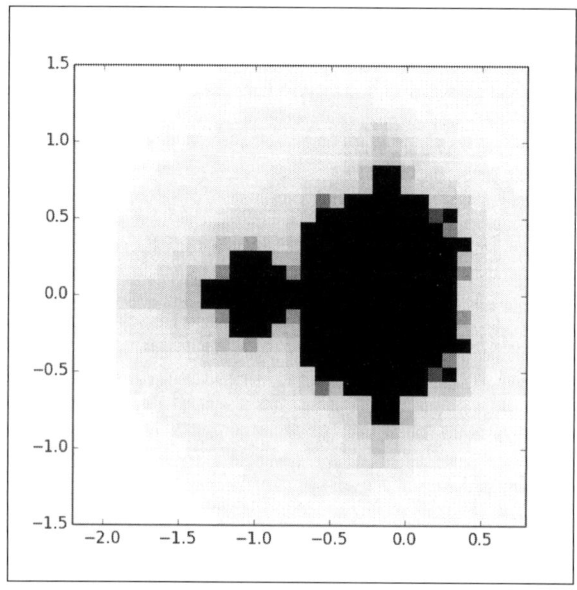

We might want to use an interpolation scheme that is more sophisticated than the punny linear interpolation. The latter is cheap to compute but produces unsightly artifacts. Let's use a bicubic interpolation, using `interpolation = 'bicubic'`. We will get a much better result:

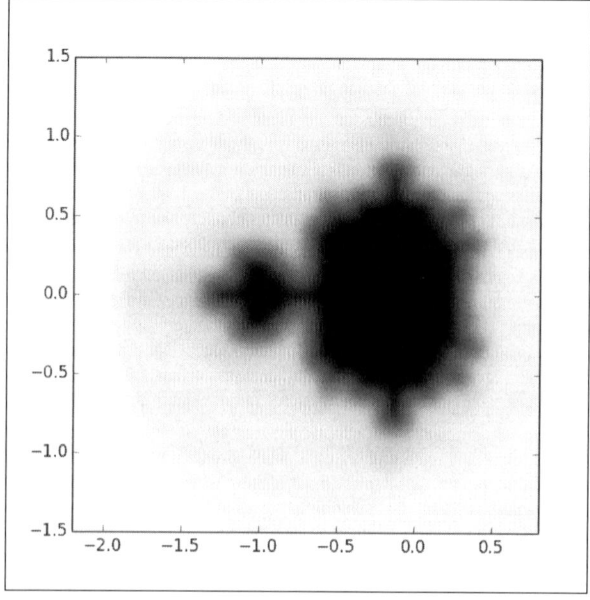

matplotlib has more sophisticated interpolation schemes such as `sinc` and `lanzcos`.

Adding a colormap legend to a figure

A colormap is a key ingredient to produce both readable and visually pleasing figures. However, we are doing science here, and esthetic is just a side objective. When using colormaps, we would like to know which value corresponds to a given color. In this recipe, we will look at a simple way to add such information to a figure.

How to do it...

We will use the same example, the Mandelbrot set. We simply add a call to `pyplot.colorbar()`:

```
import numpy as np
from matplotlib import pyplot as plt
import matplotlib.cm as cm

def iter_count(C, max_iter):
  X = C
  for n in range(max_iter):
    if abs(X) > 2.:
      return n
    X = X ** 2 + C
  return max_iter

N = 512
max_iter = 64
xmin, xmax, ymin, ymax = -2.2, .8, -1.5, 1.5
X = np.linspace(xmin, xmax, N)
Y = np.linspace(ymin, ymax, N)
Z = np.empty((N, N))

for i, y in enumerate(Y):
  for j, x in enumerate(X):
    Z[i, j] = iter_count(complex(x, y), max_iter)

plt.imshow(Z,
           cmap = cm.binary,
           interpolation = 'bicubic',
           extent=(xmin, xmax, ymin, ymax))
```

```
cb = plt.colorbar(orientation='horizontal', shrink=.75)
cb.set_label('iteration count')

plt.show()
```

The preceding code will produce the following output:

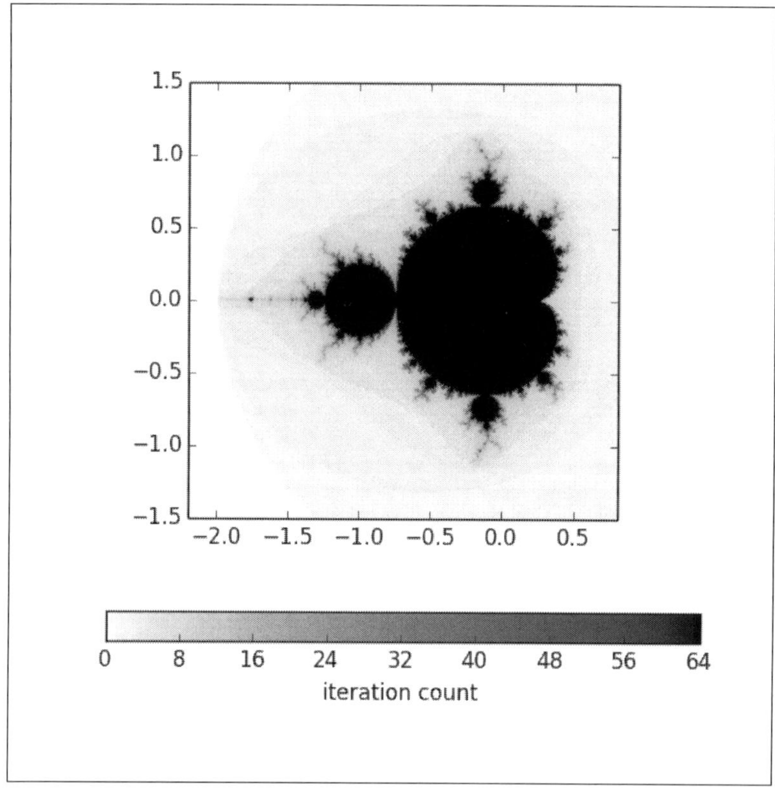

A neat color bar allows you to associate the colors from the colormap to the value of interest. Here, it is the Mandelbrot iteration count.

How it works...

Most of the script is strictly identical to the script introduced in the previous recipe. The relevant bit of the script is the following:

```
cb = plt.colorbar(orientation='horizontal', shrink=.75)
cb.set_label('iteration count')
```

The `pyplot.colorbar()` function signals matplotlib that we want a colorbar to be shown. For demonstration purposes, we use some optional parameters here. The `orientation` parameter is to choose whether the colorbar should be vertical or horizontal. It is vertical by default. The `shrink` parameter is to shrink the colorbar from its default size. A colorbar will not have a legend by default. A legend can be set, but it is a bit awkward to do so. The call to the `pyplot.colorbar()` function produces a `Colorbar` instance. We then call the `set_label()` method of that `Colorbar` instance.

Visualizing nonuniform 2D data

So far, we have assumed that we have uniformly sampled 2D data; our data is sampled with a grid pattern. However, nonuniformly sampled data is very common. For instance, we might want to visualize measurements from weather stations. Weather stations are built wherever it is possible; they are laid out into a perfect grid. When sampling functions, we might use a sophisticated sampling process (adaptive sampling, quasi-random sampling, and so on) which does not produce grid layouts. Here, we show a simple way to deal with such 2D data.

How to do it...

The script draws the Mandelbrot set sampled from the same square as in the previous recipes. However, instead of using a regular grid sampling, we randomly sample the Mandelbrot set, as shown in the following example:

```
import numpy as np
from numpy.random import uniform, seed

from matplotlib import pyplot as plt
from matplotlib.mlab import griddata
import matplotlib.cm as cm

def iter_count(C, max_iter):
  X = C
  for n in range(max_iter):
    if abs(X) > 2.:
      return n
    X = X ** 2 + C
  return max_iter

max_iter = 64
xmin, xmax, ymin, ymax = -2.2, .8, -1.5, 1.5

sample_count = 2 ** 12
A = uniform(xmin, xmax, sample_count)
B = uniform(ymin, ymax, sample_count)
C = [iter_count(complex(a, b), max_iter) for a, b in zip(A, B)]
```

```
N = 512
X = np.linspace(xmin, xmax, N)
Y = np.linspace(ymin, ymax, N)
Z = griddata(A, B, C, X, Y, interp = 'linear')

plt.scatter(A, B, color = (0., 0., 0., .5), s = .5)
plt.imshow(Z,
           cmap = cm.binary,
           interpolation = 'bicubic',
           extent=(xmin, xmax, ymin, ymax))
plt.show()
```

This script will show the randomly sampled Mandelbrot set. The sample points are shown as tiny black dots:

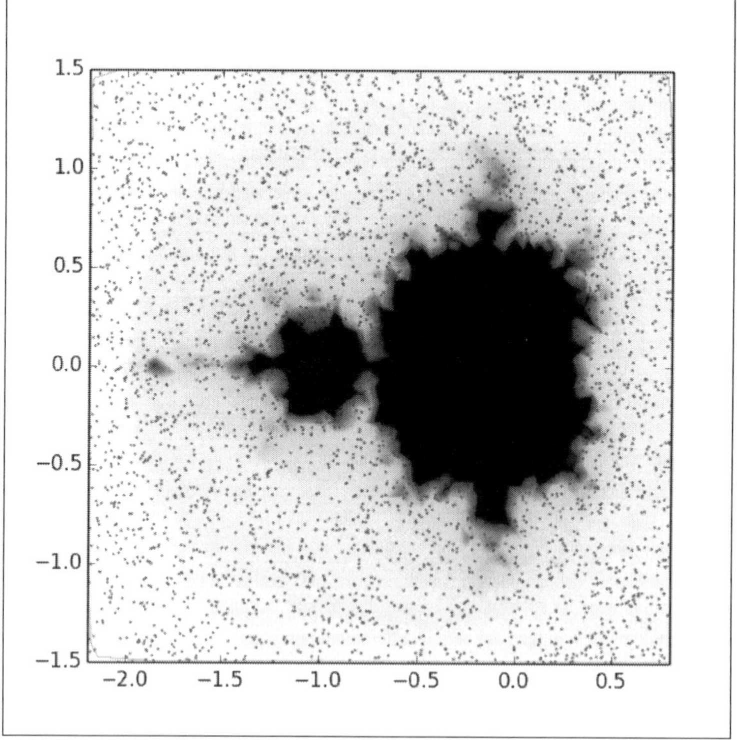

Obviously, due to the random sampling process, the result is more chaotic than what we get from a regular sampling. However, we used only 4,096 samples instead of the 262,144 samples used in the previous examples, so the result we got is honorable. With the **nonuniform sampling** capabilities of matplotlib, using an adaptive sampling approach would allow you to get a high resolution view of the Mandelbrot set at a much lower computational cost than a regular grid sampling.

How it works...

First, the script randomly samples the Mandelbrot set, which is done by the following part of the script:

```
sample_count = 2 ** 12
A = uniform(xmin, xmax, sample_count)
B = uniform(ymin, ymax, sample_count)
C = [iter_count(complex(a, b), max_iter) for a, b in zip(A, B)]
```

The arrays `A` and `B` hold the coordinates of the samples, while the list `C` contains the value for each of these samples.

Then, the script will produce a 2D array of data from the nonuniform samples, which is accomplished by the following part:

```
N = 512
X = np.linspace(xmin, xmax, N)
Y = np.linspace(ymin, ymax, N)
Z = griddata(A, B, C, X, Y, interp = 'linear')
```

The arrays `X` and `Y` define a regular grid. The array `Z` is a 2D array built by interpolating the nonuniform samples. This interpolation is done by the `griddata()` function from the `matplotlib.mlab` package. Since we now have a 2D array, we can use the `pyplot.imshow()` function to visualize it. An additional call to `pyplot.scatter()` is used to show the original sample points.

For demonstration purposes, we use a linear interpolation for `pyplot.griddata()`, with the optional parameter `interp`. By default, this parameter is set to `'nn'`, which stands for natural neighbor interpolation. The latter scheme is preferable in most cases as it is very robust.

Visualizing a 2D scalar field

matplotlib and NumPy offer some interesting mechanisms that make the visualization of a 2D scalar field convenient. In this recipe, we show a very simple way to visualize a 2D scalar field.

How to do it...

The `numpy.meshgrid()` function generates the samples from an explicit 2D function. Then, `pyplot.pcolormesh()` is used to display the function, as shown in the following code:

```
import numpy as np
from matplotlib import pyplot as plt
import matplotlib.cm as cm
```

```
n = 256
x = np.linspace(-3., 3., n)
y = np.linspace(-3., 3., n)
X, Y = np.meshgrid(x, y)

Z = X * np.sinc(X ** 2 + Y ** 2)

plt.pcolormesh(X, Y, Z, cmap = cm.gray)
plt.show()
```

The preceding script will produce the following output:

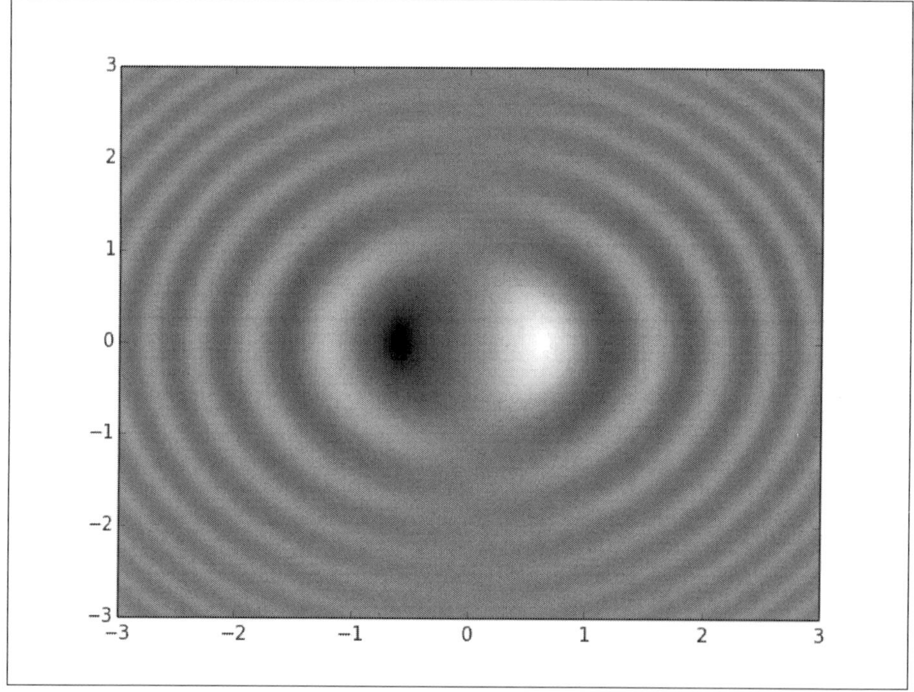

Note how a sensible choice of colormap can be helpful; here, negative values appear in black and positive values appear in white. Thus, we have the sign and magnitude information visible at a glance. Use a colormap going from red to blue with white at the middle of the scale, which does an even better job.

How it works...

The `numpy.meshgrid()` function takes two coordinates, `x` and `y`, and builds two grids of the coordinates `X` and `Y`. Because `X` and `Y` are NumPy 2D arrays, we can manipulate them as we would for a single variable. We do not have to write a loop to generate the matrix `Z`. This makes computing the scalar field concise and easy to read:

```
Z = X * numpy.sinc(X ** 2 + Y ** 2)
```

Then, the function `pyplot.pcolormesh()` is called to render the samples. We could have the same result from `pyplot.imshow()`. However, we just need to pass `X`, `Y`, and `Z` here to get the coordinate system right, rather than play with an optional parameter. Doing so makes the script easier to read. Also, for a large amount of data, `pyplot.pcolormesh()` is likely to be much faster.

Visualizing contour lines

So far, we have visualized data by coloring each data point and have thrown in some interpolation on top. matplotlib is able to provide more sophisticated representations for 2D data. **Contour lines** link all points with the same value, helping you to capture features that might not be easily seen otherwise. In this recipe, we will see how to display such contour lines.

How to do it...

The function `pyplot.contour()` allows you to generate contour annotations. To demonstrate this, let's reuse our code from the previous recipes in order to study a zoomed-in part of the Mandelbrot set:

```
import numpy as np
from matplotlib import pyplot as plt
import matplotlib.cm as cm

def iter_count(C, max_iter):
  X = C
  for n in range(max_iter):
    if abs(X) > 2.:
      return n
    X = X ** 2 + C
  return max_iter

N = 512
max_iter = 64
```

```
xmin, xmax, ymin, ymax = -0.32, -0.22, 0.8, 0.9
X = np.linspace(xmin, xmax, N)
Y = np.linspace(ymin, ymax, N)
Z = np.empty((N, N))

for i, y in enumerate(Y):
  for j, x in enumerate(X):
    Z[i, j] = iter_count(complex(x, y), max_iter)

plt.imshow(Z,
            cmap = cm.binary,
            interpolation = 'bicubic',
            origin = 'lower',
            extent=(xmin, xmax, ymin, ymax))

levels = [8, 12, 16, 20]
ct = plt.contour(X, Y, Z, levels, cmap = cm.gray)
plt.clabel(ct, fmt='%d')

plt.show()
```

The preceding script will show a detail of the Mandelbrot set with sophisticated contour annotations:

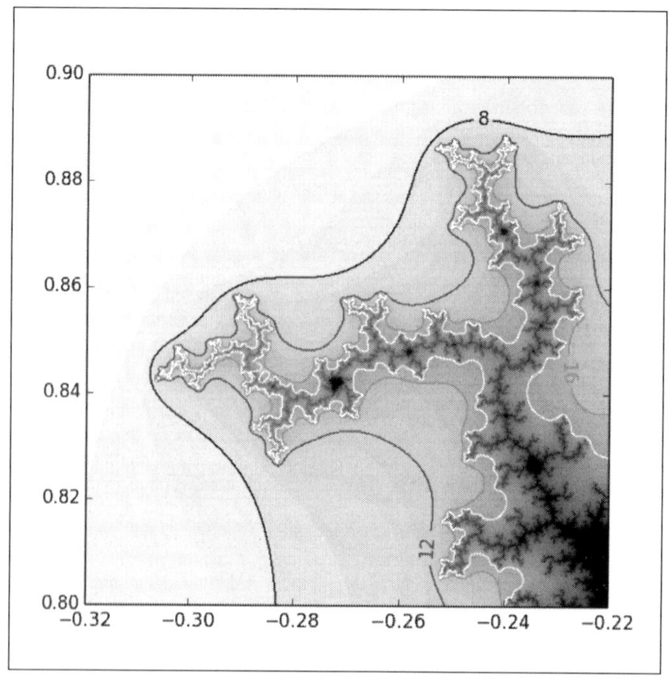

How it works...

We recognize the code used in the previous recipes demonstrated with the Mandelbrot set. The only difference here is that we zoom inside a particular detail of the Mandelbrot set by changing the value of `xmin`, `xmax`, `ymin`, and `ymax`. We use `pyplot.imshow()` to render the iteration count of each sample, as we did before.

Only one addition has been made: the call to `pyplot.contour()`. This function takes the coordinates `X` and `Y` of the sample grid and the samples stored in the matrix `Z`. The function will then render contours corresponding to the values specified in the `levels` list. The level can be colored with a colormap using the optional parameter `cmap`. We could have used the optional parameter `color` to specify one unique color for all the contours.

The level of each contour can be shown either with a colorbar or directly on the figure. The `pyplot.contour()` function returns a `Contour` instance. The `pyplot.clabel()` function takes the `Contour` instance and an optional format string to render a label per contour.

There's more...

Here, the contours are shown simply as lines. However, we can show filled contours. Let's demonstrate this on the same detail of the Mandelbrot set we used before:

```
import numpy as np
from matplotlib import pyplot as plt
import matplotlib.cm as cm

def iter_count(C, max_iter):
  X = C
  for n in range(max_iter):
    if abs(X) > 2.:
      return n
    X = X ** 2 + C
  return max_iter

N = 512
max_iter = 64
xmin, xmax, ymin, ymax = -0.32, -0.22, 0.8, 0.9
X = np.linspace(xmin, xmax, N)
Y = np.linspace(ymin, ymax, N)
Z = np.empty((N, N))

for i, y in enumerate(Y):
  for j, x in enumerate(X):
    Z[i, j] = iter_count(complex(x, y), max_iter)
```

```
levels = [0, 8, 12, 16, 20, 24, 32]
plt.contourf(X, Y, Z, levels, cmap = cm.gray, antialiased = True)
plt.show()
```

The preceding script will produce the following output:

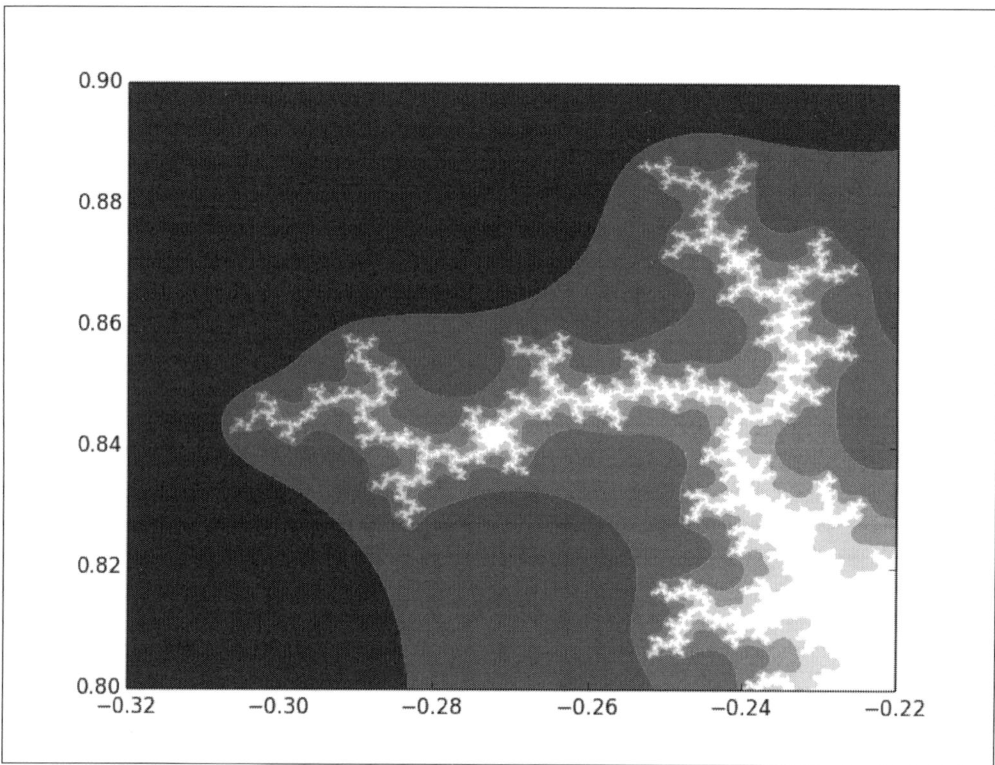

Here, we simply replaced `pyplot.contour()` with `pyplot.contourf()` and used additional levels for the contours. By default, filled contours are not antialiased. We used the `antialiased` optional parameter to get a more eye-pleasing result.

Visualizing a 2D vector field

So far, we have been working with 2D scalar fields: functions that associate a value to each point of the 2D plane. Vector fields associate a 2D vector to each point of the 2D plane. Vector fields are common in Physics as they provide solutions to differential equations. matplotlib provides functions to visualize vector fields.

Getting ready

For this example, we will need the SymPy package; a package for symbolic computations. This package has been used only to keep the example short and is not required for working with vector fields.

How to do it...

To illustrate the visualization of vector fields, let's visualize the velocity flow of an incompressible fluid around a cylinder. We do not need to bother about how to compute such a vector field but only about how to show it. The `pyplot.quiver()` function is what we need; refer to the following code:

```
import numpy as np
import sympy
from sympy.abc import x, y
from matplotlib import pyplot as plt
import matplotlib.patches as patches

def cylinder_stream_function(U = 1, R = 1):
  r = sympy.sqrt(x ** 2 + y ** 2)
  theta = sympy.atan2(y, x)
  return U * (r - R ** 2 / r) * sympy.sin(theta)

def velocity_field(psi):
  u = sympy.lambdify((x, y), psi.diff(y), 'numpy')
  v = sympy.lambdify((x, y), -psi.diff(x), 'numpy')
  return u, v

U_func, V_func = velocity_field(cylinder_stream_function() )

xmin, xmax, ymin, ymax = -2.5, 2.5, -2.5, 2.5
Y, X = np.ogrid[ymin:ymax:16j, xmin:xmax:16j]
U, V = U_func(X, Y), V_func(X, Y)

M = (X ** 2 + Y ** 2) < 1.
U = np.ma.masked_array(U, mask = M)
V = np.ma.masked_array(V, mask = M)

shape = patches.Circle((0, 0), radius = 1., lw = 2., fc = 'w', ec
  = 'k', zorder = 0)
plt.gca().add_patch(shape)

plt.quiver(X, Y, U, V, zorder = 1)

plt.axes().set_aspect('equal')
plt.show()
```

The preceding script will produce the following output:

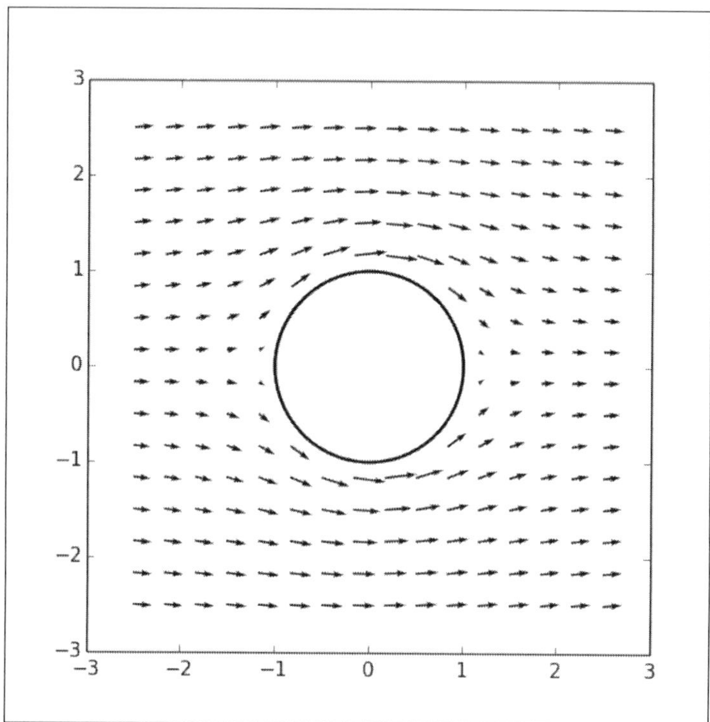

How it works...

Although the script is a bit long, the purely graphical part is simple. The vector field is stored in the matrices `U` and `V`: the coordinates of each vector we sampled from the vector field. The matrices `X` and `Y` contain the sample positions. The matrices `X`, `Y`, `U`, and `V` are passed to `pyplot.quiver()`, which renders the vector field. Note that `pyplot.quiver()` can take just `U` and `V` as parameters, but then the legend will show the indexes of the samples rather than their coordinates.

As the vector field that we used as an illustration here is the fluid flow around a cylinder, the cylinder itself is shown as follows:

```
shape = patches.Circle((0, 0), radius = 1., lw = 2., fc = 'w', ec
  = 'k', zorder = 0)
plt.gca().add_patch(shape)
```

The vector field inside the cylinder does not appear; we use a masked array. We first create a mask that defines which samples should be shown. Then, we apply this mask on `U` and `V`, as shown in the following script:

```
M = (X ** 2 + Y ** 2) < 1.
U = np.ma.masked_array(U, mask = M)
V = np.ma.masked_array(V, mask = M)
```

This allows you to hide singularities in a solution.

Visualizing the streamlines of a 2D vector field

Using arrows to represent a vector field works fairly well. But matplotlib can do better than this—it can show the streamlines of a vector field. A streamline shows how the vector field flows. In this recipe, we will show you how to create streamlines.

How to do it...

Let's use the fluid flow example of the previous recipe. We will simply replace the arrows with streamlines, as shown in the following code:

```
import numpy as np
import sympy
from sympy.abc import x, y
from matplotlib import pyplot as plt
import matplotlib.patches as patches

def cylinder_stream_function(U = 1, R = 1):
  r = sympy.sqrt(x ** 2 + y ** 2)
  theta = sympy.atan2(y, x)
  return U * (r - R ** 2 / r) * sympy.sin(theta)

def velocity_field(psi):
  u = sympy.lambdify((x, y), psi.diff(y), 'numpy')
  v = sympy.lambdify((x, y), -psi.diff(x), 'numpy')
  return u, v

psi = cylinder_stream_function()
U_func, V_func = velocity_field(psi)

xmin, xmax, ymin, ymax = -3, 3, -3, 3
Y, X = np.ogrid[ymin:ymax:128j, xmin:xmax:128j]
U, V = U_func(X, Y), V_func(X, Y)

M = (X ** 2 + Y ** 2) < 1.
U = np.ma.masked_array(U, mask = M)
V = np.ma.masked_array(V, mask = M)
```

```
shape = patches.Circle((0, 0), radius = 1., lw = 2., fc = 'w', ec
  = 'k', zorder = 0)
plt.gca().add_patch(shape)

plt.streamplot(X, Y, U, V, color = 'k')

plt.axes().set_aspect('equal')
plt.show()
```

The preceding script will display a flow around the cylinder, as shown in the following screenshot:

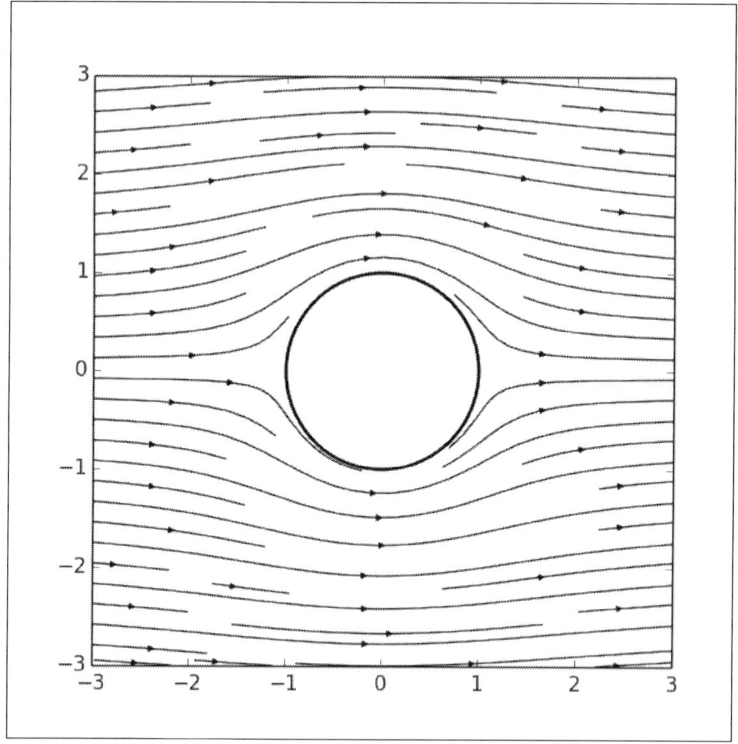

How it works...

The code generating the sample vectors' coordinates is the same as in the previous recipe. Here, we use more samples (`128*128` instead of `32*32`) to get accurate streamlines. Apart from this, the only difference is that we use `pyplot.streamlines()` instead of `pyplot.quiver()`. The four mandatory parameters are the same: the coordinates `X` and `Y` of the samples, and the coordinates `U` and `V` of the vectors. The optional parameter `color` is used to set the streamlines' colors.

There's more...

We can color the streamlines using a colormap with the optional parameter `color` and `cmap`:

```
plt.streamplot(X, Y, U, V, color = U ** 2 + V ** 2, cmap =
  cm.binary)
```

The `color` parameter takes a 2D array, which is used to color the streamlines. In this example, the color reflects the velocity of the flow as shown in the following output:

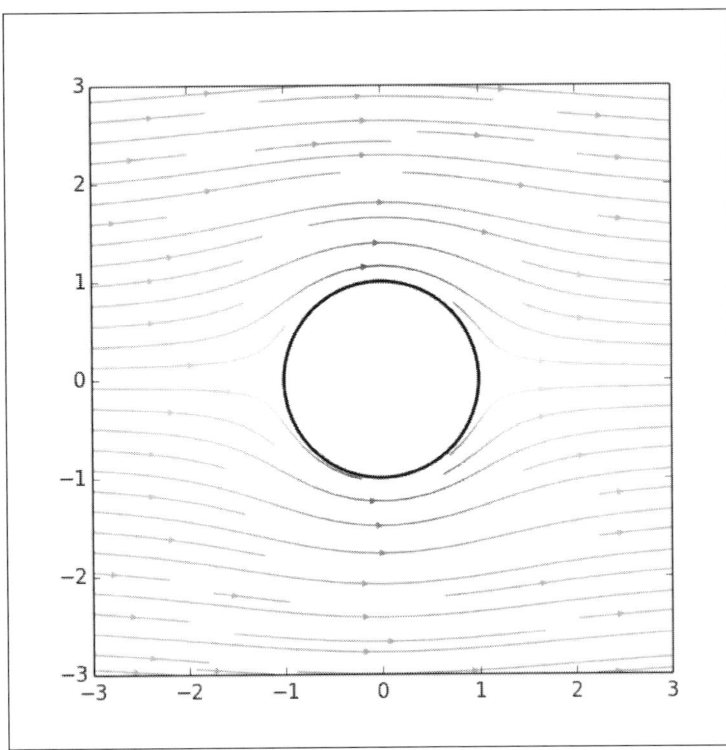

7
Working with 3D Figures

In this chapter, we will cover the following topics:

- Creating 3D scatter plots
- Creating 3D curve plots
- Plotting a scalar field in 3D
- Plotting a parametric 3D surface
- Embedding 2D figures in a 3D figure
- Creating a 3D bar plot

Introduction

matplotlib has ever-increasing support for three-dimensional plots. Since Version 1.2, the API to make 3D figures has been very similar to the 2D API. Adding one more dimension to your plots can help you to visualize more information at a glance. Also, 3D plots are quite an attention-grabber on a presentation or during a class. In this chapter, we are going to explore what matplotlib can do with a third dimension.

Creating 3D scatter plots

Scatter plots are very simple plots; for each point of your dataset, one point is shown in the figure. The coordinates of one point are simply the coordinates of the corresponding data. We have already explored scatter plots in two dimensions in *Chapter 1, First Steps*. In this recipe, we are going to see that scatter plots in three dimensions work the same way with just very minor changes.

In order to have some interesting data to visualize for this example, we are going to use the Lorenz strange attractor. This is a 3D structure that represents the solution of a simple dynamical system, coming from meteorology. This dynamical system is a famous textbook example of a chaotic system.

How to do it...

In the following code, we are going to call the figure-rendering methods from an `Axes` instance rather than calling the methods from `pyplot`:

```
import numpy as np
from mpl_toolkits.mplot3d import Axes3D
import matplotlib.pyplot as plt

# Dataset generation
a, b, c = 10., 28., 8. / 3.
def lorenz_map(X, dt = 1e-2):
  X_dt = np.array([a * (X[1] - X[0]),
                            X[0] * (b - X[2]) - X[1],
                            X[0] * X[1] - c * X[2]])
  return X + dt * X_dt

points = np.zeros((2000, 3))
X = np.array([.1, .0, .0])
for i in range(points.shape[0]):
  points[i], X = X, lorenz_map(X)

# Plotting
fig = plt.figure()
ax = fig.gca(projection = '3d')

ax.set_xlabel('X axis')
ax.set_ylabel('Y axis')
ax.set_zlabel('Z axis')
ax.set_title('Lorenz Attractor a=%0.2f b=%0.2f c=%0.2f' % (a, b,
  c))


ax.scatter(points[:, 0], points[:, 1],  points[:, 2], zdir = 'y',
  c = 'k')
plt.show()
```

The preceding code will show the now familiar user interface with the following figure:

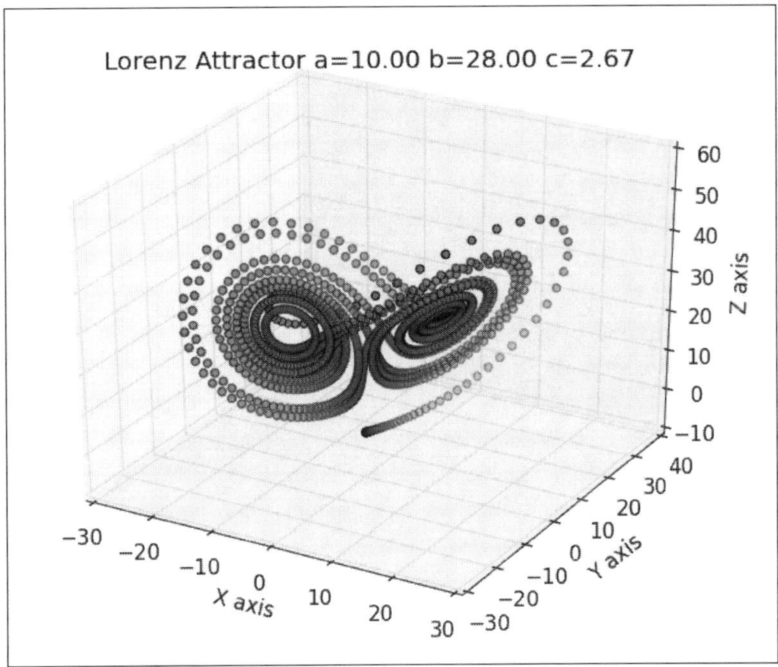

Before our eyes, the Lorenz attractor! If you drag your mouse inside the figure (move the mouse with the left button pressed), the 3D shape will rotate as if you were manipulating a trackball. You can rotate the figure and inspect the Lorenz attractor in all possible angles.

Note that although all dots are shown in blue, some points tend to be shaded toward white. matplotlib applies this fog-like effect to enhance the depth perception of scatter plots. Dots that are farther from our eyes will be dithered towards white—an old trick that painters from the Renaissance period already knew.

How it works...

We will not linger too much on the data generation for this example; that is not the point here. We just need to know that the dataset is stored in matrix points with three columns, one column per dimension.

Before doing anything three-dimensional with matplotlib, we first need to import the 3D extension for matplotlib: this is the purpose of the following import directive:

```
from mpl_toolkits.mplot3d import Axes3D
```

So far, most of the time, we have submitted all our rendering directives by calling methods from `pyplot`. However, for three-dimensional plots, things are a tad more involved, as shown in the following code:

```
fig = plt.figure()
ax = fig.gca(projection = '3d')
```

We create a `Figure` instance and attach an `Axes3D` instance to it. While the `Axes` instance is in charge of the usual 2D rendering, `Axes3D` will take care of the 3D rendering. Then, 3D scatter plots work exactly like their 2D counterparts, as shown in the following code:

```
ax.scatter(points[:, 0], points[:, 1],  points[:, 2])
```

We are giving the `X`, `Y`, and `Z` coordinates of the points to represent. Here, we simply give the three columns of the points' matrix. We could use a plain Python list, but we use a NumPy array just for its convenience. Again, note that we call the `scatter()` method of the `Axes3D` instance, not the `scatter` method from `pyplot`. Only the `scatter()` method from `Axes3D` interprets 3D data.

Finally, the functions we explored in *Chapter 3, Working with Annotations*, are also available, although they are called from the `Axes3D` instance. The title is set with `set_title()` and the axes are annotated with `set_xlabel()`, `set_ylabel()`, and `set_zlabel()`.

There's more...

As we have just seen, scatter plots in 3D work like they would in 2D. Indeed, apart from the setup code to create an `Axes3D` instance, everything seems to work like it would in 2D. This is not just an impression. For instance, customizing a scatter plot works in exactly the same way. Let's change the marker's shape and color by replacing the call to `Axes3D.scatter()` as follows:

```
ax.scatter(points[:, 0], points[:, 1],  points[:, 2],
                 marker = 's',
                 edgecolor = '.5',
             facecolor = '.5')
```

The output will now look like the following figure:

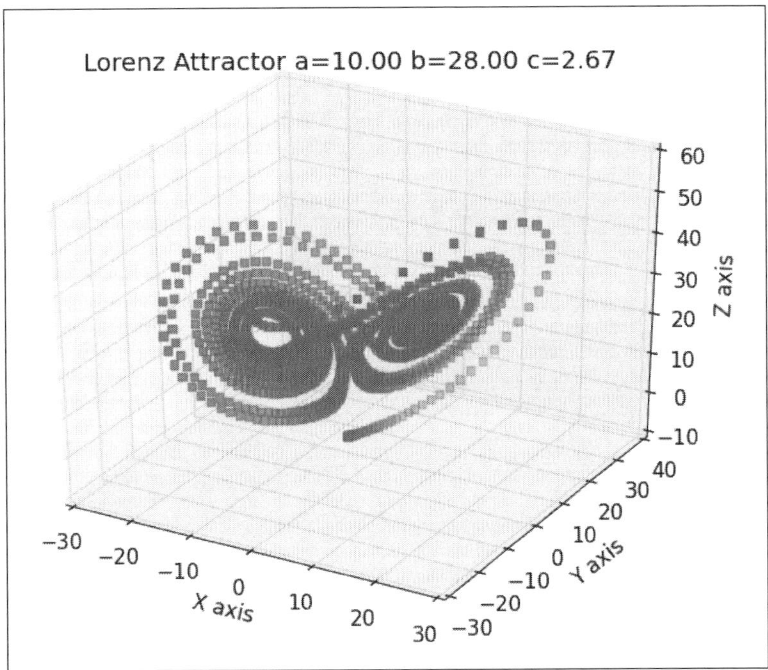

Indeed, all the tips and tricks from *Chapter 2, Customizing the Color and Styles* stand true in 3D.

Creating 3D curve plots

As the previous recipe has demonstrated, what we have learned in the previous chapters stands true when creating three-dimensional figures. Let's confirm this by plotting 3D parametric curves. In this recipe, we keep the same dataset as in the previous recipe; that is, the Lorenz attractor.

How to do it...

In 2D, we draw curves by calling `pyplot.plot()`. As the previous recipe hinted, all we have to do here is set up an `Axes3D` instance and call its `plot()` method, as shown in the following code:

```
import numpy as np
from mpl_toolkits.mplot3d import Axes3D
import matplotlib.pyplot as plt

a, b, c = 10., 28., 8. / 3.
```

```
def lorenz_map(X, dt = 1e-2):
  X_dt = np.array([a * (X[1] - X[0]),
                              X[0] * (b - X[2]) - X[1],
                              X[0] * X[1] - c * X[2]])
  return X + dt * X_dt

points = np.zeros((10000, 3))
X = np.array([.1, .0, .0])
for i in range(points.shape[0]):
  points[i], X = X, lorenz_map(X)

fig = plt.figure()
ax = fig.gca(projection = '3d')
ax.plot(points[:, 0], points[:, 1],  points[:, 2], c = 'k')
plt.show()
```

The preceding code will show the familiar Lorenz attractor, but instead of simply showing each data point, the points are linked by a curve as shown in the following figure:

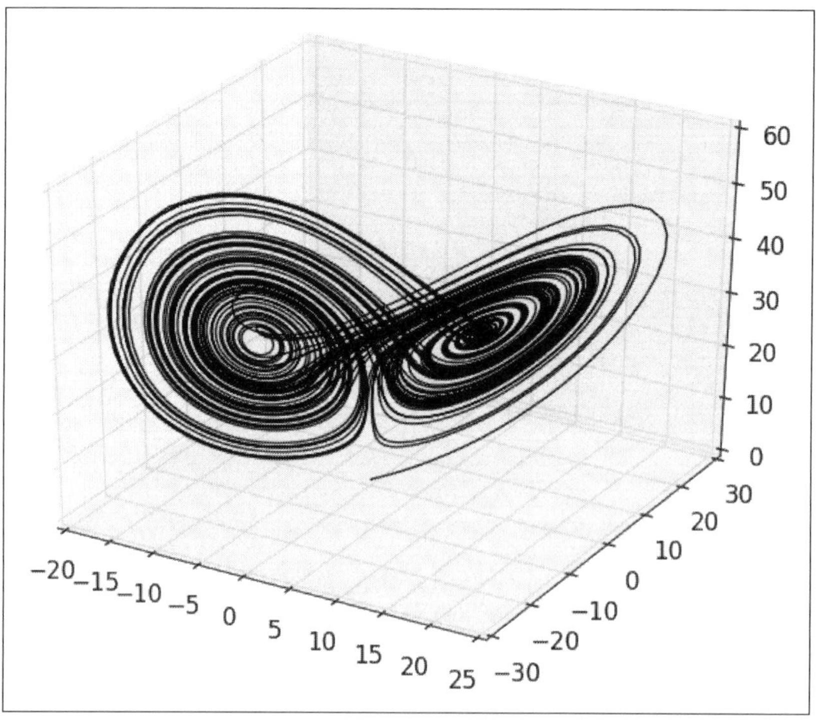

When we rotate the view with the user interface, the particular intertwined spiral structure of the Lorenz attractor is very apparent.

How it works...

As for any three-dimensional figure, we first set up an `Axes3D` instance. Then, the call to `plot()` works similar to its 2D counterpart: we give it one list per dimension and the coordinates of the points for each dimension.

Plotting a scalar field in 3D

So far, we have seen that 3D plots essentially mimic their 2D counterparts. However, there's more to matplotlib's three-dimensional plotting abilities. A lot of figures specific to the third dimension are also possible. Let's start with a simple use case: plotting a 2D scalar field as a 3D surface.

How to do it...

As usual, we are going to generate some test data, set up an `Axes3D` instance, and pass our data to it:

```
import numpy as np
from matplotlib import cm
from mpl_toolkits.mplot3d import Axes3D
import matplotlib.pyplot as plt

x = np.linspace(-3, 3, 256)
y = np.linspace(-3, 3, 256)
X, Y = np.meshgrid(x, y)
Z = np.sinc(np.sqrt(X ** 2 + Y ** 2))

fig = plt.figure()
ax = fig.gca(projection = '3d')
ax.plot_surface(X, Y, Z, cmap=cm.gray)
plt.show()
```

The preceding code will show the following figure:

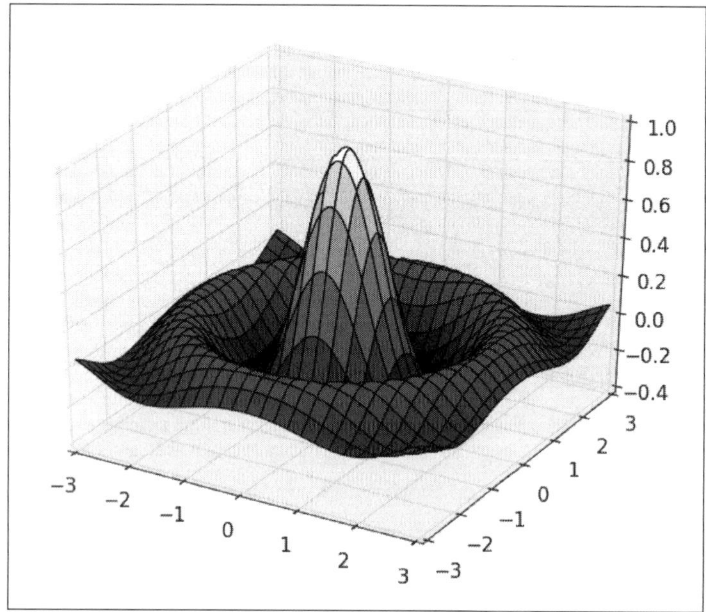

How it works...

The data generation works in exactly the same way as was demonstrated in *Chapter 6, Working with Maps*. Two matrices, `X` and `Y`, are created holding the coordinates of a regular grid. We compute the matrix `Z` and the scalar field functions of `X` and `Y`.

From here, things get very trivial; we call the `plot_surface()` method, which takes `X`, `Y`, and `Z` to display the scalar field as a 3D surface. The colors are taken from a colormap (the `cmap` optional parameter) and the matrix `Z`.

There's more...

You might not want to see the black curves shown on the 3D surface. This can be done using some additional optional parameters of `plot_surface()` as shown in the following code:

```
ax.plot_surface(X, Y, Z,
    cmap=cm.gray,
    linewidth=0,
    antialiased=False)
```

The black curves are now gone, making for a simpler figure as follows:

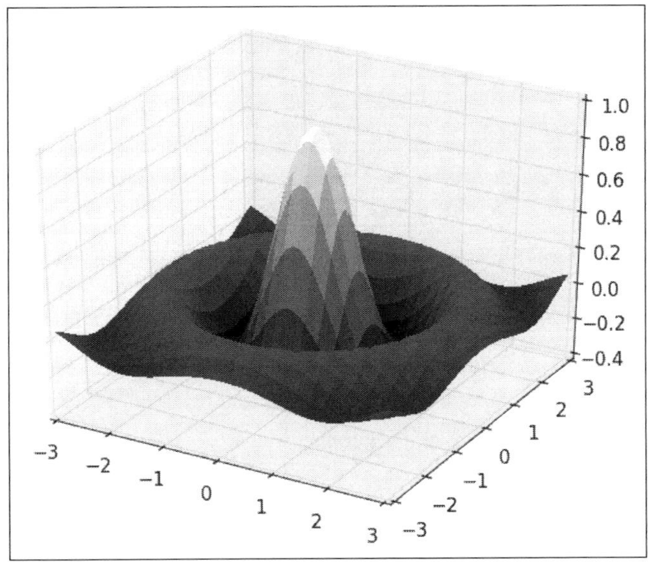

On the other hand, we might want to keep the black curves and get rid of the fancy colors. This can also be done with the optional parameters of `plot_surface()` as shown in the following code:

```
ax.plot_surface(X, Y, Z, color = 'w')
```

And only the black curves remain, making for a minimalist surface plot as shown in the following figure:

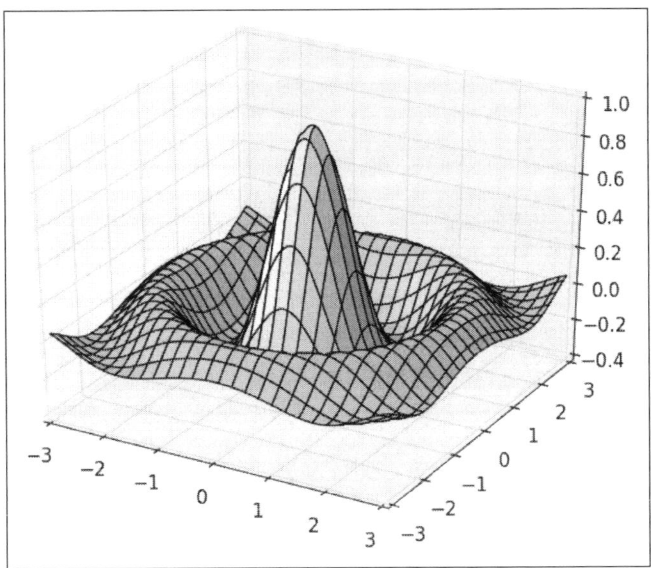

Finally, we might want to get rid of the hidden faces removal and want the surface to be made of wireframe. Now, this is not something that `plot_surface()` can achieve. However, `plot_wireframe()` was made just for this, as shown in the following code:

```
ax.plot_wireframe(X, Y, Z, cstride=8, rstride=8, color = 'k')
```

Now, the same surface is rendered in a wireframe style as shown in the following figure:

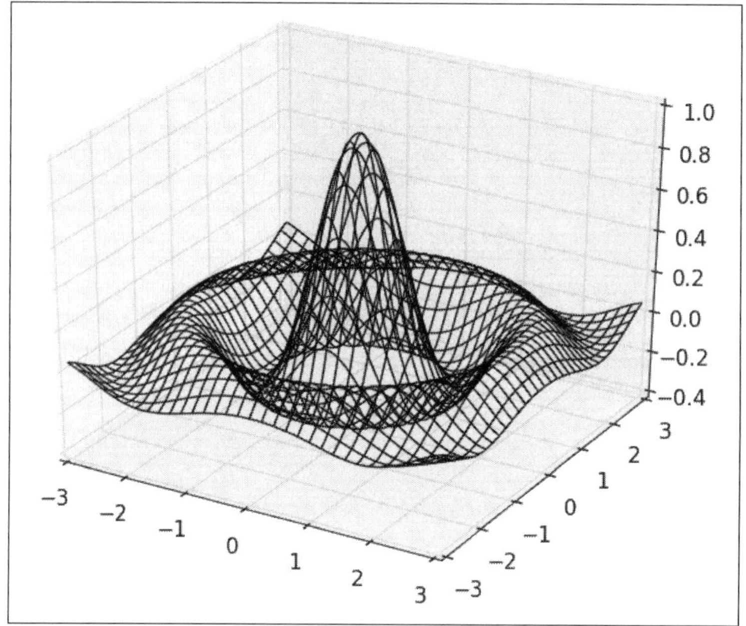

The `plot_wireframe()` parameter takes the same `X`, `Y`, and `Z` coordinates as input as the `plot_surface()` parameter. We use two optional parameters, `rstride` and `cstride`, to tell matplotlib to skip every eight coordinates on the `X` and `Y` axes. Without this, the space between the curves would be too small and we will see just a big black outline.

Plotting a parametric 3D surface

In the previous recipe, we used `plot_surface()` to plot a scalar field: that is, a function of the `f(x, y) = z` form. However, matplotlib is able to plot a generic, parametric 3D surface. Let's demonstrate this by plotting a torus, which is a fairly simple parametric surface.

How to do it...

We are going to use `plot_surface()` again to display a torus, using the following code:

```
import numpy as np
from mpl_toolkits.mplot3d import Axes3D
import matplotlib.pyplot as plt

# Generate torus mesh
angle = np.linspace(0, 2 * np.pi, 32)
theta, phi = np.meshgrid(angle, angle)
r, R = .25, 1.
X = (R + r * np.cos(phi)) * np.cos(theta)
Y = (R + r * np.cos(phi)) * np.sin(theta)
Z = r * np.sin(phi)

# Display the mesh
fig = plt.figure()
ax = fig.gca(projection = '3d')
ax.set_xlim3d(-1, 1)
ax.set_ylim3d(-1, 1)
ax.set_zlim3d(-1, 1)
ax.plot_surface(X, Y, Z, color = 'w', rstride = 1, cstride = 1)
plt.show()
```

The preceding code will display our torus as follows:

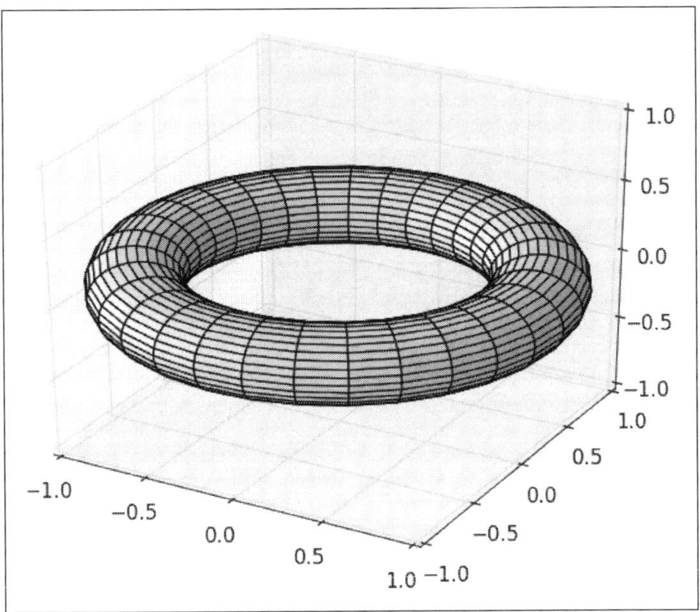

How it works...

A torus is a surface that can be parameterized with two parameters, `theta` and `phi`, varying from `0` to `2 * pi`, as shown in the following code:

```
angle = np.linspace(0, 2 * np.pi, 32)
theta, phi = np.meshgrid(angle, angle)
```

The `theta` and `phi` variables describe a regular grid layout. The 3D coordinates of the torus mesh are written as a function of `theta` and `phi`, as shown in the following code:

```
r, R = .25, 1.
X = (R + r * np.cos(phi)) * np.cos(theta)
Y = (R + r * np.cos(phi)) * np.sin(theta)
Z = r * np.sin(phi)
```

Then, we simply pass `X`, `Y`, and `Z` to the `plot_surface()` method. The `plot_surface()` method assumes that `X`, `Y`, and `Z` are gridded data. We need to set the optional parameters `rstride` and `cstride` to make it clear that `X`, `Y`, and `Z` are gridded data.

We explicitly set the axes' limit to the `[-1, 1]` range. By default, while creating 3D plots, matplotlib will automatically scale each axis. Our torus extends in the `[-1, 1]` range on the `X` and `Y` axes, but only in the `[-.25, .25]` range on the `Z` axis. If we let matplotlib scale the axis, the torus will appear stretched on the `Z` axis as shown in the following figure:

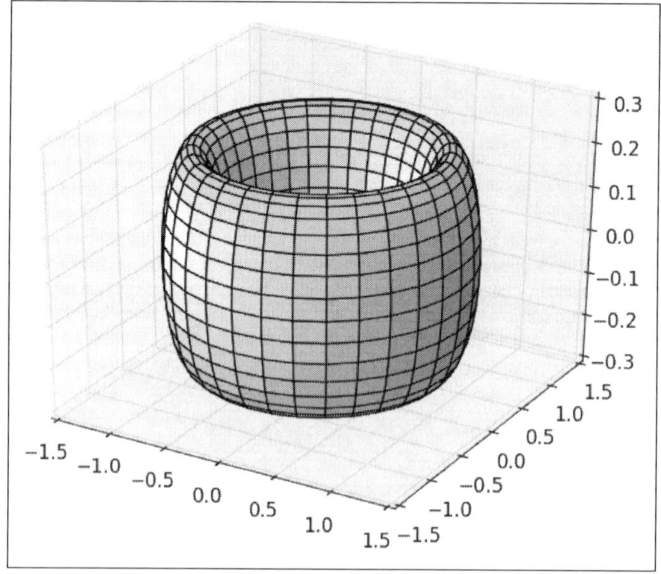

Thus, when plotting a 3D surface, we have to manually set each axis range to get a properly scaled view.

There's more...

As shown in the previous recipe, we can replace the call to `plot_surface()` with a call to `plot_wireframe()` in order to get a wireframe view of the torus using the following code:

```
ax.plot_wireframe(X, Y, Z, color = 'k', rstride = 1, cstride = 1)
```

This simple change is enough to get a wireframe view as shown in the following figure:

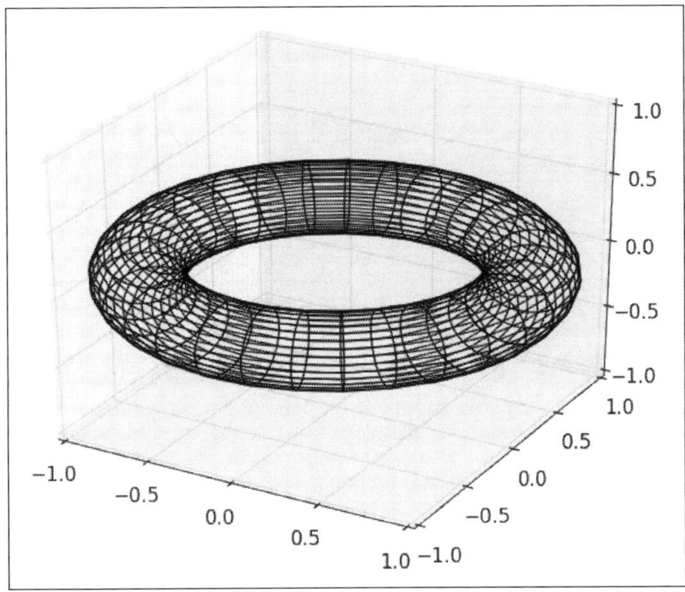

Embedding 2D figures in a 3D figure

We have seen in *Chapter 3*, *Working with Annotations*, how to annotate figures. A powerful way to annotate a three-dimensional figure is to simply use two-dimensional figures. This recipe is a simple example to illustrate this possibility.

How to do it...

To illustrate the idea, we are going to plot a simple 3D surface and two curves using only the primitives that we have already seen before, as shown in the following code:

```
import numpy as np
from mpl_toolkits.mplot3d import Axes3D
import matplotlib.pyplot as plt
```

```
x = np.linspace(-3, 3, 256)
y = np.linspace(-3, 3, 256)
X, Y = np.meshgrid(x, y)
Z = np.exp(-(X ** 2 + Y ** 2))
u = np.exp(-(x ** 2))

fig = plt.figure()
ax = fig.gca(projection = '3d')
ax.set_zlim3d(0, 3)
ax.plot(x, u, zs=3, zdir='y', lw = 2, color = '.75')
ax.plot(x, u, zs=-3, zdir='x', lw = 2., color = 'k')
ax.plot_surface(X, Y, Z, color = 'w')

plt.show()
```

The preceding code will produce the following figure:

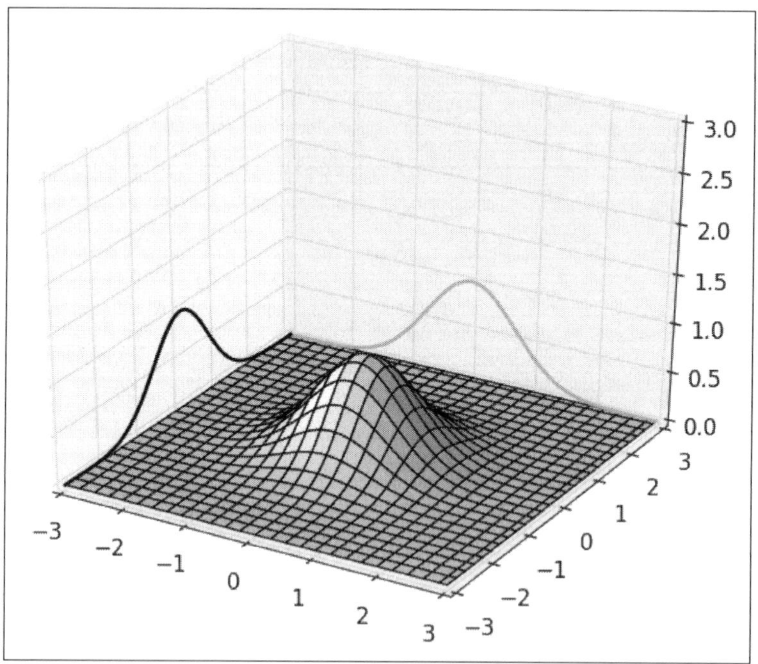

The black and gray curves are drawn as 2D curves projected on a plane.

How it works...

The 3D surface is generated as shown in the previous recipes. The `Axes3D` instance, `ax`, supports the usual 2D rendering commands such as `plot()`, as shown in the following code:

```
ax.plot(x, u, zs=3, zdir='y', lw = 2, color = '.75')
```

However, the call to `plot()` has two new optional parameters: `zs` and `zdir`:

- `Zdir`: This determines on which plane the 2D plot will be drawn, X, Y, or Z
- `Zs`: This determines the offset of the plane

Thus, to embed 2D figures in a 3D figure, we simply need to remember that all the 2D primitives are available with `Axes3D`. We just have two optional parameters, `zdir` and `zs`, to set to place the plane on which the figures need to be rendered.

There's more...

Embedding 2D figures in a 3D figure is very simple, but it opens up a lot of possibilities to create sophisticated figures using the simple primitives we have explored so far. For instance, we already know everything to make a layered bar graph using the following code:

```
import numpy as np
from matplotlib import cm
import matplotlib.colors as col
from mpl_toolkits.mplot3d import Axes3D
import matplotlib.pyplot as plt

# Data generation
alpha = 1. / np.linspace(1, 8, 5)
t = np.linspace(0, 5, 16)
T, A = np.meshgrid(t, alpha)
data = np.exp(-T * A)

# Plotting
fig = plt.figure()
ax = fig.gca(projection = '3d')
cmap = cm.ScalarMappable(col.Normalize(0, len(alpha)), cm.gray)
for i, row in enumerate(data):
  ax.bar(4 * t, row, zs=i, zdir='y', alpha=0.8, color=cmap.to_rgba(i))
plt.show()
```

The preceding code will produce the following figure:

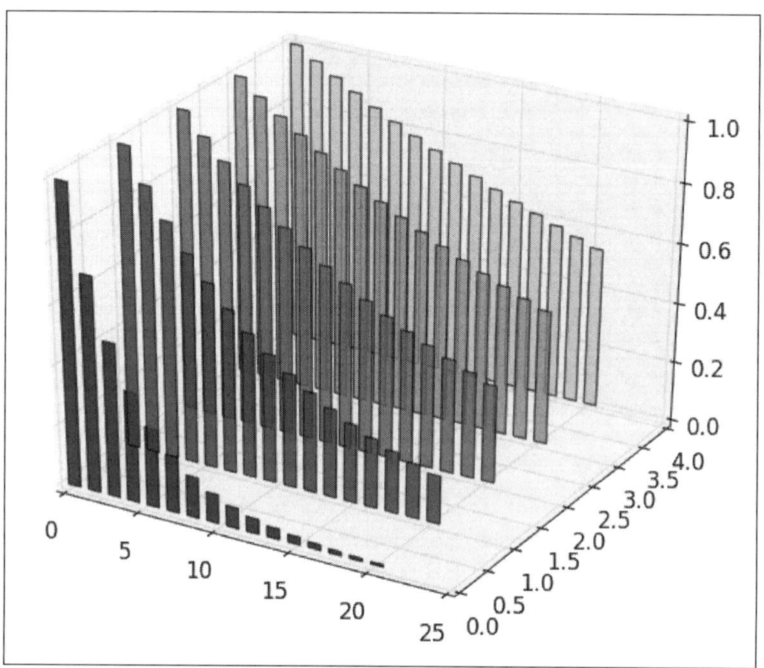

We can see that the preceding code uses features introduced in the previous chapters:

- The creation of a bar graph has been covered in *Chapter 1, First Steps*
- The coloring of bar graphs using a colormap has been covered in *Chapter 2, Customizing the Color and Styles*
- The layering of bar graphs has been covered in the present recipe

Creating a 3D bar plot

Using several 2D layers in a 3D figure, we can plot multiple bar plots. However, we can also go full 3D and plot bar plots with actual 3D bars.

How to do it...

To demonstrate 3D bar plots, we will use the simple, synthetic dataset from the previous recipe as shown in the following code:

```
import numpy as np
from mpl_toolkits.mplot3d import Axes3D
```

```
import matplotlib.pyplot as plt

# Data generation
alpha = np.linspace(1, 8, 5)
t = np.linspace(0, 5, 16)
T, A = np.meshgrid(t, alpha)
data = np.exp(-T * (1. / A))

# Plotting
fig = plt.figure()
ax = fig.gca(projection = '3d')

Xi = T.flatten()
Yi = A.flatten()
Zi = np.zeros(data.size)

dx = .25 * np.ones(data.size)
dy = .25 * np.ones(data.size)
dz = data.flatten()

ax.set_xlabel('T')
ax.set_ylabel('Alpha')
ax.bar3d(Xi, Yi, Zi, dx, dy, dz, color = 'w')

plt.show()
```

This time, the bars appear as 3D blocks as shown in the following figure:

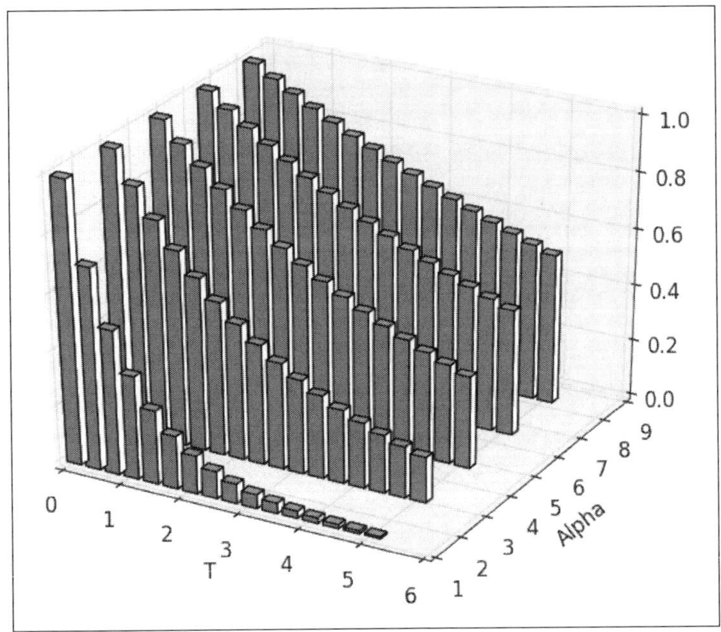

How it works...

The bars are positioned with a grid layout. The `bar3d()` method takes six mandatory parameters as the input. The first three parameters are the `X`, `Y`, and `Z` coordinates of the lower end of each bar. Here, we build the coordinates of the bars from the dataset as follows:

```
Xi = T.flatten()
Yi = A.flatten()
Zi = np.zeros(data.size)
```

Each bar will start at the same level, `0`. The `X` and `Y` coordinates are those of the dataset. The `bar3d()` method takes the list of coordinates as the input, not the gridded coordinates, which is why we call the `flatten` method on the matrices `A` and `T`.

The next three mandatory parameters of the `bar3d()` method are the dimensions of each bar on each dimension. Here, the height of the bars is taken from the `data` matrix. The bar width and depth are set to `.25`, as shown in the following code:

```
dx = .25 * np.ones(data.size)
dy = .25 * np.ones(data.size)
dz = data.flatten()
```

We can now call `bar3d()` using the following code:

```
ax.bar3d(Xi, Yi, Zi, dx, dy, dz, color = 'w')
```

8
User Interface

In this chapter, we will cover:

- Making a user-controllable plot
- Integrating a plot into the Tkinter user interface
- Integrating a plot into the wxWidgets user interface
- Integrating a plot into the GTK user interface
- Integrating a plot into a Pyglet application

Introduction

matplotlib can do more than plot figures; it can plot figures you can interact with. An interactive visualization can be a great way to explore some data and discover some interesting patterns. Also, an interactive figure can be a great support for teaching purposes. In this chapter, we are going to explore the different options we have to create such **interactive plots**.

Making a user-controllable plot

Out of the box, without requiring any additional packages, matplotlib offers primitives to add controllers on a figure so that a user can interact with it. In this recipe, we are going to see how to plot a famous parametric curve: the SuperShape curve. This curve is controlled by six parameters: A, B, M, N1, N2, and N3. These parameters determine the shape of the curve. They can be set interactively by the user by moving the cursor on the figure.

How to do it...

The following code will display a curve using `pyplot.plot()`, which at this point should be simple. However, we now use user interface elements (more commonly called **widgets**), that is, sliders. This can be done with the following steps:

1. We start with the necessary import directives as follows:

```
import numpy as np
from matplotlib import pyplot as plt
from matplotlib.widgets import Slider
```

2. The SuperShape curve is defined by the following function:

```
def supershape_radius(phi, a, b, m, n1, n2, n3):
  theta = .25 * m * phi
  cos = np.fabs(np.cos(theta) / a) ** n2
  sin = np.fabs(np.sin(theta) / b) ** n3
  r = (cos + sin) ** (-1. / n1)
  r /= np.max(r)
  return r
```

3. We then define the initial values for the parameters of the SuperShape curve using the following code:

```
phi = np.linspace(0, 2 * np.pi, 1024)
m_init = 3
n1_init = 2
n2_init = 18
n3_init = 18
```

4. We define the plot and place sliders as follows:

```
fig = plt.figure()
ax = fig.add_subplot(111, polar = True)

ax_m  = plt.axes([0.05, 0.05, 0.25, 0.025])
ax_n1 = plt.axes([0.05, 0.10, 0.25, 0.025])
ax_n2 = plt.axes([0.7, 0.05, 0.25, 0.025])
ax_n3 = plt.axes([0.7, 0.10, 0.25, 0.025])

slider_m  = Slider(ax_m,  'm',  1, 20, valinit = m_init)
slider_n1 = Slider(ax_n1, 'n1', .1, 10, valinit = n1_init)
slider_n2 = Slider(ax_n2, 'n2', .1, 20, valinit = n2_init)
slider_n3 = Slider(ax_n3, 'n3', .1, 20, valinit = n3_init)
```

5. We render the curve once by using the following code:

```
r = supershape_radius(phi, 1, 1, m_init, n1_init, n2_init,
  n3_init)
lines, = ax.plot(phi, r, lw = 3.)
```

6. We specify what to do when a slider is updated by the user, as shown in the following code:

```
def update(val):
    r = supershape_radius(phi, 1, 1, np.floor(slider_m.val),
slider_n1.val, slider_n2.val, slider_n3.val)
    lines.set_ydata(r)
    fig.canvas.draw_idle()

slider_n1.on_changed(update)
slider_n2.on_changed(update)
slider_n3.on_changed(update)
slider_m.on_changed(update)
```

7. We are now done and can conclude our script with the following:

```
plt.show()
```

8. The preceding code will display a curve as expected, with (rudimentary) slider controls, as shown in the following figure:

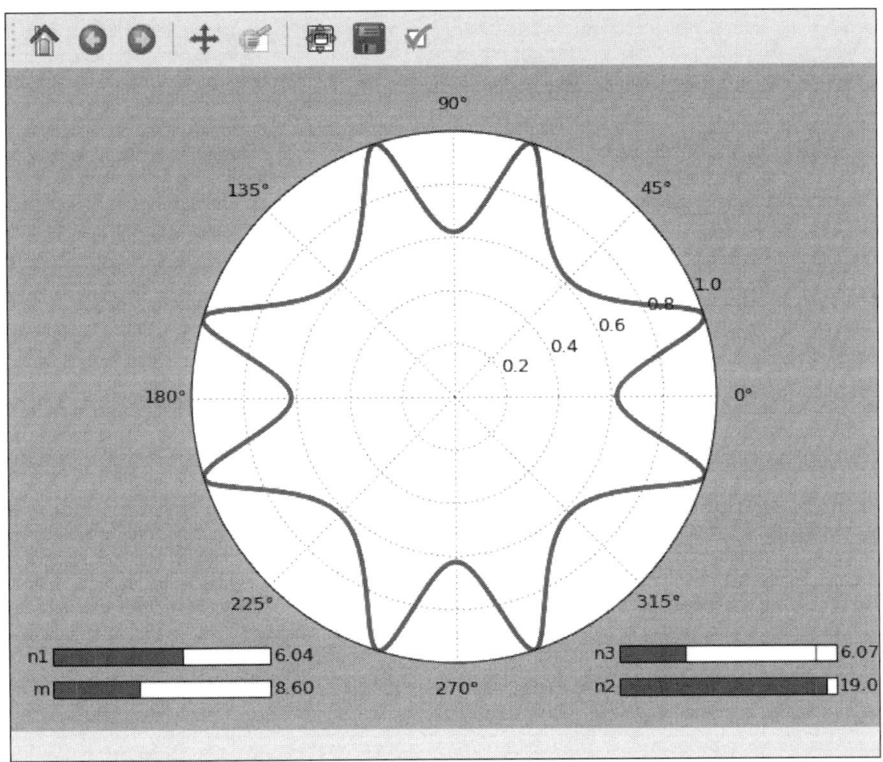

You can drag the sliders on the left or the right and see the curve change. Note that on older computers, the animation feels noticeably sluggish.

How it works...

The code is a bit longer than usual. Let's break it up!

The SuperShape curve is a polar curve. The `supershape_radius` function computes a radius for every angle in the `[0, 2 * pi]` interval. The function takes as an input an array of angles and the six parameters of the SuperShape curve.

We create a `Figure` instance, `fig`, and an `Axes` instance, `ax`, explicitly as shown in the following code:

```
fig = plt.figure()
ax = fig.add_subplot(111, polar = True)
```

All widgets are defined in the `matplotlib.widgets` package. We place four slider widgets on the figure for the parameters M, N1, N2, and N3.

Each slider is associated with a subfigure created by a call to `plot.axes()`. Each `Slider` instance is created by a call to the `Slider` constructor. The constructor takes four mandatory parameters: a subfigure instance, a label, a minimum value, and a maximum value. We use the optional parameter `valinit` to set the initial position of each slider, as shown in the following code:

```
ax_m  = plt.axes([0.05, 0.05, 0.25, 0.025])
ax_n1 = plt.axes([0.05, 0.10, 0.25, 0.025])
ax_n2 = plt.axes([0.7, 0.05, 0.25, 0.025])
ax_n3 = plt.axes([0.7, 0.10, 0.25, 0.025])

slider_m  = Slider(ax_m,  'm',  1, 20, valinit = m_init)
slider_n1 = Slider(ax_n1, 'n1', .1, 10, valinit = n1_init)
slider_n2 = Slider(ax_n2, 'n2', .1, 20, valinit = n2_init)
slider_n3 = Slider(ax_n3, 'n3', .1, 20, valinit = n3_init)
```

We plot the curve itself, but we keep track of what will be rendered: a collection of lines stored in the `lines` variable, which is done using the following code:

```
lines, = ax.plot(phi, r, lw = 3.)
```

We define the behavior of each slider when their positions are changed: they will call a function named `update`:

```
slider_n1.on_changed(update)
slider_n2.on_changed(update)
slider_n3.on_changed(update)
slider_m.on_changed(update)
```

The `update` function reads the position of each slider and the position of each point of the curve to be displayed is updated, the collection of lines is updated, and finally, the `Figure` instance `fig` is notified of the change, as shown in the following code:

```
def update(val):
    lines.set_ydata(supershape_radius(phi, 1, 1, np.floor(slider_m.
      val), slider_n1.val, slider_n2.val, slider_n3.val))
    fig.canvas.draw_idle()
```

Finally, we are ready to plot everything using the following:

```
plt.show()
```

There's more...

Although slider controls are definitely a nice way to adjust a parameter interactively, there are more widgets available in the `matplotlib.widgets` package. Buttons and checkboxes are also available.

Integrating a plot to a Tkinter user interface

matplotlib provides rudimentary widgets to build interactive figures. However, those widgets are very rudimentary and do not scale well for anything that needs more than a couple of controllers. A real graphical user interface library is more adapted to creating sophisticated interactions. Fortunately, Python comes with such a library: **Tkinter**. Tkinter allows you to create some widgets and give them a windows layout. Even better, matplotlib provides a convenient hook to integrate plots to a user interface made with Tkinter. In this recipe, we will be reproducing the previous example, but using Tkinter for the user interface part.

How to do it...

Conveniently, matplotlib provides a special Tkinter widget that we can use to render figures. Updating the figure inside that special widget is done as in the previous recipe. Here are the steps that we need to follow:

1. We start with the mandatory import directives as follows:

   ```
   import numpy as np
   from tkinter import *

   from matplotlib.backends.backend_tkagg import
     FigureCanvasTkAgg
   from matplotlib.figure import Figure
   ```

   Note that the import directive for Tkinter here is valid for Python 3. If you are using Python 2, then you should replace `tkinter` with `Tkinter`.

2. Then, we define the function for the SuperShape curve using the following code:

```
def supershape_radius(phi, a, b, m, n1, n2, n3):
  theta = .25 * m * phi
  cos = np.fabs(np.cos(theta) / a) ** n2
  sin = np.fabs(np.sin(theta) / b) ** n3
  r = (cos + sin) ** (-1. / n1)

  r /= np.max(r)
  return r
```

3. We define a utility object to linearly scale a range into another as follows:

```
class LinearScaling(object):
  def __init__(self, src_range, dst_range):
    self.src_start, src_diff = src_range[0], src_range[1] -
      src_range[0]
    self.dst_start, dst_diff = dst_range[0], dst_range[1] - dst_
      range[0]
    self.src_to_dst_coeff = dst_diff / src_diff
    self.dst_to_src_coeff = src_diff / dst_diff

  def src_to_dst(self, X):
    return (X - self.src_start) * self.src_to_dst_coeff +
      self.dst_start

  def dst_to_src(self, X):
    return (X - self.dst_start) *
      self.dst_to_src_coeff + self.src_start
```

4. Now comes the user interface, which is coded as follows:

```
class SuperShapeFrame(Frame):
  def __init__(self, master = None):
    Frame.__init__(self, master)
    self.grid()
    self.m = 3
    self.n1 = 2
    self.n1_scaling = LinearScaling((.1, 20), (0, 200))
    self.n2 = 18
    self.n2_scaling = LinearScaling((.1, 20), (0, 200))
    self.n3 = 18
    self.n3_scaling = LinearScaling((.1, 20), (0, 200))

    self.fig = Figure((6, 6), dpi = 80)
    canvas = FigureCanvasTkAgg(self.fig, master = self)
    canvas.get_tk_widget().grid(row = 0, column = 0, columnspan =
      4)
```

```
label = Label(self, text = 'M')
label.grid(row = 1, column = 1)
self.m_slider = Scale(self, from_ = 1, to = 20, orient =
  HORIZONTAL, command = lambda i : self.update_m())

self.m_slider.grid(row = 1, column = 2)

label = Label(self, text = 'N1')
label.grid(row = 2, column = 1)
self.n1_slider = Scale(self, from_ = 0, to = 200, orient =
  HORIZONTAL, command = lambda i : self.update_n1())
self.n1_slider.grid(row = 2, column = 2)

label = Label(self, text = 'N2')
label.grid(row = 3, column = 1)
self.n2_slider = Scale(self, from_ = 0, to = 200, orient =
  HORIZONTAL, command = lambda i : self.update_n2())
self.n2_slider.grid(row = 3, column = 2)

label = Label(self, text = 'N3')
label.grid(row = 4, column = 1)
self.n3_slider = Scale(self, from_ = 0, to = 200, orient =
  HORIZONTAL, command = lambda i : self.update_n3())
self.n3_slider.grid(row = 4, column = 2)

self.draw_figure()

def update_m(self):
  self.m = self.m_slider.get()
  self.refresh_figure()

def update_n1(self):
  self.n1 = self.n1_scaling.dst_to_src(self.n1_slider.get())
  self.refresh_figure()

def update_n2(self):
  self.n2 = self.n2_scaling.dst_to_src(self.n2_slider.get())
  self.refresh_figure()

def update_n3(self):
  self.n3 = self.n3_scaling.dst_to_src(self.n3_slider.get())
  self.refresh_figure()

def refresh_figure(self):
  r = supershape_radius(self.phi, 1, 1, self.m, self.n1, self.
  n2, self.n3)
  self.lines.set_ydata(r)
  self.fig.canvas.draw_idle()
```

```
def draw_figure(self):
  self.phi = np.linspace(0, 2 * numpy.pi, 1024)
  r = supershape_radius(self.phi, 1, 1, self.m, self.n1, self.
  n2, self.n3)
  ax = self.fig.add_subplot(111, polar = True)
  self.lines, = ax.plot(self.phi, r, lw = 3.)
  self.fig.canvas.draw()
```

5. Finally, we set up and start our user interface as follows:

```
app = SuperShapeFrame()
app.master.title('SuperShape')
app.mainloop()
```

6. The SuperShape curve is drawn and can be controlled with four slider widgets as shown in the following figure:

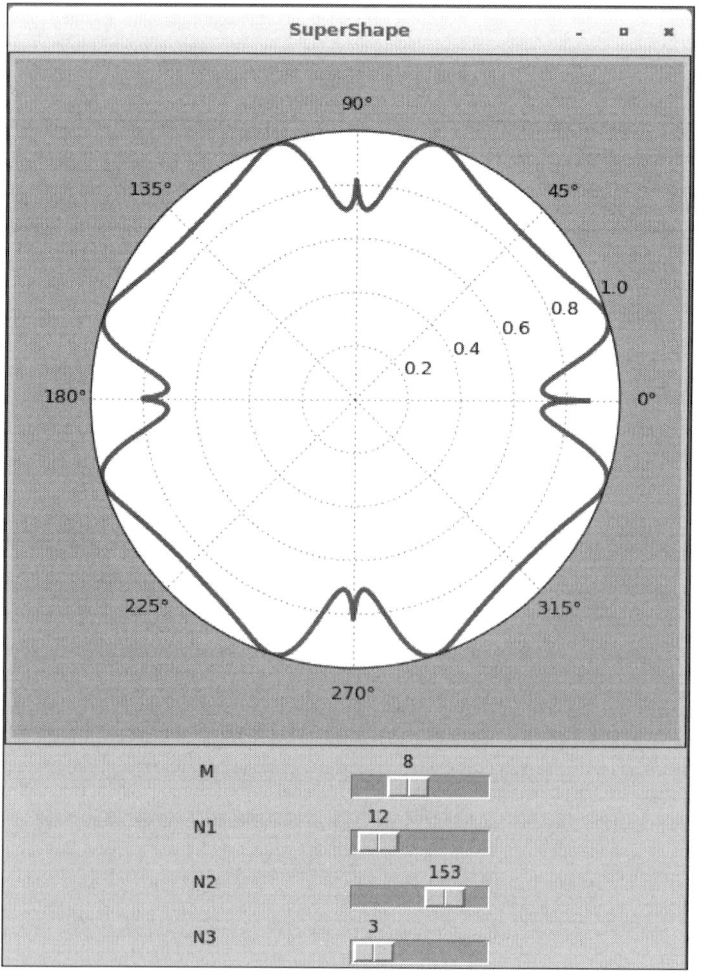

How it works...

In this example, all the work is done by the `SuperShapeFrame` object, which is a subclass of the `TKinter Frame` class. A `Frame` object is simply a window, in Tkinter lexicon.

matplotlib provides a `FigureCanvasTKAgg` object as part of the `matplotlib.backends.backend_tkagg` module. A `FigureCanvasTKAgg` object encapsulates a `Figure` instance and behaves like a Tkinter object. Thus, in this example, we create a window (the `Frame` object) and we populate it with widgets: four slider instances and a `FigureCanvasTKAgg` instance. The canvas is created as follows:

```
self.fig = Figure((6, 6), dpi = 80)
canvas = FigureCanvasTkAgg(self.fig, master = self)
```

We first create a matplotlib figure and simply pass it as a parameter to the `FigureCanvasTkAgg` constructor. We do not need to keep track of the canvas itself; we just need to keep track of the figure. The size of the canvas depends on the size of the figure and its resolution. Here, our figure is a square of six units at 80 dpi: 480 pixels.

There are two operations we need to implement: drawing the figure, and refreshing it. We only need to draw the figure once. Then, when the user changes some parameters of the curve we have displayed, we have to refresh the figure.

The figure is drawn using the `draw_figure()` method as follows:

```
def draw_figure(self):
  self.phi = np.linspace(0, 2 * np.pi, 1024)
  r = supershape_radius(self.phi, 1, 1, self.m, self.n1, self.n2,
  self.n3)
  ax = self.fig.add_subplot(111, polar = True)
  self.lines, = ax.plot(self.phi, r, lw = 3.)
  self.fig.canvas.draw()
```

We attach an `Axes` instance, `ax`, to our `Figure` instance. We render our curve and keep a track of the result of this operation: a collection of lines. Finally, we tell the canvas to render the figure.

The figure is refreshed using the `refresh_figure()` method as follows:

```
def refresh_figure(self):
  r = supershape_radius(self.phi, 1, 1, self.m, self.n1, self.n2,
  self.n3)
  self.lines.set_ydata(r)
  self.fig.canvas.draw_idle()
```

When refreshing the figure, we do not re-plot everything (but it can be done that way); we simply update the collection of lines and notify the canvas to update the figure. Every time a slider is modified by the user, we refresh the figure by calling `refresh_figure()`.

One quirk of using Tkinter sliders is that those sliders return only integer values; however, in practice, at least in a science or engineering context, we need floating point values. To work around this issue, we implement a `LinearScaling` class, linearly scaling values from one range to the other. The sliders are given a range of 0 to 200. One instance of `LinearScaling` is created for each of the four parameters to convert the slider positions to the actual value of the parameter.

Integrating a plot to a wxWidgets user interface

Using Tkinter, we can combine the plotting abilities of matplotlib and a fully featured GUI library. This solution has the advantage of relying on standard Python only. However, a classical argument against Tkinter is how it looks: the user interface has a look and feel of its own, not the look and feel of the platform it runs on.

The wxWidgets user interface is another GUI module for Python, binding the wx library. The wx library exposes a common API to create graphical interfaces on Windows, OS X, and Linux. The graphical interfaces created with wx will have the look and feel of the platform they run on. In this recipe, we will look at how we can interface wxWidgets with matplotlib.

How to do it...

The general idea is very similar to what has been done with the matplotlib/Tkinter integration. matplotlib provides a special wxWidget widget that embeds a `Figure` object. Creating and updating that `Figure` object works the same way as before, as shown in the following steps:

1. We start with the import directives as follows:

```
import wx
import numpy as np

from matplotlib.backends.backend_wxagg import
  FigureCanvasWxAgg
from matplotlib.figure import Figure
```

2. We add the function to define a SuperShape curve using the following code:

```
def supershape_radius(phi, a, b, m, n1, n2, n3):
  theta = .25 * m * phi

  cos = np.fabs(np.cos(theta) / a) ** n2
```

```
  sin = np.fabs(np.sin(theta) / b) ** n3
  r = (cos + sin) ** (-1. / n1)
  r /= np.max(r)
  return r
```

3. We are going to need a utility object to scale linearly from one range to the other as follows:

```
class LinearScaling(object):
  def __init__(self, src_range, dst_range):
    self.src_start, src_diff = src_range[0], src_range[1] - src_
      range[0]
    self.dst_start, dst_diff = dst_range[0], dst_range[1] - dst_
      range[0]
    self.src_to_dst_coeff = dst_diff / src_diff
    self.dst_to_src_coeff = src_diff / dst_diff

  def src_to_dst(self, X):
    return (X - self.src_start) * self.src_to_dst_coeff + self.
      dst_start

  def dst_to_src(self, X):
    return (X - self.dst_start) * self.dst_to_src_coeff + self.
      src_start
```

4. We define our user interface using the following code:

```
class SuperShapeFrame(wx.Frame):
  def __init__(self, parent, id, title):
    wx.Frame.__init__(self, parent, id, title,
      style = wx.DEFAULT_FRAME_STYLE ^ wx.RESIZE_BORDER,
      size = (480, 640))
    self.m = 3
    self.n1 = 2
    self.n1_scaling = LinearScaling((.01, 20), (0, 200))

    self.n2 = 18
    self.n2_scaling = LinearScaling((.01, 20), (0, 200))

    self.n3 = 18
    self.n3_scaling = LinearScaling((.01, 20), (0, 200))

    self.fig = Figure((6, 6), dpi = 80)

    panel = wx.Panel(self, -1)
```

```
    self.m_slider = wx.Slider(panel, -1, self.m, 1, 20, size =
      (250, -1), style = wx.SL_AUTOTICKS | wx.SL_HORIZONTAL |
      wx.SL_LABELS)

    self.n1_slider = wx.Slider(panel, -1, self.n1_scaling.src_to_
      dst(self.n1), 0, 200, size = (250, -1), style = wx.SL_
      AUTOTICKS | wx.SL_HORIZONTAL | wx.SL_LABELS)

    self.n2_slider = wx.Slider(panel, -1, self.n1_scaling.src_to_
      dst(self.n2), 0, 200, size = (250, -1), style = wx.SL_
      AUTOTICKS | wx.SL_HORIZONTAL | wx.SL_LABELS)

    self.n3_slider = wx.Slider(panel, -1, self.n1_scaling.src_to_
      dst(self.n3), 0, 200, size = (250, -1), style = wx.SL_
      AUTOTICKS | wx.SL_HORIZONTAL | wx.SL_LABELS)

    self.m_slider.Bind(wx.EVT_SCROLL, self.on_m_slide)
    self.n1_slider.Bind(wx.EVT_SCROLL, self.on_n1_slide)
    self.n2_slider.Bind(wx.EVT_SCROLL, self.on_n2_slide)
    self.n3_slider.Bind(wx.EVT_SCROLL, self.on_n3_slide)

    sizer = wx.BoxSizer(wx.VERTICAL)
    sizer.Add(FigureCanvasWxAgg(panel, -1, self.fig), 0, wx.TOP)
    sizer.Add(self.m_slider,  0, wx.ALIGN_CENTER)
    sizer.Add(self.n1_slider, 0, wx.ALIGN_CENTER)
    sizer.Add(self.n2_slider, 0, wx.ALIGN_CENTER)
    sizer.Add(self.n3_slider, 0, wx.ALIGN_CENTER)
    panel.SetSizer(sizer)

    self.draw_figure()

  def on_m_slide(self, event):
    self.m = self.m_slider.GetValue()
    self.refresh_figure()

  def on_n1_slide(self, event):

    self.n1 = self.n1_scaling.dst_to_src(self.n1_slider.
    GetValue())
    self.refresh_figure()

  def on_n2_slide(self, event):
    self.n2 = self.n2_scaling.dst_to_src(self.n2_slider.
    GetValue())
    self.refresh_figure()
```

```
def on_n3_slide(self, event):
  self.n3 = self.n3_scaling.dst_to_src(self.n3_slider.
  GetValue())
  self.refresh_figure()

def refresh_figure(self):
  r = supershape_radius(self.phi, 1, 1, self.m, self.n1, self.
  n2, self.n3)
  self.lines.set_ydata(r)
  self.fig.canvas.draw_idle()

def draw_figure(self):
  self.phi = np.linspace(0, 2 * np.pi, 1024)
  r = supershape_radius(self.phi, 1, 1, self.m, self.n1, self.
  n2, self.n3)
  ax = self.fig.add_subplot(111, polar = True)
  self.lines, = ax.plot(self.phi, r, lw = 3.)

  self.fig.canvas.draw()
```

5. We can now initialize and start the user interface as follows:

```
app = wx.App(redirect = True)
top = SuperShapeFrame(None, -1, 'SuperShape')
top.Show()
app.MainLoop()
```

6. This script produces a window showing the SuperShape curve. As in the previous recipes of this chapter, moving the sliders will modify the curve's shape, as shown in the following figure:

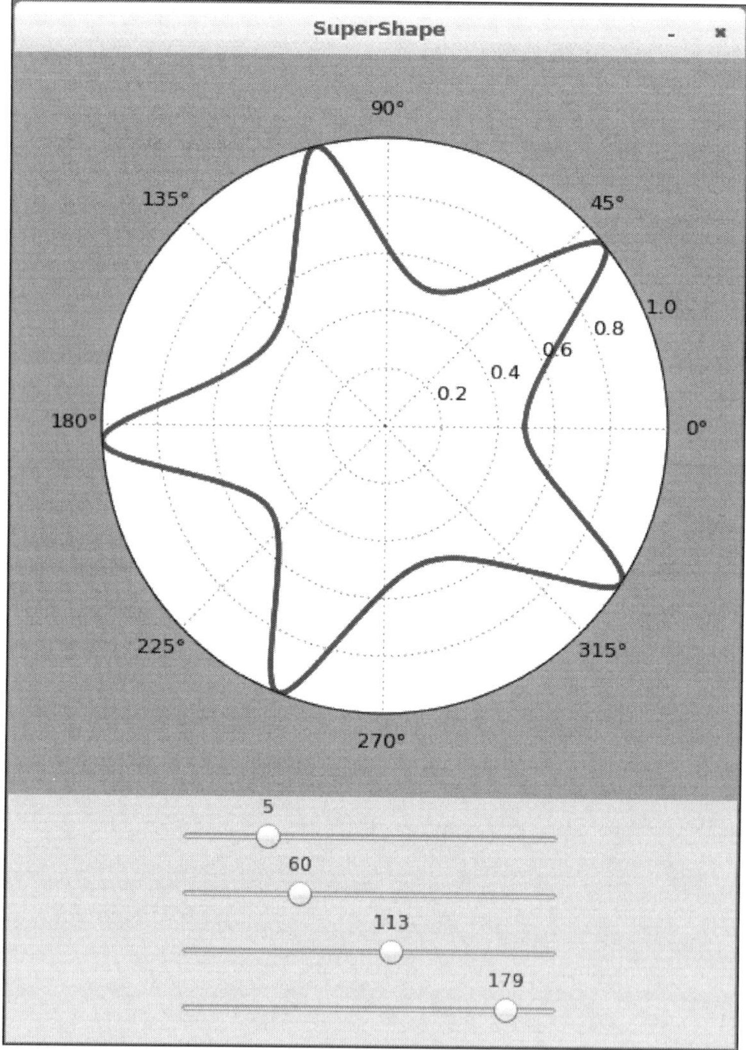

The appearance of the user interface will change depending on which platform you are running the script on: Linux, Windows, OS X, and so on.

How it works...

matplotlib provides the `FigureCanvasWxAgg` object in the `matplotlib.backends.backend_wxagg` module. The `FigureCanvasWxAgg` object is a wxWidget widget that contains a matplotlib figure. The actual size of that widget depends on the figure it contains. Here, we create a `Figure` instance of 6 x 6 units, with 80 pixels per unit: 480 x 480 pixels. Creating the `Figure` instance and its widget is as easy as running the following code:

```
self.fig = Figure((6, 6), dpi = 80)
canvas = FigureCanvasWxAgg(canvas_container, -1, self.fig)
```

As in the Tkinter example, there are two steps to handle with the matplotlib widget. We have to draw the figure and update it. Again, we create the `draw_figure()` and `refresh_figure()` methods to handle those steps.

The `draw_figure()` method creates an `Axes` instance, plots the curve, and keeps track of the result, that is, a set of lines. Finally, the plot is rendered as follows:

```
def draw_figure(self):
  self.phi = np.linspace(0, 2 * np.pi, 1024)
  r = supershape_radius(self.phi, 1, 1, self.m, self.n1, self.n2,
  self.n3)
  ax = self.fig.add_subplot(111, polar = True)
  self.lines, = ax.plot(self.phi, r, lw = 3.)

  self.fig.canvas.draw()
```

Then, every time the figure needs to be refreshed, because of some user input, we call `refresh_figure()`. The `refresh_figure()` method updates the set of lines that the plot is made of, using the following code:

```
def refresh_figure(self):
  r = supershape_radius(self.phi, 1, 1, self.m, self.n1, self.n2,
  self.n3)
  self.lines.set_ydata(r)
  self.fig.canvas.draw_idle()
```

So, as we can see, using wxWidget or Tkinter does not introduce any noticeable difference on the matplotlib side. Note that, just as for Tkinter, wxWidgets sliders can output only integer-valued positions, and we have to use the `LinearScaling` object of the previous recipe to get real-valued positions.

Integrating a plot to a GTK user interface

GTK is a user interface library that is especially popular on Linux environments. GTK is very complete, and its PyGObject binding for Python is especially convenient to use. In this recipe, we demonstrate how to interface GTK with matplotlib. We use the SuperShape application for this demonstration.

Getting ready

This recipe demonstrates how to use the latest Python binding for GTK, PyGObject. Thus, you will need to install PyGObject (most Linux distributions have a standard package for it) and obviously, GTK, if you don't have them already.

How to do it...

By now, if you have gone through the previous recipes on Tkinter and WxWidget, you will see a pattern in the way matplotlib integrates with the user interface. The pattern is the same here: Matplolib provides a canvas object specific to GTK, which embeds a `Figure` instance. Integrating a plot to the GTK user interface can be done with the following steps:

1. We start with the necessary import directives as follows:

```
from gi.repository import Gtk
import numpy as np
from matplotlib.figure import Figure
from matplotlib.backends.backend_gtk3agg import
FigureCanvasGTK3Agg
```

2. We add the following definition of the SuperShape curve:

```
def supershape_radius(phi, a, b, m, n1, n2, n3):
  theta = .25 * m * phi
  cos = np.fabs(np.cos(theta) / a) ** n2
  sin = np.fabs(np.sin(theta) / b) ** n3
  r = (cos + sin) ** (-1. / n1)
  r /= np.max(r)
  return r
```

3. Then we define our user interface using the following code:

```
class SuperShapeWindow(Gtk.Window):
  def __init__(self):
    Gtk.Window.__init__(self, title = 'SuperShape')

    layout_box = Gtk.Box.new(Gtk.Orientation.VERTICAL, 0)
    self.add(layout_box)
```

```
    self.m = 3
    self.n1 = 2
    self.n2 = 18
    self.n3 = 18

    self.fig = Figure((6, 6), dpi = 80)
    w, h = self.fig.get_size_inches()
    dpi_res = self.fig.get_dpi()
    w, h = int(np.ceil(w * dpi_res)), int(np.ceil(h * dpi_res))

    canvas = FigureCanvasGTK3Agg(self.fig)
    canvas.set_size_request(w, h)
    layout_box.add(canvas)

    self.m_slider = Gtk.HScale.new(Gtk.Adjustment(self.m, 1, 20,
      1., .1, 1))
    self.m_slider.connect('value-changed', self.on_m_slide)
    layout_box.add(self.m_slider)

    self.n1_slider = Gtk.HScale.new(Gtk.Adjustment(self.n1, .01,
      20, 1., .1, 1))
    self.n1_slider.connect('value-changed', self.on_n1_slide)
    layout_box.add(self.n1_slider)

    self.n2_slider = Gtk.HScale.new(Gtk.Adjustment(self.n2, .01,
      20, 1., .1, 1))
    self.n2_slider.connect('value-changed', self.on_n2_slide)
    layout_box.add(self.n2_slider)

    self.n3_slider = Gtk.HScale.new(Gtk.Adjustment(self.n3, .01,
      20, 1., .1, 1))
    self.n3_slider.connect('value-changed', self.on_n3_slide)
    layout_box.add(self.n3_slider)

    self.draw_figure()
  def on_m_slide(self, event):
    self.m = self.m_slider.get_value()

    self.refresh_figure()

  def on_n1_slide(self, event):
    self.n1 = self.n1_slider.get_value()
    self.refresh_figure()
```

```
    def on_n2_slide(self, event):
      self.n2 = self.n2_slider.get_value()
      self.refresh_figure()

    def on_n3_slide(self, event):
      self.n3 = self.n3_slider.get_value()
      self.refresh_figure()

    def draw_figure(self):
      self.phi = np.linspace(0, 2 * np.pi, 1024)
      ax = self.fig.add_subplot(111, polar = True)
      r = supershape_radius(self.phi, 1, 1, self.m, self.n1, self.
        n2, self.n3)
      self.lines, = ax.plot(self.phi, r, lw = 3.)
      self.fig.canvas.draw()

    def refresh_figure(self):
      r = supershape_radius(self.phi, 1, 1, self.m, self.n1, self.
        n2, self.n3)
      self.lines.set_ydata(r)
      self.fig.canvas.draw_idle()
```

4. To conclude, we set up our application and start it using the following code:

```
win = SuperShapeWindow()
win.connect('delete-event', Gtk.main_quit)
win.show_all()
Gtk.main()
```

5. The SuperShape curve is shown in a window, and the parameters of the curve can be adjusted with the sliders, as shown in the following figure:

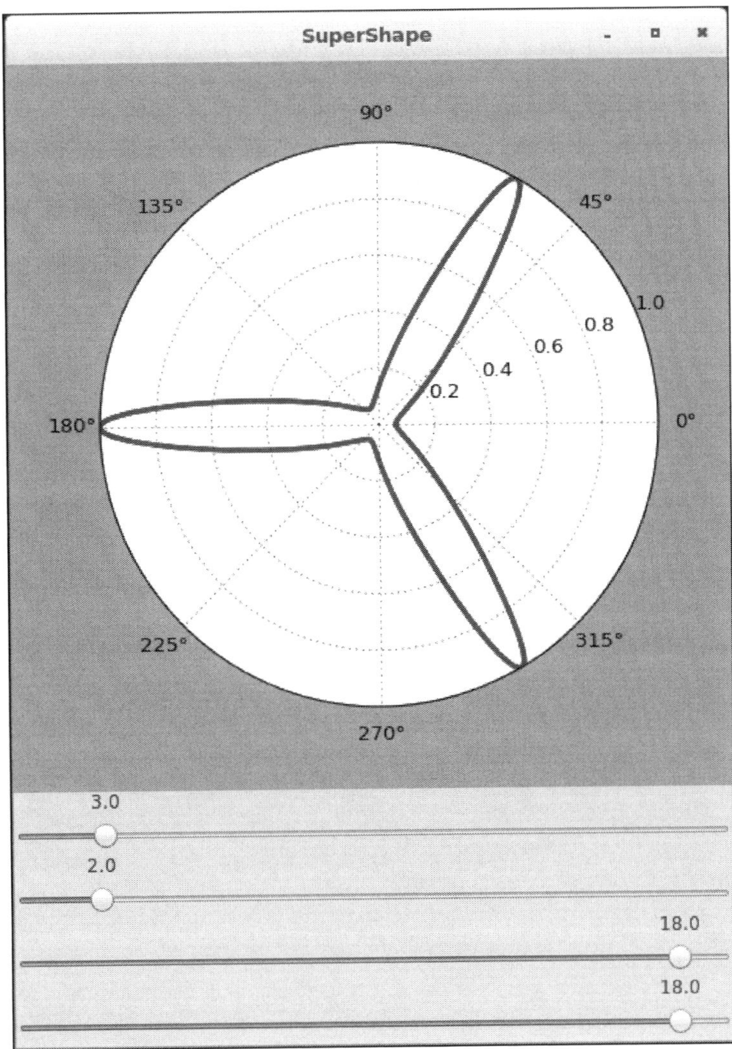

How it works...

matplotlib provides the `FigureCanvasGTK3Agg` object in the `matplotlib.backends.backend_gtk3agg` module. The `FigureCanvasGtk3Agg` object is a GTK widget that contains a matplotlib figure. We have to set up the size of the canvas object using the following code:

```
self.fig = Figure((6, 6), dpi = 80)

w, h = self.fig.get_size_inches()
```

```
    dpi_res = self.fig.get_dpi()
    w, h = int(np.ceil(w * dpi_res)), int(np.ceil(h * dpi_res))

    canvas = FigureCanvasGTK3Agg(self.fig)
    canvas.set_size_request(w, h)
```

From there, we are back to a familiar organization. We have a `draw_figure()` method to create the plot and a `refresh_figure()` method to update it. Those methods are identical to those of the WxWidget recipe. The few minor differences with the WxWidget recipe comes from the GTK API specifications. For instance, the slider widgets in GTK work with floating point units.

Integrating a plot in a Pyglet application

Pyglet is a very well written Python module to use OpenGL on any platform. Using Pyglet (and thus OpenGL) allows you to use the graphic hardware of your computer to its maximum. For instance, it would be fairly easy with Pyglet to show figures on three adjacent screens with fancy transition effects. In this recipe, we are going to see how to interface matplotlib with Pyglet. As in the previous example, we are going to display the SuperShape curve on the full screen and without any widgets.

How to do it...

Pyglet does not have the same functionality with widgets as Tkinter and wxWidgets have. This script will render a curve to an in-memory image. That image will then be simply shown on the whole screen surface. Thus, the figure will be shown on a full screen mode. Let's see how this is done using the following code:

```
import pyglet, StringIO
import numpy as np

from matplotlib.figure import Figure
from matplotlib.backends.backend_agg import FigureCanvasAgg

def render_figure(fig):
  w, h = fig.get_size_inches()
  dpi_res = fig.get_dpi()
  w, h = int(np.ceil(w * dpi_res)), int(np.ceil(h * dpi_res))

  canvas = FigureCanvasAgg(fig)
  pic_data = StringIO.StringIO()
  canvas.print_raw(pic_data, dpi = dpi_res)
  return pyglet.image.ImageData(w, h, 'RGBA', pic_data.getvalue(), -4
    * w)
```

```
def draw_figure(fig):
  X = np.linspace(-6, 6, 1024)
  Y = np.sinc(X)

  ax = fig.add_subplot(111)
  ax.plot(X, Y, lw = 2, color = 'k')

window = pyglet.window.Window(fullscreen = True)
dpi_res = min(window.width, window.height) / 10
fig = Figure((window.width / dpi_res, window.height / dpi_res), dpi =
dpi_res)

draw_figure(fig)
image = render_figure(fig)

@window.event
def on_draw():
  window.clear()
  image.blit(0, 0)

pyglet.app.run()
```

This script will display a curve in full screen mode, exploiting the entire surface of your screen. Note that you have to press the *Esc* key to close the application.

How it works...

matplotlib provides a special object, `FigureCanvasAgg`, as part of the `matplotlib.backends.backend_agg` module. This object constructor takes a figure as input and can render the result to a file. Using the `print_raw` method, the file will contain the raw pixel data. The standard `StringIO` module allows us to create an in-memory file. So we simply ask `FigureCanvasAgg` to render to a `StringIO` file as follows:

```
canvas = FigureCanvasAgg(fig)
pic_data = StringIO.StringIO()
canvas.print_raw(pic_data, dpi = dpi_res)
```

Then, we can retrieve the in-memory data and use it to create a Pyglet `Image` object as follows:

```
pyglet.image.ImageData(w, h, 'RGBA', pic_data.getvalue(), -4 * w)
```

Note that we have to specify the width, `w`, and the height, `h`, of a picture. They can be deduced from the dimension of the `Figure` instance and its resolution using the following code:

```
w, h = fig.get_size_inches()
dpi_res = fig.get_dpi()
w, h = int(np.ceil(w * dpi_res)), int(np.ceil(h * dpi_res))
```

This recipe shows you more generally how to render a matplotlib figure to an in-memory buffer. For instance, one can write a script that renders several figures in memory and feed them to a module to create a video. Because all this happens in memory, it is faster than merely saving pictures files on a hard disk and later compiling the pictures into a video.

Index

Symbols

A

B

C

D

E

F

G

H

I

L

M

N

O

P

Q

R

S

T

U

V

W

Thank you for buying
matplotlib Plotting Cookbook

About Packt Publishing

Packt, pronounced 'packed', published its first book "*Mastering phpMyAdmin for Effective MySQL Management*" in April 2004 and subsequently continued to specialize in publishing highly focused books on specific technologies and solutions.

Our books and publications share the experiences of your fellow IT professionals in adapting and customizing today's systems, applications, and frameworks. Our solution based books give you the knowledge and power to customize the software and technologies you're using to get the job done. Packt books are more specific and less general than the IT books you have seen in the past. Our unique business model allows us to bring you more focused information, giving you more of what you need to know, and less of what you don't.

Packt is a modern, yet unique publishing company, which focuses on producing quality, cutting-edge books for communities of developers, administrators, and newbies alike. For more information, please visit our website: `www.packtpub.com`.

About Packt Open Source

In 2010, Packt launched two new brands, Packt Open Source and Packt Enterprise, in order to continue its focus on specialization. This book is part of the Packt Open Source brand, home to books published on software built around Open Source licences, and offering information to anybody from advanced developers to budding web designers. The Open Source brand also runs Packt's Open Source Royalty Scheme, by which Packt gives a royalty to each Open Source project about whose software a book is sold.

Writing for Packt

We welcome all inquiries from people who are interested in authoring. Book proposals should be sent to `author@packtpub.com`. If your book idea is still at an early stage and you would like to discuss it first before writing a formal book proposal, contact us; one of our commissioning editors will get in touch with you.

We're not just looking for published authors; if you have strong technical skills but no writing experience, our experienced editors can help you develop a writing career, or simply get some additional reward for your expertise.

[PACKT] open source
community experience distilled
PUBLISHING

NumPy Beginner's Guide Second Edition

ISBN: 978-1-78216-608-5 Paperback: 310 pages

An action packed guide using real world examples of the easy to use, high performance, free open source NumPy mathematical library

1. Perform high performance calculations with clean and efficient NumPy code.
2. Analyze large data sets with statistical functions.
3. Execute complex linear algebra and mathematical computations.

Learning SciPy for Numerical and Scientific Computing

ISBN: 978-1-78216-162-2 Paperback: 150 pages

A practical tutorial that guarantees fast, accurate, and easy-to-code solutions to your numerical and scientific computing problems with the power of SciPy and Python

1. Perform complex operations with large matrices, including eigenvalue problems, matrix decompositions, or solution to large systems of equations.
2. Step-by-step examples to easily implement statistical analysis and data mining that rivals in performance any of the costly specialized software suites.
3. Plenty of examples of state-of-the-art research problems from all disciplines of science, that prove how simple, yet effective, is to provide solutions based on SciPy.

Please check **www.PacktPub.com** for information on our titles

15199344R00126

Made in the USA
San Bernardino, CA
17 September 2014